THE WRITINGS OF ANNA FREUD
Volume VIII

PSYCHOANALYTIC PSYCHOLOGY OF NORMAL DEVELOPMENT

1970–1980

THE WRITINGS OF ANNA FREUD
VOLUME VIII

PSYCHOANALYTIC PSYCHOLOGY OF NORMAL DEVELOPMENT

1970–1980

INTERNATIONAL UNIVERSITIES PRESS, INC.

NEW YORK

Library of Congress Cataloging in Publication Data
Freud, Anna, 1895-
    Psychoanalytic psychology of normal development.

    (The Writings of Anna Freud; v. 8)
    Bibliography: p.
    Includes Index.
    1. Child psychology — Addresses, essays, lectures.
2. Developmental psychology — Addresses, essays,
lectures. 3. Psychoanalysis — Addresses, essays,
lectures. 4. Child analysis — Addresses, essays,
lectures. 5. Child psychology — Addresses,
essays, lectures. I. Title. II. Series: Freud,
Anna, 1895-   . Works. English; v. 8.
[DNLM: 1. Child development. 2. Child psychology.
3. Psychoanalytic theory. WS 105 F899p]
BF721.F692   vol. 8   618.92'89s   [618.92'89]   81-11809
ISBN 0-8236-6877-0   AACR2

Manufactured in the United States of America

Acknowledgments

The material in this book was collected at the Hampstead Child-Therapy Clinic, an organization which at present is maintained by the G. G. Bunzl Fund, London; Herman A. and Amelia S. Ehrmann Foundation, New York; Field Foundation, New York; Freud Centenary Fund, London; Anna Freud Foundation, New York; Paul Mellon, Washington; New-Land Foundation, New York; Leo Oppenheimer and Flora Oppenheimer Haas Trust, New York; and a number of private supporters. The author expresses her gratitude for their generous support over many years.

Contents

vii

Part II
Contributions to Psychoanalytic Symposia

Part III
Introductions to Freud's Writings

Part IV
Applications of Psychoanalysis and Brief Writings

Part I

Normal Child Development

Part 1

Normal Child Development

1

Introduction

After years of working on the one hand as analysts of adults and on the other hand as child analysts, with children of all ages, all descriptions, and all degrees of mental health and illness, we have come to the conclusion that there may be room within the psychoanalytic discipline for a subsection of theoretical and clinical formulations which can serve as a basis for a psychoanalytic psychology of child development. By saying this, we do not mean to belittle the contributions made so far to the knowledge of childhood by work with adult patients. Rather, we point to certain differences in the view of childhood processes as they are seen either from the vantage point of the analyst of adults or from that of the child analyst.

As analysts of adults we attempt to revive our patients' childhood by a variety of methods: by means of remnants

This paper is published here for the first time. It also appears in *Die Schriften der Anna Freud,* Volume 10. Munich: Kindler Verlag, 1980.

of the past which survive in conscious memory or reveal themselves as ingrained personal characteristics; by lifting to consciousness repressed impulses and experiences; by the analysis of dreams; by means of interpreting transference behavior, transference fantasies, and the transference neurosis. As a result we obtain what, as analysts of adults, we take as a fair picture of the patient's early years, i.e., of his first interactions with the caretaking figures in his environment; of the division of a primarily undivided self into the inner agencies of id, ego, and later superego; of the sequence of libidinal phases and concomitant development of aggression; of the barriers against drive and wish fulfillment as evolved in the maturing defense organization.

Nevertheless, as child analysts, we are less satisfied with the reconstructed picture. We distrust conscious memories of childhood experiences even beyond the familiar notion of "cover memories" since we know how in the course of their growth children falsify their memories in the service of denial, wishful thinking, and avoidance of unpleasure. We know from ongoing observation that traumatic and other pathogenic events usually occur over extended periods and are seldom as tied to a specific moment in time as it appears later. We do not believe that regression during adult analysis produces wholly reliable evidence of the past states to which the patient is attempting to return, i.e., to the original infantile position without additions and overlays from later stages of development. While we think of psychosexual development as a sequence of phases, we believe that it is possible to subdivide development, especially that of the libidinal stages, far beyond the rather global divisions perceived from the aspect of the adult personality. Still more important than the foregoing is our conviction that whatever becomes visible in reconstruction is weighted heavily toward the side of pathology, with a comparative neglect of normal progressive development. Unfulfilled childhood longings for relatedness, narcissistic wounds, incompletely repressed strivings, unsolved conflicts vie with each other for expression in dreams and in the transference. In contrast, there is no such upsurge from the past or the repressed unconscious on the side of those psychic strivings, conflicts, and experiences which have been dealt with adequately, i.e., for which satisfactory solutions have been found. These have been added to the existing framework of the personality and have been turned into stepping stones toward further growth.

Some of this has, of course, been taken for granted in analytic work with adult patients. When analyzing an obsessional neurosis, we expect to reconstruct a wealth of detailed data concerning the vicissitudes of the anal-sadistic phase and to learn comparatively little about orality and phallic sexuality. Conversely, when we analyze phobias and hysterias, the oral and phallic events loom large, with the anal-sadistic phase remaining in obscurity. In both instances it is the existence of fixation points and inadequately solved conflicts which determines which material is offered by the patients for purposes of reconstruction.

We can offer even better illustrations from the analysis of sleeping, eating, and learning disturbances or the disturbance of any of the functions of the adult such as interference with object relationships, management of physical health, development of secondary process thinking, etc.

We have learned that in all these respects a long developmental line leads up to the final result and that any point on the line can become a focal point for arrest, fixation, or distortion of development. In adulthood then, it will be this particular station on the line which will appear in the analysis with all its details, while those steps which have been negotiated without causing disruption and have made smooth entry into the fabric of the personality may remain silent. They will, however, be accessible to the child analyst or to the analytic observer of children, both of whom have the opportunity to witness the developmental processes while they are ongoing.

To investigate the happenings on the developmental lines may help not only to trace the child's advances or his failures but also to assemble the data necessary for constructing a developmental psychology of childhood which is in line with psychoanalytic thinking. As analysts, when dealing with neurotic symptoms, we understand these as the result of interaction between conflicting internal forces, i.e., as compromise formations. What is true for pathology may be equally true for the child's developmental achievements. At any time during his moves toward maturity the child can be shown to be under pressure. Internally, his maturing higher functions battle with his primitive drive derivatives and try to limit satisfaction and wish fulfillment. Externally, the loved persons on whom he is dependent urge submission to the demands of reality. From step to step the child has to reconcile these influences and has to find solutions which are acceptable in the inner as well as in the outer world. Basically, this is a view of developmental functioning which is available to every analyst.

In short, a psychoanalytic child psychology cannot limit itself to any one side of the child's nature — neither to his drives, nor to his object relationships, nor to his intellectual, moral, or social growth as such. Every forward move is a question of interplay between all of them, added to interplay with the environment. Every station on any of the developmental lines represents a compromise, i.e., the best possible solution of conflicting influences which is available to the child at a particular moment in time. Such solutions may have adaptive value in the inner and outer world, or fail to do so. This will decide whether they serve progressive development or are pathogenic. In any case, observation in the service of a developmental psychology should be impartially directed toward both occurrences.

We have previously made the point that as analysts of adults we view mental health on the basis of our experiences with psychopathology, and that analytic work with children creates an opportunity for taking an opposite stand: to view pathological manifestations on the basis of our understanding of normal progressive growth.

2

The Widening Scope
of Psychoanalytic
Child Psychology,
Normal and Abnormal
[1972]

In our time, when the first years of life have become an independent and even preferred field of exploration, it is not
easy for analysts to realize that at the beginning of the psychoanalytic era the study of childhood and its disturbances
was not an aim in itself but merely a by-product of very

A short draft version of this paper entitled "The Infantile Neurosis:
Genetic and Dynamic Considerations" was published as chap. 11 in Volume 7 of my *Writings;* and in *The Psychoanalytic Study of the Child,*
26:79–90. New York: Quadrangle Books, 1971. The full version of this
paper is published here for the first time. German translation: Der
wachsende Wirkungskreis der psychoanalytischen Kinderpsychologie:
Normal und abnorm. *Die Schriften der Anna Freud,* Volume 10.
Munich: Kindler Verlag, 1980.

different endeavors. What was essential then was to acquire a first understanding of the meaning of the adult neuroses as manifestations of a dynamic unconscious; to learn to translate their symbolic and distorted language into conscious thought; to define the working of basic psychic mechanisms such as repression, reaction formation, and projection. There were important tasks such as establishing the links between the neuroses and character formation on the one hand and with the perversions on the other; to show up the similarities and differences between neuroses and psychoses and to explore the therapeutic possibilities in both areas.

Within these concerns, the study of the infantile neurosis occupied a place similar to that of the study of children's dreams in relation to dream interpretation in general. It was hoped that the simpler organization of the child's mind would allow for easier glimpses into the working of the mental apparatus and thereby render transparent what it obscured in later life by the increasing psychic complexities.

What needed and found confirmation, above all, were several hypotheses concerning adult neurotics: that their troubles, whether hysterical, phobic, or obsessional, are rooted in early childhood experiences and can be traced back to them; that interactions between conscious and unconscious forces in the mind, i.e., the defensive maneuvers which keep unconscious content from rising to the surface, are equally initiated in childhood; that, altogether, conflicts within the mind begin early in life, as soon as the mental apparatus becomes differentiated into separate agencies which serve purposes besides that of direct drive satisfaction, namely, reality-adaptive, moral, and aesthetic aims.

Questions such as these were answered by the correspondences between the adult and the infantile neurosis, as they were established at the time. The precipitating conflicts for the former were seen in the clashes between active and passive sexual strivings; between heterosexuality and homosexuality; between object love and death wishes against the loved persons; between primitive instinctual trends of all kinds and opposing ego and superego concerns. In the childhood neurosis these were equaled by the events of the phallic-oedipal period with almost identical swings between incompatible active and passive oedipal attitudes; between masculine and feminine identifications; between castration fears and castration wishes; between love and hate; between striving for unrestrained wish fulfillment and ego and superego demands.

There also was little difference to be found between the adult's and the child's attempts to cope with these internal contradictions. When faced with emotional dilemmas which could not be solved by rational thinking and conscious effort, both could be shown to deny, repress, displace, or project the psychic contents that caused anxiety, and consequently to produce the same hysterical, phobic, or obsessional symptoms.

Since, in most other respects, adults and children, as mature and immature human beings, are widely different from each other, this identity in their psychopathology was unexpected and surprising in the first instance. It was subsequently resolved by the realization that neither adult nor child neurotics deal with their problems on the developmental level on which they arise. Faced by losses, disappointments, frustrations, or conflicts in his mature sex life, the adult neurotic abandons his genitality and returns, i.e., regresses, to the polymorphously perverse infantile sexual urges which have preceded it. The child, in similar quandaries, does likewise and returns from the oedipal-phallic level to its precursors. Both, then, adult and child find themselves in the same situation. They are confronted by urges and fantasies which had been age-adequate at the oral or anal-sadistic level of development, but which, re-cathected at this later stage, are rejected by the personality as unacceptable and therefore arouse deep-seated anxieties. These latter have to be defended against and their content compromised with. To bring about the compromise formations which are symptomatic for the neuroses at all ages, adults and children employ defense mechanisms which (as previously described) are more or less identical.

In Freud's writings we are given two examples of infantile neuroses, one seen and studied at the time of its occurrence, the other seen in retrospect, i..e., reconstructed during the analysis of an adult patient. These two case histories have held the stage during more than fifty years as being representative illustrations for the concept of the infantile neurosis. The discussions which they contain of their causation, their content, and the psychic processes active in them can be taken as evidence of the then-reigning ideas concerning this pathological manifestation.

The story of "A Phobia in a Five-Year-Old Boy" was published in 1909 to fulfill the psychoanalyst's wish "for a more direct and less roundabout proof of the fundamental theorems" laid down in *The Three Essays on the Theory of Sexuality* several years before (1905b). What the revelations made by the child were meant to provide was "a possibility of observing in children at first hand and in all the freshness of life the sexual impulses and wishes which we dig out so laboriously in adults" (1909a, p. 6).

Little Hans, the hero of the story, fulfilled these requirements to the utmost. From the descriptions of his father who treated him,[1] the picture of Hans emerged as that of a cheerful, amiable, affectionate, active-minded little boy who negotiated the first stages of development without noticeable difficulties. He enjoyed the body care given to him by his mother in his infancy, deriving especial pleasure from "cutaneous contact." He found his way from such more autoerotic enjoyments "to object love in the usual manner." He gave evidence of exhibitionistic and scoptophilic wishes as well as evidence of excretory pleasure. There is speculation whether he may have been "one of those children who like retaining their excreta till they can derive a voluptuous sensation from the evacuation" (p. 108).

On the other hand, "no trace was observed in him of any inclination to play with his excrement" and he took the required steps toward coping with his prephallic impulses without much trouble. "He early became clean in his habits" (p. 108). He did not "give free play to the propensity towards cruelty and violence which is a constituent of human nature. On the contrary, . . . the transformation of aggressive tendencies into feelings of pity took place in him at a very early age" (p. 112). He reacted to the birth of a baby sister with the not unusual "outburst of sexual pleasure and sexual curiosity" (p. 113), accompanied by the usual ambivalence of feel-

[1]"Under supervision," as we would say today.

lings toward the new arrival.

Clashes between instinctual wishes and opposing forces did not become pathogenic for him until he entered into the phallic phase of infantile sexuality. Then a lively interest and pleasure in his sexual organ were matched by fear for its safety and the strength of his oedipal-aggressive wishes for the sole possession of his mother by hate and death wishes toward the father who, by now, had become a rival. "But this father, whom he could not help hating as a rival, was the same father whom he had always loved and was bound to go on loving, who had been his model, had been his first playmate, and had looked after him from his earliest infancy" (p. 134).

Starting from this conflict of feelings, for which no solution could be found, the child's development began to take a regressive course. Phallic masturbation, which had been pleasurable until then, was given up. Pleasure in free movement was lost and replaced by avoidance and restriction. Fear of retribution by the father was displaced onto the horse, which formerly had been appreciated as a moving, kicking, masculine-aggressive being. Ideas of biting and the fear of being bitten appeared from a forgotten past, obviously as a return to the most primitive form of aggression during the oral stage. Recathexis of anal wishes and fantasies provided the material for fantasies of pregnancy, anal birth, and anal babies. Masculine identification with a father who owns the mother and produces babies with her began to change into feminine identification with the mother herself who handles the babies, takes them to the toilet, and enjoys their bodily functions. With this, even the masterful oedipal wishes for ownership of the mother changed into an infantile clinging to her presence and protection.

In short, Hans had developed a phobia which interrupted the smooth progress of his forward development, interfered with his actions and occupations, and was as distressing to the patient himself as it was to his parents.

In the further course, during the treatment he received, this crippling state gradually gave way to the unraveling of its conflicting elements. Repression, as an "automatic and excessive" process, was replaced by conscious understanding and "condemnation" (p. 145) by the higher agencies of the mind. Regression was undone and finally and almost triumphantly the boy reclaimed his lost masculine aspirations via the fantasy of the plumber who restored his sexual organ. This signified the victory of manhood over feminine trends, of activity over passivity, and of progressive over regressive tendencies.

There is considerable difference between this phobia and the disturbances reconstructed and described in "The History of an Infantile Neurosis" (1918). While "Hans's illness may perhaps have been no more serious than that of many other children" (p. 143), i.e., no more than a temporary exacerbation of the unavoidable difficulties by which all children are confronted, the so-called Wolf Man's development, traced in the paper, was threatened from the beginning by much graver factors. There was evidence that the early observation of parental intercourse, the primal scene, had already started him on the course of double identification, the passive-feminine role being, from then onward, as desirable as, or more desirable to him than, the active-masculine one. This predilection for passivity then seemed to govern his orality and, instead of promoting pleasure in eating and oral aggression, resulted in difficulties of food intake and anxiety-laden fantasies of being devoured. A passing phase of urethral erotism helped toward identification with the father's masculinity but was brought to an abrupt end by the experience of seduction which inevitably served to reinforce the passive strivings. There followed on the anal stage a battle between the usual passive-receptive trends and the phase-adequate anal sadism; but here, too, the predominance of passivity assured that the latter was short-lived and, due to fear and guilt feelings, soon transformed into masochism. The Wolf Man, at this time, seemed well on the way to passive homosexuality, and he would have succumbed to this but for his entry into the phallic phase. What helped him here, though, were not the pleasurable manly strivings, which would have been timely, but the castration fears; these, however precariously, enabled him to keep a hold on his masculinity. Altogether, the conflicts between active and passive, between the strivings of a normal and an inverted oedipus complex, found expression in the wolf dream, followed by the wolf phobia.

Contrary to Hans's return to normal masculine development, the Wolf Man's battles against his conflicting infantile urges were doomed to continue. His anxiety hysteria gradually acquired an obsessional overlay directed especially against sadism and aggression. Passivity triumphed. His enjoyment of life remained severely disturbed. An intolerance for narcissistic frustration remained and increased. It was the latter which finally played its role toward reactivating the infantile neurosis in adult life.

During the discussion of these two case histories, Freud arrived at some more general formulations, such as the following:

— that troubles such as an infantile phobia are "quite extraordinarily frequent" (1909a, p. 142);
— that in "later life these children either become neurotic or remain healthy" (p. 142);
— that the infantile neurosis is more frequent, i.e., more normal as an occurrence than its adult counterpart;
— that the finding that every adult neurosis is preceded by an infantile one is therefore not reversible: not every infantile neurosis is followed by neurotic illness in later life;
— that many infantile neuroses are open to a spontaneous cure which occurs at the transition point between the phallic-oedipal and the latency period;
— that it depends on the experiences of adult life whether the childhood conflicts will be reactivated, i.e., whether a new neurosis will be formed.

THE STATUS OF THE INFANTILE NEUROSIS WITHIN THE PSYCHOANALYTIC CHILD PSYCHOLOGY OF TODAY

There is a world of difference between those investigations of the infantile neurosis as a "type and model" for adult neuroses and our present explorations of normal and abnormal child development which aim at the enumeration, description, and exploration of any interference with optimal mental growth. Instead of comparing the psychopathology of childhood with that of adults, we have taught ourselves to view it against the background of a normal process of maturing and unfolding mental functioning, however hypothetical and subject to variation such a concept of normality may be. Instead of classifying the various types of disturbance according to the diagnostic categories used for adults, we have introduced a diagnostic scheme in which interference with development is the main criterion. So far as symptomatology is concerned, we are mindful of Freud's (1909a) early warning "that we concentrate too much upon symptoms and concern ourselves too little with their causes" (p. 143). Following in this spirit, we are discarding the descriptive approach to the symptomatology of childhood and replacing it by a metapsychological one, i.e., by grouping symptoms not according to their manifest phenomenology but according to the latent processes which underlie them. The material under study by us therefore extends far beyond the area of the infantile neuroses, which we classify as the disorders caused by conflict and shaped by the various types of compromise between the conflicting forces. It includes the deviations from the norm caused by the child's reaction to adverse environmental circumstances, i.e., the atypical developments; the infantilisms caused by delays of growth or by undefended regressions; the character disorders caused by imbalances between instinctual forces and their controlling counterpart in ego and superego; the deviations of development due to sensory defects such as absence of vision; the complete arrests of growth for unknown reasons, as in the autistic children, etc.

It is a point not to be overlooked that this widening of our field of work takes us beyond the area of psychopathology and adds to it the whole realm of child psychology and personality formation. What we learn to trace are lines of development which lead in discernible steps from the infant's primitive, undifferentiated or even prepsychological state to such mature achievements as constant object relatedness, companionship, control of intake and output, body management, and working ability.

What I am emphasizing is that, by now, our interest is drawn in three directions. There are, for one, the circumstances, forces, and processes which create the basis on which the individual personality is built, i.e., the pleasure-pain, frustration-satisfaction experiences to which the infant's mental apparatus is subjected. There is, secondly, the growth toward differentiation within the mental apparatus which proceeds via imitation, identification with, and introjection of the object world and leads to the establishment of different internal agencies. Thirdly, with increasing ego and superego functioning, with the need for reality adaptation and with the intolerance for indiscriminate wish fulfillment, there is disparity of aims, i.e., conflict. The two former sets of phenomena are above all significant for determining the type of personality development and the nonneurotic deviations from the norm. The third and last-named one is instrumental in creating the neuroses. Obviously, it is our present task to pursue all three, on the one hand to differentiate between them and on the other hand to show up their interactions.

The Psychosomatic Early Reaction Type of Infancy

The distinctions between personality background, differentiations within the personality, and conflict-determined neurotic pathology can be traced through all phases of development beginning from the earliest reactions of the infant. The earliest disorders to be met appear in the somatic areas of breathing, sleeping, feeding, elimination, and skin sensitivity. So far as they have no purely organic cause, they can be traced to interaction of inborn modes of functioning with the mother's handling of these given potentialities, i.e., her more or less skillful or insensitive, well- or ill-timed response to the infant's needs; or they can be traced to the infant's high sensitivity to the mother's emotional states, her anxieties, her moods, her predilections, and her avoidances. Unpleasure or distress due to either cause can find discharge only in two manners: either through crying, or by way of physical pathways within the somatic areas mentioned above.

Even though such disturbances of smooth functioning have a symptomatic character, it seems extremely important not to confuse them with the later symptomatic manifestations as they appear within the context of the neuroses. The infant is exposed to environmental influence and interacts with it. But we do not regard it as being in "conflict" or as "compromising" either with external or with internal forces. Both are psychic reactions of which, according to our assumptions, the mental apparatus is not capable until a later age. What we have before us at this time of life is, I believe, something different. It is the physical discharge of psychological distress through skin eruptions, feeding and sleeping difficulties, digestive upsets, etc., which is as natural for the infant as, vice versa, the psychological discharge of physical distress through crying, grizzling, or unhappiness. There is, at this time, an easy access of mind to body and body to mind—an access which is the basis for the infantile psychosomatic reactions and which remains the habitual manner of discharge of tension until, with progressing mental development, new pathways will be opened up via thought, speech, and purposeful action.[2]

What is important for our present context are the developmental implications of this early psychosomatic era for personality building as well as for neurotogenesis.

So far as personality building is concerned, these influences are threefold, and are mediated via the *pleasure-pain, satisfaction-frustration* experiences. For one, it is the quantitative balance between these which has repercussions. Infants, in whose experience unpleasure dominates over pleasure, tend to show delay in ego growth since normally the ego organizes itself around a nucleus of pleasurable experience as the "pleasure ego." In its turn, delay in the emergence of the ego agency from the undifferentiated id-ego matrix may lead to all kinds of ego defects, deficiencies, and distortions, as we know them from the atypical, borderline, and psychotic clinical pictures. According to our present assumptions, these are not caused by conflict, as the neuroses are, but by what Balint (1968) called "basic faults," i.e., by deviations in development. We ascribe, secondly, similar importance to the method of *dealing with unpleasure* to which the individual child is introduced.

---

[2]It is well known, though of lesser relevance here, that these more sophisticated pathways are not always fully used. Discharge of tension via the body may remain the preferred method which is the basis of psychosomatic pathology in later childhood and adulthood.

Where a mother, for whatever reason, is unable to give adequate comfort to her infant, this may have a lasting effect on this individual's own capacity to cope with even normal amounts of unpleasure, pain, and anxiety, i.e., on his frustration tolerance. Such children remain easily dissatisfied and excessively demanding. In later childhood, once the ego's defense mechanisms are established, the children also tend to use these defenses excessively when faced with any kind of unpleasure, and this opens up the path to neurotic symptomatology. Last, but not of lesser importance, is the fact that it is the smooth satisfaction of early body needs which paves the way from autoerotism and narcissism to the first form of object relationship, the anaclitic one. Where need satisfaction is diminished or interfered with, this transition may remain incomplete or be completed belatedly, with lasting effects on the individual's general capacity for object relationship.

So far as the later infantile and adult neuroses are concerned, the early psychosomatic events also contribute to them in a very direct manner. From the *Studies on Hysteria* onward, it has always been considered a problem why the patient selects specific body parts or organ systems for the symbolic representation of his psychic conflicts and for the conversion of psychic tension into physical pain. The answer given to the question was by means of the concept of a "somatic compliance" which renders certain body parts or physical functions (skin, intestinal tract, breathing, limbs, movement) more useful for this purpose than are others. In this context it is tempting to think that, in fact, the selection of the body part to be used later for hysterical conversion occurs during the early psychosomatic phase. Whichever physical pathway for discharge has been preferred at that time may remain more vulnerable ever after and more prone to receive psychic cathexis which is displaced from ongoing conflicts. Detailed comparisons between later hysterical symptomatology and upheavals in the first year of life will have to prove or disprove the validity of such an assumption.

The Prephallic, Preoedipal Parent-Infant Relationship

The same difference between primary effect on personality building and secondary consequences for nonneurotic and neurotic psychopathology needs to be followed through all aspects of the infant-parent relationship in the whole period of prephallic emotional and instinctual development. The psychoanalytic literature of recent decades is rich in supplying descriptions, findings, and theories concerning these stages, especially with reference to the interactions between infant and mother and their relevance for ego growth.[3]

We know from the analyses of adults how many different conscious and unconscious meanings parenthood may have to them, the infant which they have produced representing for them a continuation of their own personality, confirmation of their sexual identity, fulfillment of ideals, reincarnation of loved or hated figures of the past, either a welcome or an unwelcome addition to the family, a burden, etc. We also know, from direct observation and from reconstruction, how many roles the parents, and especially

[3]See, for example, Winnicott (1958, 1965), Spitz (1965), Provence (1962, 1967, 1977) and many others.

the mother, have to fulfill for the child: as providers, as stimulators, as anaclitic objects, as protective shields against overstimulation, as auxiliary egos, as targets for the child's oral and anal, sadistic, aggressive, and loving impulses.

For our purposes, it is not only these roles in themselves which are significant but the variety of ways in which the functions are fulfilled by the parent and reacted to by the child. Deprivation and neglect, seduction and separation, nonavailability of objects, lack of their proper responses are environmental interferences with normality. Furthermore, according to the circumstances mentioned above, parents may cathect the body and person of the child narcissistically or with object libido; with libido or aggression; consistently or with interruptions. On his side, the child may answer to the parental involvement, subject to his inborn capacities, in passive-receptive or active ways; with pleasurable or painful sensations; satisfied and comfortable or complaining and demanding; submissive or revolting; loving, hating, ambivalent, etc. There are on both sides multiple possibilities of relating to each other, and the variety of resulting combinations is virtually countless. To put it in other words: the complexity of interaction between these parental and infantile attitudes forms the basis for the unending individual differences between people's personalities.

So far as basic personal qualities are concerned, it is an early psychoanalytic finding that the experience of being well loved and highly estimated in early childhood is responsible for "primary narcissism," i.e., the child's libidinal investment in himself, and that it creates for all later life an unshakable feeling of security and confidence. We meet the same attributes in the more modern literature under the terms of self-regard, self-esteem or, in relation to the environment, as "basic trust." For the personality this is decisive for the individual's balance between narcissism and object relatedness as well as for such characteristics as optimism or pessimism, courageousness or timidity, outgoing or withdrawn attitudes, all of which remain for life. But, secondarily, such personal characteristics also have a definite relevance for psychopathology. Whoever is pessimistic by nature will be more prone to develop depressions; whoever is timid by nature will react to anxiety and unpleasure preferably with avoidance and phobic mechanisms. The same is true of the strength and constancy of the early object ties which the child develops in relation to the parents. Primarily these facilitate identifications and internalizations and enrich the personality. But secondarily, by strengthening ego and superego development, they promote the differentiation within the personality and thereby prepare the ground for internal conflict and neurotic symptomatology.

We may attempt to view the *prephallic instinctual trends* themselves under the same double aspect, but in their case the resulting impression is a different one. It is well known, of course, that derivatives of them also enter into and shape the personality, partly as unchanged remnants of orality and anal sadism (in the form of stimulus hunger, greed, demandingness, possessiveness, untidiness, aggressivity, brutality), partly as transformations into the opposite (in the form of compliance, self-abnegation, pity, orderliness, cleanliness). But the importance of these contributions, deeply rooted as they are, is overshadowed by those made by the prephallic trends to psychopathology via *arrests, fixations,* preparation for *regressions,* and *compromise formations.*

As mentioned before, we assume that no neurotic conflict in later life is dealt with on the developmental level on which it arises and that its symptomatic solution is invariably preceded by a retreat (regression) to earlier stages of growth. If this clinical finding is correct, the importance of the earlier levels and the amounts of attraction exerted by them can hardly be overestimated.

We know how disastrous it is for a child's normality when, either for organic or traumatic reasons, progressive growth is *arrested* and either the drives, or ego and superego, or both sides of the personality are brought to a standstill instead of completing their development. Clinical pictures such as those of the mentally deficient, the autistic, the infantilisms, perhaps the morally deficient bear witness to such happenings.

The psychoanalytic concept of *fixation* to one of the early developmental levels is, of course, not synonymous with that of such arrests. It implies merely that at a particular stage of infantile sexuality the child's experience has been anything but optimal: that he has been starved of satisfaction by those who took care of him; or overfed with it; that he has been subjected to seduction, which meant inappropriate and untimely overstimulation on that level; that he has overstimulated himself autoerotically by excessive use of this particular erotogenic zone for purposes of pleasure gain and comfort. Where this happens, it is difficult for the child to renounce these forms of satisfaction at the time when they normally should become obsolete and give way to new ones, i.e., when thumb sucking should be exchanged for anal interests and these, in their turn, for phallic masturbation. Eventually, the forward step is made, but not without lingering regret for what has been given up. To put it in dynamic-economic terms: some of the sexual and aggressive energy with which the prephallic satisfactions had been cathected is left behind on the points concerned, remains latent on them, and can be reactivated easily according to need, i.e., whenever difficulties, conflicts, and frustrations arise in later life. What the prephallic infantile trends supply in this manner are the *fixation points* to which later *regressions* will take place. Although fixation as such is not yet pathological, pathological potentialities are contained in it. If too much drive energy remains fixed to the earliest stages, not enough impetus will be available for the later ones, or for sublimation, both becoming impoverished. Worse than that is the fact that a past which remains cathected with too much drive energy will exert a powerful attraction that may pull the child backward, cause him to lose important developmental gains, and involve him once more in the pursuit of primitive fantasies and wish-fulfilling activities which he had outgrown. Where regressions of this kind already happen on the prephallic level, the resulting clinical pictures (such as infantilisms) are difficult to distinguish diagnostically from those which are produced by true arrests.

So far as neurotic symptoms in the prephallic phases are concerned, there is no doubt that these occur, even though it has always been debated how their formation can be explained at a time when identifications and internalizations with the object world are still ongoing and the interactions between the inner agencies are not yet fully internalized. Clinical evidence shows that during the oral and anal phases, children already produce manifest symptoms of hysterical, phobic, and obsessional nature such as the affliction of limbs; phobic reactions to food intake; phobic interference with elimination; phobic anxiety concerning going to sleep or being bathed; inhibitions of touch or of motility; rigid insistence on repetition, regularity, and any absence of change; intolerance for dirt and cruelty. Manifestly, these symptoms are identical with those of a full-blown infantile neurosis, and it needs a closer scrutiny during child analysis to arrive at a number of important differences between the two.

It seems to me that the *conflicts* on which this earliest symptomatology is based are not the later internal ones, but are clashes which arise between the child's wish to pursue and satisfy his prephallic urges and the parental influences which go in the opposite direction, i.e., which attempt to prohibit or to inhibit the fulfillment of these same urges. Thus the child at this time is involved, above all, in conflicts with external authority, and the *dangers* by which his ego feels threatened are not attributable to fear of the superego, i.e., guilt, but to fear of the object world, i.e., either of punishment or of loss of love. An exception in this respect are the conflicts caused by the child's ambivalence toward the parents, i.e., the alternation of love and hate toward them, which is objected to internally as soon as the ego has developed sufficiently to take notice of the incompatibility of trends and to be intolerant toward them. But here, too, the anxieties which arise are not on moral grounds; they are due to fear of object loss.

It is an important further difference that the symptomatology of this early stage need not be interconnected and organized into syndromes, as it will be later, but that the various symptoms are isolated and exist independently of each other. Further, they are not the permanent structures of the later neuroses. They are transitory, subject to changes in environmental influence, to changes in object relations, and, above all, to the developmental alterations in the importance and dominance of the instinctual trends by which they are caused.

Nevertheless, conflicts with the external world also need to be solved, and their solution proceeds—as with later purely internal ones—by means of compromises.

In part, the child yields to pressure and withdraws from the free pursuit of early drive activity. For another part he saves for himself whatever amount of pleasure he can still extract from it, even in disguised and distorted form, and for this all the defense mechanisms come into action which are at the disposal of the ego at this early time: denial, repression, displacement, projection, identification with the aggressor, etc.

Altogether, we may say that symptom (i.e., compromise) formation in the prephallic phase is a prestage of the infantile neurosis. It represents the first attempts of the maturing ego to come to terms with instinctual frustration.[4]

The Phallic-Oedipal Stage and the Infantile Neuroses

There is considerable variation in the chronological age at

[4]See in this and many other respects H. Nagera (1966).

which the stage of phallic sexuality is reached. We usually place it around the age of three, though it is equally normal for it to happen somewhat earlier or later. In any case, the main features of the individual child's *personality* have been laid down by then and what we expect further in this respect are modifications and rearrangements of basic attitudes rather than additions to them. Drastic changes appear in the area of *object relationship*. The child's attitudes to the important people in his environment are no longer governed by primitive clinging, clamoring for immediate need and wish fulfillment, violent swings between love and hate, one-sided torturing and controlling. There appears regard for the object and a first give-and-take in the relationship. Even though at the beginning of this phase, the parents may merely be the targets for the child's exhibitionistic and scoptophilic wishes, this changes presently to the semiadult forms of selective love for a partner in the triangular oedipal setting, i.e., a jealous, possessive passion accompanied by death wishes for the parental rival. It is these trends which, after subsiding, contribute to the child's mental apparatus the internalizations, identifications, and introjections which strengthen, confirm, and render independent whatever prestructures and forerunners of the superego had been established at the earlier times.

It is these advances in the ego and superego sphere which impose a different shape on the child's psychopathology. Disapproval by the object world now loses its role as a direct pathogenic agent and pathology becomes at the same time more complex, more intricate, and wholly based on the workings of the mental apparatus. When the child meets frustration of phallic wishes or threats to the phallic organ, he acts like the adult does in comparable situations: he drops his age-adequate concerns and revives the fixations to anality or orality, which then arouse internal disapproval, i.e., guilt. Again, compromise formations have to be found to relieve the tension, but this time the turmoil is an internal one, is removed from environmental influence, impervious to environmental changes, and, in its severer forms, may inhibit, distort, or block further growth instead of being "outgrown" due to progressive development.

Further, the true infantile neurosis which the child has acquired now is no longer the ego's answer to the frustration of single instinctual trends. Rather, it is an elaborate attempt to deal with a massive and complex upheaval caused by the clashes between opposing drive derivatives; between conflicting, exciting, pleasurable, and painful affects and mutually exclusive attitudes toward objects. Although the precipitating events belong to the area of the oedipus and castration complexes, the whole neurotic involvement is contributed to by the residues of past stages, from infancy onward, and quite especially by the libidinal fixations which have left their mark on the individual during his development.

Insight into these complex interactions between past and present, background and actuality, instinctual trends and ego functioning, conflicting id tendencies and identifications, etc., is revealed to us in every analysis of an infantile neurosis.

Child analysts hold a multiple view of the infantile neurosis. On the one hand, we regard it as belonging to the realm of psychopathology and realize that in its severer forms it can be crippling, as it has been, actually, in the case of the Wolf Man. On the other hand, we also know that it has its regular place in the childhood of many individuals whose future adaptation to life is successful, and that the conflicts underlying it are the normal ones, as they were with Little Hans. There is even more to it than this if we look at it from the developmental point of view. The infantile neurosis represents doubtless positive evidence of personality growth, a progression from primitive to more sophisticated reaction patterns. We can take it as a sign that the child's capacity for object relationship is intact; that his identifications and internalizations have been effective enough to complete the inner structuralization of his personality; that his ego is adequately defended against irruptions from the id and neither immature, nor deformed, nor distorted. Children who do not achieve these developmental advances, after all, develop not infantile neuroses but clinical states on the border to psychosis, or mental deficiency, or present pictures of the disjointed neurotic symptom formation which is characteristic for those who remain arrested on a preoedipal level of personality organization.

At the time when it was compared with the adult neuroses, the infantile neurosis was placed at the lower end of pathological events. Contrasting with this, in the picture given above, it now is placed at the culminating point of infantile psychopathology.

CONCLUSION

The present-day inquiries into the antecedents of the infantile neurosis have initiated an era in psychoanalysis which deserves to be called "The Widening Scope of Psychoanalytic Child Psychology, Normal and Abnormal." Among the many gains in knowledge which it has brought with it, one particular one seems to me to deserve especial emphasis: we have learned during these researches to distinguish between the reversible and the irreversible.

As analysts, we are proud to possess a therapeutic technique by means of which psychic processes can be undone, and even apparently stable psychic structures can be dissolved into their elements. The analytic dissection of identifications, the undoing of repressions, the repetition of past emotional experience, the general lifting of unconscious psychic content to consciousness, are powerful weapons in the therapeutic battle against the patient's inadequate compromises with external and internal forces which underlie his neurotic symptomatology. What analysis tries to reverse here, and usually succeeds in reversing, are the immature ego's misguided decisions which were made under the pressure of danger and anxiety. These are remade under new conditions and in the safer atmosphere of the therapeutic setting. As Freud (1909a) described for the case of Little Hans: "Analysis replaces the process of repression, which is an automatic and excessive one, by a temperate and purposeful control on the part of the highest agencies of the mind" (p. 145). What is true of repression has been proved equally true with regard to the other defense mechanisms amd defensive maneuvers of the ego. Identifications can be undone; regressions reversed; projected psychic content reaccepted as the individual's own; displacements can be set right; reaction formations can be toned down, while the instinctual trends held down by them are recognized and receive some access to the surface.

Unfortunately, this removal of damage done applies only to the ego's operations in the areas of external and internal conflict. It does not apply equally to the conditions under which the ego has developed or to the earliest mother-infant interactions by which the personality is shaped. Areas in body and mind, once made vulnerable, retain their vulnerability as a latent potentiality, even if their manifest involvement in pathology is checked by analysis. Fixation points retain their cathexis, even where regression to them is reversed. Basic personal characteristics such as temperament, or frustration tolerance, or the potential for object love, and the sublimation potential remain almost untouched, even though the affects engendered during the early mother-infant interchange may find an outlet in the analytic transference.

In short, there is no undoing of the past itself, even if—as many analysts claim—it can be repeated almost unchanged within the analytic situation. It has exerted its influence on development and left permanent traces. What analysis can do is to assist the patient's ego to come to new terms with these residues.

Patients entering analysis, or parents bringing a child for analytic treatment, often express the fear that analytic intervention will remove or destroy the individual characteristics of the personality. Actually, it has no power to do so. If acquired early enough, they are almost as firmly entrenched in the psychic constitution as are the individual's inborn givens.

3

Diagnosis and Assessment of Childhood Disturbances

(1974 [1954])

When Dr. Waelder suggested the topic of the application of psychoanalytic knowledge acquired in the analytic treatment of children to the wider problems of childhood disturbances seen in the child guidance clinic, I was glad to agree. I have been in analytic work with children and their

This paper is based on the first Freud Memorial Lecture held in Philadelphia in 1954. It remained unpublished until, in 1974, the author delivered the twentieth Freud Memorial Lecture (see chap. 4), when both lectures appeared in the same issue of the *Journal of the Philadelphia Association of Psychoanalysis,* 1:55–68, 1974. German translation: Diagnose und Bewertung von Störungen in der Kindheit. *Die Schriften der Anna Freud,* Volume 10. Munich: Kindler Verlag, 1980.

The author has frequently dealt with the topic of this paper; see, for example, Volume 5, chaps. 3, 17, 21, 22, 27; Volume 6, chaps. 3, 4, 5; Volume 7, chap. 10.

parents for many years and have had the good fortune to become the organizer of an analytic child guidance clinic. On the other side of the Atlantic real psychoanalytic child guidance clinics are still rare, though the application of psychoanalytic principles and knowledge to child guidance work is fairly frequent. The difference, as I see it, between the usual, analytically oriented child guidance clinic and what I would call an analytic clinic is that we are not content with treating the severe disturbances of childhood with methods which were designed for much milder disturbances.

The analyst entering upon this kind of work is in some respects in a more favorable position than the analytically oriented psychiatrist, and in other respects he finds himself at a disadvantage. Certainly, where deep treatment is concerned, the analyst is better off. Equally certainly, it seems to me, the analyst is in a more difficult position where diagnosis and assessment of disturbances are concerned. We are confronted by the necessity to make up our minds quickly—usually after a few interviews, sometimes after a short period of observation—and assess the nature of the child's disturbance and select the appropriate method of treatment. As analysts, we are used to taking a long time to acquire material from our patients, and we base our assessment of disturbances on that material. Having decided to analyze a child, we gradually gain access to his fantasy life; we examine his relations to the various members of his family; we follow the disturbance to its roots. We work in that way sometimes for years, and when we are ready to hand the child back to his parents, our diagnosis of the disturbance is ready, though by that time the child is much improved or cured.

But in a child guidance clinic, it is necessary to arrive at a diagnosis more quickly because the latter will determine our choice of treatment: whether to give guidance only to the mother, or to take the child into daily or weekly treatment; or perhaps to change the child's school life; or in extreme cases to separate the child from parents and siblings. All these weighty decisions have to be arrived at rather quickly, and they must be made at a time when the analyst really does not yet have sufficient data to make up his mind.

It seemed to me worthwhile therefore to describe the considerations we take into account in arriving at diagnoses at the Hampstead Clinic. The first consideration is the age of the child. There is a great difference between the diagnosis of disturbances in very young chilidren under five and that of latency children, that is, children between five and twelve to thirteen years of age.

DIAGNOSIS OF THE SCHOOLCHILD

Isolation of Symptoms

One would expect that the diagnosis of mental disturbances in latency and preadolescent children does not really differ very much from that of adults. As everybody who has been in touch with psychiatry knows, diagnosis in adult cases is arrived at rather quickly and easily. I still remember the time when I at the very beginning of my work was a guest student at the psychiatric clinic in Vienna where I used to listen to the young interns as they quickly went through the case sheets of patients who had arrived the evening before. They read only a few sentences in each; for instance, a patient complained that the neighbors were talking about her—paranoia, obviously. Or a patient complained that she was really not the least good to her family— well, a melancholia. I thought that was simply marvelous, and I looked forward to the time when I, though not a psychiatrist myself, would acquire sufficient knowledge to do that in my work with children.

We know of course why we can arrive—all of us—with such ease at the diagnosis of the typical disturbances of the adult. When we find a specific symptom, we have the right to expect that it is part of a specific syndrome, and it is very rare that our expectation in this respect is not fulfilled. This is the first difference in diagnosis and assessment between adults and children because in the case of childhood disturbances a specific symptom is definitely not indicative of a specific neurosis or whole syndrome. Here are some examples from my own experience:

One of the cases described to me recently by a mother was that of a little girl who could not go to sleep except when her slippers were placed exactly side by side in front of her bed. This is part of the so-called bedtime ritual, which one would be tempted to ascribe to an obsessional neurosis. But this diagnosis would be wrong. This little girl was in fact completely disorganized, restless, with uncontrolled motility; she had disturbances in every area of her life, but no other obsessional symptom.

I once treated a hysterical boy who suffered from a definite compulsion to count, a symptom that again belongs in the context of an obsessional neurosis, but he had this compulsion in the midst of phobic and hysterical disturbances.

I remember another latency boy whose main disturbance was an obsessional neurosis, but who had a whole host of psychosomatic and hysterical symptoms.

This means that in children symptoms are isolated, with symptoms of one kind appearing in the middle of neurotic disturbances of another kind. It is not always easy for the interviewer to assess the significance of such symptoms. He must ask himself whether a particular symptom is indicative of an obsessional neurosis in the making, where anxiety and hysterical symptoms still persist from earlier times, or whether he is really dealing with a hysterical disturbance that is obscured by the fact that in the anal-sadistic stage the child has acquired one or two of the symptoms which are characteristic of this stage. It seems to me that the isolation of symptoms, this mixture of disturbances, is well worth more attention. It definitely accounts for many of our difficulties in diagnosing.

Surface Appearance and Origin of Symptoms

There is another difficulty. Symptoms as they appear in the child and are revealed in the diagnostic interview rarely give the psychiatrist or analyst any clues to the underlying disturbance. There is the fact that two completely contrasting symptoms may be due to the same inner disturbance, or, the other way around, symptoms that on the surface appear to be very similar may owe their origin to very different causes. Here are some examples:

We find delinquent children with identical symptoms,

such as stealing, in whom the disturbance is due to a lack of ego and superego development, or the absence of an active father figure in their early life. This means there is a moral defect in the building up of their personalities due to environmental defects, specifically the absence of the proper educational influences. However, we also find the identical disturbance with a history of a completely contrasting nature: a father figure too present, his influence too emphatic, the identification with him and the resulting superego too strict, so that the child then is in full revolt against this pressure on him from both outside and inside. This means that the same delinquent symptoms may be due either to amorality or to supermorality.

Or consider a symptom like bed wetting, which in Europe is very prevalent in child guidance clinics. The symptom itself does not give us the slightest clue to its origin. It may be due to the parent's having neglected to train the child. Or the child may have been properly toilet trained and lost bladder control after a traumatic experience of separation from his mother, and will regain it quickly when the worst shock of the traumatic separation has passed. But it may also be the expression of a complicated internal conflict, e.g., a struggle between masculinity and femininity. In this case, no change in the environmental circumstances, no change in the educational handling of the child will make the slightest difference.

We are especially led astray by cases of aggressive boys in the latency period, boys who are so aggressive, so masculine that they become a menace to their school community and are extremely difficult for the family to cope with. The mere observation from outside, or the mere report given about their behavior, does not tell us whether in these children this is a direct expression of an excessive aggressive masculinity or exactly the opposite, whether these are passive-feminine boys who are so afraid of their feminine tendencies that they overemphasize their aggressive masculinity to reassure themselves that they really are boys.

Recently a little boy was brought to our clinic about whom the neighborhood complained because he exhibited his male organ actively to all the little girls in the neighborhood. Opinions in the staff conference were quite divided. Some felt that this was age-appropriate behavior; perhaps a bit too much, or the neighborhood would not complain. They maintained that he was just an active little boy who had not been much restrained; that there was very little wrong with him; advice to the mother about his handling probably was all that was required. Others took exactly the opposite view. It turned out that this little boy had gone through several operations in his life; something had been wrong with his finger which had to be set right. At another time his big toenail had to be operated on. And, worst of all, he developed a lump under the foreskin of his penis which had to be removed in the hospital. The striking thing was that after the child came home, he demanded insistently from the mother that this lump should be given back to him. These data give a completely different aspect to the case. Evidently, he was in a state of intense anxiety that he had been damaged genitally by the operation and he exhibited really, not to the little girls, but to himself, to reassure himself. Again no amount of educational handling would cure a case of this kind. The only thing that can help him is making the anxiety which enforces his behavior conscious and removing it by analytic treatment.

Inaccessibility of Material in Diagnostic Interviews

How can we be sure that we will always arrive at the right distinction? On what should we base our diagnosis if diagnosis by way of symptom is so unreliable at this stage of life? The next thing we base our hopes on is the diagnostic interview. Analysts have quite a reputation with the lay public of being very good at diagnostic interviews. Some people even believe that an analyst need only look at a complete stranger to know everything about him. Nothing could be further from the truth. No analyst can make these snap decisions about what goes on inside another person, and no analyst should. He waits until the material rises to the surface and convinces him of the state that reigns inside. But for the diagnostic interview, that is most unfortunate, because whoever has dealt with schoolchildren in such situations knows very well that children betray hardly anything to the interviewing psychiatrist. They hide their feelings. Very often they are resentful about having been brought to the clinic; they are suspicious, and quite rightly; the more normal they are, the less they like strangers prying into the intimacies of their life.

It is so rare that we get deeper unconscious material in a diagnostic interview that I went through all our case files to select the very few cases in which this occurred. These were latency children who did betray something about the center of their inner disturbances in the diagnostic interview.

There was a boy of ten who in the first interview with me was most restless in his behavior. He fidgeted, he sat and stood up, and sat down again; there was nothing on my desk that he did not touch. He did not say a thing. I asked him about the semidelinquent symptoms for which he had been sent. I tried to ask him about his family; his parents had been divorced under rather unhappy circumstances. But all he said was very politely, "I would not like to give you wrong impressions." In his carefulness not to give me wrong impressions, he gave me no impressions at all, until by chance he saw on my desk a tape measure that can be wound up, and began to play with it. He pulled it out and snapped it back, restlessly repeating this many times over; he did not stop until it broke. When it broke, his whole behavior changed. He was a different boy. He became most cooperative, nearly cringing in his appeal to me, and asked me over and over again whether I could mend it again. I think this particular boy revealed the reason for his disturbance in that particular interview. His worries evidently centered on masturbation. His fears were that he would damage himself. The change in his behavior from distrust, suspicion, occasional overbearingness to passive appeal occurred whenever he feared he had damaged himself by his masturbatory activity. But such cases are rare—so rare, in fact, that at the Hampstead Clinic we are now trying to compare diagnostic interviews with what we learned from the subsequent analyses.

There was another interesting case, a boy of twelve and a half. He was of Greek extraction, a little stranger in London who had the unlucky experience to have the house he lived in with his parents burgled in the night. He and his sister were awakened by the disturbance. They stood at the window and saw the thieves make off with their possessions.

From that moment on the boy developed a state of intense anxiety and could not be induced to leave the room alone, to go out into the street alone without his mother, or to go to school. The question was why a comparatively harmless experience of this kind should have such a traumatic influence on him. In the diagnostic interview with the psychiatrist in charge, he described the incident most vividly: he had seen a man with a white bundle climb over the fence, and he said he knew very well what was hidden under the bundle, a long, sharp knife; he was very much afraid for his sister because he had read in the paper that there are men who stick sharp knives into little girls. (Actually there had been reports in the London papers of two cases of rape where little girls had been killed.) In his description of the incident he was safe—all the threats had been toward his little sister. Then he went on talking about other things that he had read in the papers. There had been mail-van robberies and bags of valuable mail had been stolen from these vans. He said that made him very anxious, "I really don't know why, because after all I am not a mail van." Then he said, "Sometimes my uncle gives me a letter to take to my father and then I really am a mail van." I think in that way he had guided us straight to the reason why the apparently small burglary had acquired such immense significance for him. It had aroused his passive fantasy in which he saw himself as a woman raped, attacked, and killed by a man—just as by carrying the mail, he was turned into a van that then became the victim of attack.

Another case is that of a boy who in the bombing of London had been wounded together with his mother. Although she never recovered physically, they both had overcome the shock, except that he subsequently acquired a severe anxiety state. This particular boy revealed in the diagnostic interview that he thought that every airplane that now came over London in peacetime really contained. in it his father, who had divorced his mother, and that at any moment his father might throw bombs from the airplane. This again reveals very clearly that this boy suffered from a passive attitude toward his father and expected an attack from him.

A simpler story, perhaps, is that of a little girl who had ceased to function in school and at home. Her parents were divorced and she lived with her grandparents. She was clearly torn by the circumstances in her life, which were really very sad, but in the diagnostic interview she told the psychiatrist that she knew where her disturbance came from. Her grandparents, she said, insist on her having breakfast at home before going to school; then when she goes to school, she is supposed to have breakfast at school. She has lunch at school, and when she comes home she is supposed to have lunch once more with her grandmother. She said, "No stomach can have two breakfasts and two lunches of two different kinds." Actually this child's loyalties were divided between father and mother and the grandparents on either side.

Psychological Tests As Diagnostic Aids

If diagnostic interviews in the latency period were always as revealing as those cited, we would have no trouble. But I would like to stress once more that usually the opposite is the case. I think it is this particular state of affairs which has led to the wide use of tests in child guidance clinics. Psychological tests are meant to be a shortcut to reveal what the child hides, willingly or unwillingly, and what the psychiatrist is unable to see. Actually, I find that in conjunction with other investigations the various intelligence tests are useful, especially when there is a wide divergence between the child's behavior in school and the test result. A child with a high IQ who appears to be stupid in school should certainly be further investigated. The projective tests also may give us clues, but this matter is much too large to discuss here; besides, I am no expert in testing.

Links between Surface Behavior and Underlying Conflict

I would rather turn to another aid in diagnosis and assessment which seems to me useful and is one that increases with our experience and our skill. I believe that as analysts we have made insufficient use of observation of behavior. Behavior is, after all, the *surface* expression of the child's inner life. While behavior can be misleading and be indicative of many hidden causes, there nevertheless exist certain types or patterns of childhood behavior which are invariably coupled with certain underlying causes and which therefore permit us to draw direct conclusions about the child's central unconscious conflict.

Analysts are familiar with such links from their study of character types, e.g., the anal character of the child. These children show certain typical traits that belong together: orderliness, tidiness, strong concern with the truth, a very clean outer appearance, a good sense of time, proper handling of money, and a trait not quite so pleasing to parents, a great slowing up in functioning and a difficulty in making up their minds. If one wants to know whether these character traits can be found in a child, it is useful to ask the mother how long the child takes to get dressed in the morning; if we hear half an hour or an hour or more, it is worthwhile to find out whether any other of the patterns of behavior mentioned are present as well. The difficulty in making up their minds is frequently reflected in their continually asking mother to decide for them. Analytic work with adult patients and with children has taught us that whenever we find these forms of behavior, the underlying conflict is centered in the anal-sadistic phase of development. We then also know that such a child has special trouble in fighting; that his wish for aggressive action and his normal desire for dirtiness have undergone too much repression.

In the course of time, our ability to assess pure behavior as shown in character traits has increased. There are certain patterns of behavior shown by children in their school life. For example, a teacher will be concerned about the child who is very shy, too shy to speak. These are the children who have to be asked continually to perform some task in front of others, to take part in dramatics or recitation, to work where others can observe them. We now know that these children's conflict is centered around their original exhibitionism. Their wish to expose their bodies, their faculties, their achievements, their goodness or their badness is so great they must defend themselves against it by developing these reaction formations. That is an easy diagnosis. When these children are not only shy, but unable to compete, they push themselves into the background and we know they struggle not only against their exhibitionism, but also against their aggressive wishes to outdo everybody else. We can diagnose another type of behavior. Children who compulsively play the fool and can never stop making everybody laugh were originally highly ambitious; their leading wish is to be a great hero, to dominate all the others, to perform enormous feats. Their central problem is rooted in the phallic stage. When these phallic wishes have broken down, one remains: they are still the center of attention, but they are now laughed at instead of admired. Whenever we hear of such behavior, we can infer what is the matter with that child.

We also have learned what to do with children who complain that everybody is against them, who describe teachers and classmates alike as being down on them, hurting their feelings, not wanting them around, discriminating against them. We do not believe that such a child will be helped by going to another school. We will diagnose that this child suffers from passive fantasies which are fulfilled in this apparently offending behavior of the people in his environment.

Similarly, we know what it means when children are concerned for the health of their parents and siblings; and I think that today we no longer need a child guidance clinic to diagnose why a little boy of seven leaves his bed in the early morning and listens at the door where his little brother sleeps, fearful that he might not breathe, that he might have died in the night.

Boredom is another type of behavior which we can recognize. We know from analytic treatment of children that boredom invariably means that the child has repressed a very important wish to do something, to give way to some important impulse. Very often it is the wish to masturbate. Sometimes it is the wish to follow an important libidinal fantasy which is forbidden for inner reasons. If the child succeeds in suppressing or repressing the desired activity, nothing else seems of any interest to him. This means he will then perform the actions, but the zest has gone out of them. It will return only if in treatment we have restored at least the originally desired activity to consciousness.

There is a further indication. Some children have a flat taste in their mouths whenever they feel bored. Everything then tastes dull. This happens when the repressed fantasy is an oral fantasy and has something to do with mouth pleasure, with eating, with oral connections with the love object. The flat taste corresponds to the bored feeling in the child's mind.

Another area where we get many clues is the observation of children's behavior during a bodily illness. When a teacher in the Clinic describes to us how the child behaves when he has cut his knee and is bleeding, or how he behaves when he has a high temperature, the various types of behavior revealed will give us good indications about the inner conflicts of the child. I shall select one example; I spoke before of the difficulty of separating out the violently aggressive boys who are aggressive only because they are afraid of their own passivity. This becomes easy when one hears about their behavior during bodily illness. Consider two manly, strong-looking, aggressive boys. They both fall ill or they both bleed from a little wound. The really active boy, the manly boy, will not mind at all. He will laugh about it; he will behave bravely and courageously — after all, what is a little cut? But the other one will be pricked like a balloon. His aggression, his manliness will disappear altogether, and he will be full of anxiety because the fear of damage, of femininity, of passivity which until then he has warded off successfully with the help of masculine behavior will overwhelm him. There are many more indications of this kind.

I have made so much of this point because I hope that as we become more knowledgeable, we will be able to make better diagnoses from behavior patterns in the future. I hope that every year analytic work with children will teach us to understand at least one new pattern of behavior, or one new character trait. In the end we will be able to read off many more behaviors and translate them into inner disturbances, and then we will not need to ask the child so many questions in the diagnostic interview. But perhaps that is too optimistic.

DIAGNOSIS OF THE YOUNG CHILD

Accessibility of Material

Just as everything is hidden behind defenses in the latency child, so everything is open to view in the young child, particularly in the diagnostic interview. What is the exception with the schoolchild is the rule with the little one. Every child is ready to play out his conflicts before the eyes of the psychiatrist either with the help of toys or without toys merely by his behavior. The little boy full of castration fear will go all around the room to look for broken switches; he will find all sorts of things that are damaged, which will further heighten his anxiety.

I will never forget watching a boy of four who came from a very unhappy family in which there were constant fights. He played with toy furniture that had been offered to him. It was furniture for the various rooms of a house. Most children place it in the appropriate rooms. What he did instead was to make pieces of furniture fight with each other. The tables began to fight with the chairs, and the wardrobes with the tables. There was the greatest upheaval in the rooms of the little dollhouse and it all ended up with the kitchen sink attacking the stove. And this really is the rule: children show their concerns as openly as that.

Assessment of Childhood Symptomatology

But in spite of this easy accessibility of conflicts in diagnostic interviews, the proper assessment of the real infantile disturbances is difficult. Perhaps in times past mothers brought their children only when they were suffering from a distinct neurosis; now they bring them with disturbances of all kinds. Have we, perhaps, in the guidance clinic encouraged the mother not to handle disturbances on her own? Should we encourage her to be concerned about every problem and seek advice? On the other hand, we want mothers to seek advice and to receive it. What we actually see are disturbances of every function in the child's life. There are the disturbances of sleep; the child either wakes up in the middle of the night or is unable to go to sleep. We see every conceivable disturbance of eating: eating too much, eating too little, the various food fads, the various conditions that the child makes for eating. There are difficulties of achieving bowel and bladder control and the year-long fight that mothers have over it with the child. There are the mothers who complain about their children's restlessness and overactivity with which they cannot cope. These are disturbances in the control of motility. There is listlessness, which means that the mother cannot interest the child in the environment and induce him to function as he should. There are the children who are destructive and attack everything in their environment. There are, perhaps worst of all, the children who are self-destructive, who are accident-prone, who hurt themselves continually. There are those who concentrate on only one toy and cannot be separated from it. And there are others who simply go from toy to toy throwing them aside one after the other.

Thus, we see disturbances in all functions; but how should we classify them? Are disturbances of this kind neuroses? Or do we call them neuroses only when they have reached a certain severity, a state of inner conflict? Should our decision be determined by the amount of disturbance caused in the environment? Or should it be determined by the amount of suffering which the disturbance causes the child?

It seems to me that at present the mass of infantile disturbances is a wide open field, in which a great many people are trying to make order. What people have done so far, in all countries really, is to separate off the most severe disturbances; the children who are near psychotic, who are wholly divorced from the environment, who are unable to make the proper link with their mothers or with other children, who do not learn to talk, who show defects in their intelligence. These are the children who in some places are called autistic and, in others, schizophrenic.

If we separate off this unhappy group, we are left with those disturbances which show some similarity with the neurotic disturbances of later times. We have children who develop phobic reactions of a certain kind with fears concentrated on one object or one process. It might be fear of noise, or a fear of an animal. Recently and interestingly the bogey man of former years has been replaced by the vacuum cleaner or by some other electric appliance in the house. These are phobic children and whatever they choose symbolizes for them the main danger. It was difficult to classify these well-known and almost ubiquitous phobic reactions.

There are the children who at an early age show certain obsessions, most commonly the bedtime ceremonials. But as mentioned before, such rituals may pass when toilet training is fully completed. Of special interest at bedtime is the young child's use of animals either as objects of fear or as objects of admiration, protection, and reassurance. Often animals serve both functions at the same time. I remember a little boy who could not go to sleep without a certain dog, a real dog, perhaps because the dog was to protect him against the burglars who would come in. But when he was safely in bed with his dog, he was afraid the dog would bite him and then he could not go to sleep. This shows two meanings of the same animal in quick succession. Such manifestations are indicative of the child's ambivalence conflicts.

Then there are all the psychosomatic symptoms which

one can sort out at that time. But I have the feeling that we do not get very far with our diagnostic attempts as long as we merely enumerate symptoms or list items that have some passing similarity to an adult neurosis. Such lists of symptoms give us no clue to the severity of the disturbance in the child. I think assessment should follow different principles altogether, and I would recommend three main points of view. If we learn to use not one but all three, we can feel fairly safe. If we use only one, we usually go wrong in our assessment.

Three Principles of Assessment

The first point of view, or the first aspect, would be to look at the child's disturbance from the point of view of progression or retardation of normal development, slowing up or complete arrest of development, and development backward — regression. When we hear a mother's complaints, we would have to assess in our mind where this child stands compared with normal development, on the one hand of his drives, on the other hand of his ego. This presupposes some knowledge of the sequence of the libidinal phases in the first years of life, the oral, anal, and phallic; and on the other hand, knowledge of the development of the various ego functions, such as memory, the distinction between inside and outside, the integration of sensations and perceptions, the control of motility. We should know roughly where the child should stand according to his age and then assess what has happened. Has he stopped developing? Is he too slow? Has he gone too fast? Or has he gone backward? In the more severe disturbances we always find that the child instead of going forward in his development has gone backward. I think we might even adopt the point of view that so long as development is progressive and not regressive, treatment is not really necessary; we may trust to time. When development is either at a standstill or regressive, the child should receive help.

The second aspect would be to look how the child behaves so far as his relationship to the love objects in the environment is concerned. In recent years we have learned much about precisely this point, especially about the various phases of the child's attachment to his mother. His closeness to her may be too close or not enough; there is a time when the child should separate himself from the mother and be able to go further with his affections. We consider his ability to transfer libido from the first love object to the father, to the siblings, his ability to separate from people and to find them again. If we have sound knowledge of the child's object relationships as they are normally, and we understand the wide range of normality, we can assess the disturbance. But we are wrong if we assess a child's disturbance exclusively in terms of object relationships, or exclusively in terms of development. We must also consider the third point of view.

A child may be in conflict with the mother or with the environment. He wants one thing, or his drives impel him toward one thing, and the environment interferes. A conflict arises, and so does anxiety in the child. Such external conflicts can be altered decisively when the environment or the behavior of the environment alters. Therefore we take them less seriously. But conflicts of this kind can also become internalized when the child identifies with the wishes of the environment. Then the conflict goes on inside between drive and defense. No alteration in the behavior of the environment will now alter the disturbance of the child. There are even more serious conflicts, e.g., battles between two drives in the child, his masculinity and femininity, his love and his hate, his wish to retain his love objects or to attack them. These, of course, have nothing to do with the environment. They are truly internal conflicts.

I will give an example to illustrate that the division of conflicts into external, internalized, and truly internal has direct practical implications. Let us consider eating disturbances. There are children who do not eat because they fight their mothers. This is an external conflict. Remove the child from the mother, let him eat in nursery school or in the hospital, that is, in the absence of the mother, and the disturbance will disappear. But there are children who do not eat because they believe what they eat is alive and they do not want to kill it. We see this very often when we give children something to eat that has the shape of an animal. There are children who do not eat because they think what they have before them is anal matter and they have taught themselves or have been taught by the environment not to touch it. This may be the cause of many food fads. These conflicts are already internalized. There are, though fortunately somewhat later in life, children who do not eat primarily because of self-destructive drives, because they do not want to live. There the wish to live and the wish to destroy themselves work against each other.

I think you will agree that the disturbances of these three different types need completely different types of treatment. It would be useless to advise the mother when the child has an internal conflict. On the other hand, it also would make no sense to analyze the child if his conflict is still an external one and can be altered by advising the mother. This means to me that correct assessment in the child guidance clinic is necessary is order to recommend the right kind of treatment. All the knowledge that we can collect to make assessment easier and more complete is, of course, necessary and welcome.

4

A Psychoanalytic View of Developmental Psychopathology

(1974 [1973])

I am grateful to Dr. Ecker for his gracious introduction as well as to Governor Shapp for the official honor conferred on me by his welcoming letter. I wish to thank the inaugurators of this annual event in memory of my father and those members of the audience who regularly take part in it.

As you have heard from Dr. Ecker, this is the twentieth lecture in the series of Freud Memorial Lectures, of which I have given the first in 1954. Nineteen years is a long time

The twentieth Freud Memorial Lecture, Philadelphia, 1973. First published in the *Journal of the Philadelphia Association for Psychoanalysis,* 1:7–17, 1974. Italian translation: Un'opinione psicoanalitica sulla psicopatologia evolutiva. *Opere,* 3:1137–1152. Turin: Paolo Boringhieri, 1979. German translation: Entwicklungs-Psychopathologie aus psychoanalytischer Sicht. *Die Schriften der Anna Freud,* Volume 10. Munich: Kindler Verlag, 1980.

measured in terms of personal life or the life of a psycho-analytic society. It is an astonishingly short period when applied to the study of a specific subject. Progress in psychoanalytic inquiries especially is of necessity slow since many individual cases need to be examined and analyzed before new knowledge emerges and allows for general application. It is all the slower if the subjects under investigation are not adults but children whose alliance with the analyst's work is frequently minimal. I cite this fact to explain why title and content of my paper tonight are not significantly different from the one offered here before, i.e., why I and my co-workers in the Hampstead Clinic are still concerned predominantly with the assessment of infantile psychopathology.

COMPARISON BETWEEN PAST AND PRESENT

I begin by listing for myself and the audience some of the happenings during the intervening years. There is one respect where matters have remained unchanged. We were asked then why as child analysts we were so concerned with the problem of diagnosis before treatment, that is, with a topic considered of little importance by the analysts of adults and, moreover, one not even included in the curriculum of our psychoanalytic institutes. Our answer is now, as it was then, that the child analysts' responsibility when deciding for or against therapy is much greater than the corresponding one in the case of adults. The adult sufferer from a neurosis or allied disorder does not present himself for analysis before he has convinced himself that his disturbance is severe enough to justify this course;

above all, that without therapeutic help it would remain permanent. Also, usually, he has tried all manners of external measures before deciding on internal interference. This is different with children. Even with increasing experience of assessing their psychopathology, we always remain in doubt how far their symptoms remain influenceable by external management or how far they are open to spontaneous cure via developmental alterations, i.e., how far they are transitory. Thus, we are faced by the dilemma whether, by suggesting treatment, we are perhaps involving child and parents in much discomfort, trouble, time, and expense which might be unnecessary; or whether, by refusing it, we are perhaps condemning the child to a lifetime of suffering and failure.

Sufficient as this reason for early assessment may be by itself, a further motive for pursuance of the problem has appeared in recent years. We now believe that errors in the understanding of childhood abnormality are widespread and also that they exert an impact on our view of adult psychopathology. Improvement of insight into the early processes may rectify the situation, as will be shown later.

To continue with the comparison of past and present. What has, quite obviously, remained unchanged are the *sources of information* about the children who are presented to us at the Clinic. As before, we have to take account of what we are told by the *parents,* however biased and unreliable their descriptions are in many cases. We still note with regret that young children have little or no *insight* into their own mental state and tend to obscure rather than reveal their need for therapeutic help. We rely on *diagnostic interviews,* knowing full well that the picture emerging from them is open to distortion by the parents' anxiety imparted to the child and by the child's own distrust and fear of the stranger's intervention. We gather samples of *behavior* at home and in school and of the child's general functioning or malfunctioning. A list of *symptoms* is provided for us in the form of parental complaints. As before, we use a variety of intelligence and projective tests to furnish circumscribed knowledge about different aspects of the child's personality.

Nevertheless, it is only the quality and extent of information at our disposal which have remained the same. What has progressed significantly is the use to which we are able to put it.

We have learned more than we did in the past about the *translation of behavior* patterns into their unconscious motivations. We have made ourselves increasingly *independent of the psychiatric categories* used for diagnosing the mental disorders of adult patients, and have established our own series of diagnostic entities, based on *developmental* considerations. We have trained ourselves to compose comprehensive character images of our children, so-called *Profiles,* in which the diagnostician's thinking is directed away from purely symptomatic aspects and toward the genetic, dynamic, economic, and adaptive modalities of the child's personality. More important than all that is another advance: we have broken with the tradition according to which every mental difficulty is seen and explained by comparison with severe pathological patterns and, instead, try to see it against the background of the *norm,* expectable for the particular child's age, and to measure its distance from it. We have thus redirected the main bulk of our inquiries from interest in pathology toward a study of the norm.

A PSYCHOANALYTIC STUDY OF THE NORM

As analysts of adults, we have taken the path from inquiry into the pathological manifestations to a gradual understanding of the normal ones and of decreasing the alleged gap between them. As child analysts we may do better by taking the opposite road, i.e., by getting a firm grasp of the facts of normal development and by viewing the abnormal outcomes as more or less significant deviations from this course. Not that this recommendation is by any means a popular or generally accepted one. Not unlike their colleagues in the adult field, child analysts too feel the urge to widen the scope of their therapeutic efforts and to proceed from the more benign to the severest manifestations, i.e., from the infantile neuroses to the borderline, the autistic and psychotic states.

Moreover, those who manage to turn in the suggested direction, toward the norm, are faced by the disappointing realization that the existing analytic knowledge about normal child development is much more scant than they had estimated. There is, of course, a wealth of single facts unearthed from the beginnings of psychoanalysis up to the present day: the sequence of libidinal stages as the normal precursor of mature sexuality; the ubiquity of the oedipus and castration complexes; the legitimacy of narcissism as forerunner of and adjunct to object love; the developmental stages of the ego with its mechanisms, functions, and contents; the stages of the aggressive drive; the overriding general impact of the mother-infant relationship, etc.

Nevertheless, these acquisitions, as by-products of therapeutic analyses, are more or less isolated facts, not fully interrelated with each other. Also, they are global rather than circumstantial, spanning, as the libidinal phases do, for example, periods as long as a year or more. For these reasons, they do not really satisfy our need for a detailed, orderly picture of the growth of the child's integrated personality.

There are, though, two notable exceptions from this picture in the psychoanalytic literature. René Spitz (1965), in his study of the first year of life, does not content himself with tracing the infant-mother relationship on the one hand and ego growth on the other, but demonstrates step by step how every single advance in ego functioning and awareness is placed in the service of the infant's libidinal processes to alter and shape them, both libido and ego interacting at the same time with the responses of the mother. Margaret Mahler (1968), in her turn, when faced in her work with infants with the stage of biological unity between mother and child, subdivides what appears at first glance as an entity into a significant sequence of developmental phases: the symbiotic, the autistic, and the separation-individuation phases.

THE CONCEPT OF DEVELOPMENTAL LINES

The principles of interaction of agencies and subdivision of stages, applied by these two authors to infancy, can, I believe, with profit be carried further and used to shed light on the child's whole path from immaturity to maturity. I have attempted to do this by introducing the concept of Lines of Development. What these lines represent are ladders leading up to every one of the expected achievements of the child's personality, each step on them being the result of interaction between id, ego, and environment, the way leading upward in the course of normal, progressive growth, or downward whenever regression occurs.

I repeat here briefly what I described previously (1965) as examples of such lines.

On the line from *Biological Unity with the Mother to the Adolescent Revolt* against parental influence, we expect the normal child to negotiate a large number of libidinal and aggressive substations such as: the symbiotic, autistic, separation-individuation phases (Mahler); the part-object (Melanie Klein), need-fulfilling, anaclitic relationship; the stage of object constancy; anal-sadistic ambivalence; the triangular phallic-oedipal relationship; the latency extension of ties to peers, teachers, the community, and impersonal ideals; preadolescent regressions; adolescent struggle against infantile ties and search for objects outside the family.

What has to accompany these forward moves of the drives on the ego side are an increase of awareness and understanding of environmental happenings, expanding empathy with fellow beings, progress in identifications and internalizations, in secondary process thinking, in appreciation of cause and consequence, of the reality principle in general, of adaptation to community standards, etc.

What the environment is expected to contribute are the provision of appropriate human objects, their accepting, promoting, stimulating, and controlling attitudes toward the child.

On the line from *Being Nursed to Rational Eating,* the substations are: food equals mother; food symbolizes oral, anal, sadistic, impregnation, poisoning, and birth fantasies; the mother's handling of the feeding situation has a far-reaching influence on eating and appetite becoming gradually free from these irrational concomitants.

The advance from *Wetting and Soiling to Bowel and Bladder Control* shows most clearly its determination from three sides: on the instinctual side, the child has to pass beyond his urethral and anal interests; on the environmental side, training for cleanliness has to be handled gently and gradually to prevent breakdowns and regressions; the child's ego has to outgrow its original high valuation of the body products; the superego has to incorporate the adult's devaluation of them into its own structure.

The previously described lines toward *Body Management,* toward *Companionship with Peers,* and toward the capacity to *Work* are characterized similarly as the result of interaction between the id, the maturing ego, the rudimentary superego, and the stimulating, encouraging, and controlling influences of the environment. But the list given was by no means considered to be complete; rather, it was in fact meant as an invitation to the readers of the book to make their own additions to it. Since this challenge has so far not been taken up by any other author, I offer in what follows some supplementary prototypes, constructed on the basis of the same principle.

From Physical to Mental Pathways of Discharge

At the beginning of life, every excitation, whether physical or mental, takes its path through the body and is discharged via processes in the area of sleep, food intake, intestinal movement. Also, during the whole of the first year, while psychological life expands, the access between body and mind remains an easy one. Every upheaval in the bodily sphere causes mental distress, crying, etc., while every mental upset such as shock, frustration, anxiety causes physical upheaval. This truly psychosomatic period comes to an end as, with advancing age, more and more mental pathways open up for the child and the discharge of mental tension is allocated to them. In the second year the use of the mind for the purpose of tension discharge increases considerably until, approximately in the third year, due to the perfection of secondary process thinking and speech, the division becomes decisive, mental excitation from then onward being discharged mentally and bodily excitation physically.

There are, though, some important flaws as well as frequent regressions which affect the smooth advance on this vital line. I allude here to the familiar fact that not all mental content is accepted by the ego and allowed discharge via consciousness; i.e., that repressed libidinal fantasies and aggressive impulses find the way blocked to psychological expression and for this reason continue with, or regress to, physical discharge in the form of psychosomatic or hysterical manifestations.

From Animate to Inanimate Objects

To construct any developmental line in its entirety is an arduous task; and even where great attention is paid to detail, as for instance in the advance toward emotional independence (first line of the previous enumeration), complications and offshoots are easily neglected.

I turn here to Winnicott's (1953) concept of the "transitional object" as characterization of a stage when the infant, after concentrating his libidinal and aggressive impulses on the mother, accepts a toy, partly as an addition, partly as symbolic substitute for her. While the child's love-hate relationship to human beings develops further through the stages described above, there branches off here, it seems to me, a normal sideline which carries varying quantities of libido and aggression away from their targets in the human environment and attaches them otherwise. We realize that this move is greatly encouraged by the provision of appropriate toys, cuddly animals such as teddy bears and dolls. We also know that these subsitutes are gladly accepted by the child for two reasons: as libidinal objects, they are more under the child's possessive control than the living ones; as objects of aggression, they do not take offense or retaliate. Both qualities are shared to some degree by certain animals, especially placid dogs who are "good with children." What we do not know is why specific persons, from childhood onward, change what should normally be a sideline into the main channels for their libido and aggression. We are left with guesses as to the reasons for this deviation. Contributions to it from the environmental side may be lack of appropriate objects for emotional attachment and/or rejection of the child, and these may interact with a child's specially low tolerance for frustration and specially great need for impulse discharge in the anal-sadistic phase. In any case, the result could be two distortions visible in the developmental line. With respect to the libido, the steps would lead to a greater role played by animals in the individual's life; or, more frequently, to the overvaluation of material goods, their acquisition, collection, and possession. With respect to aggression, the line would lead from the child's maltreatment of his own toys to the torturing of defenseless animals and from there to massive destructiveness turned against inanimate objects.

From Irresponsibility to Guilt

This particular line traces the child's path from his original state of happy irresponsibility in moral matters to the experience of painful guilt feelings whenever the moral code has been infringed. It is our analytic understanding that this happens by way of identification with the controlling and prohibiting influences in the external world, an explanation which covers the total road toward the expected end result.

We are well aware of some of the substations through which the child passes on his way after the first open clashes between his primitive id impulses and the external barriers to their unhindered fulfillment. We are alerted to the compliance enforced on the infantile ego by the child's physical and emotional dependency on the object world, i.e., by his fear of losing the object, or the object's love, or of incurring punishment. We can follow the changed ego attitudes toward the id which are produced first by imitation of the objects and their demands, then by the identifications with and internalizations of them which structure the superego. What we tend to miss is an intermediate stage which owes its existence to the young child's unwillingness to submit to the painful experience of internal conflict, i.e., to acknowledge the simultaneous presence within the structure of his personality of impulsive wishes and their condemnation. Since the critical faculties of his superego already are, at this time, inescapable, he resorts to the defenses of denying awareness of his own wish and allocating it via externalization to another person, usually a child. This makes him critical and censorious of his peers, until he matures sufficiently to take the final step, that is, to admit that both wish and prohibition are his own and that there is reason to feel guilt.

As with all developmental lines, it is important for our view of the adult personality that any stage of the sequence, instead of being transitory, can become a point for permanent arrest, and that the progressive steps upward can also be taken in the downward direction regressively. Thus, individuals, due to arrest or regression on this particular line, may obey the moral code only when compelled by external authority; or when observed and supported by authority; or they may remain censorious of others, i.e., hypocritical, instead of being self-critical.

EARLY DEVELOPMENT SEEN FROM THE ASPECT OF DEVELOPMENTAL LINES

Taking the totality of developmental lines as described to date and as to be constructed in the future, we arrive at a new view of child development. We can imagine an ideal norm, according to which each such line proceeds unhindered and at an even pace and reaches its highest point at the age appropriate for it, in some instances before age five years, in others not before the end of childhood, i.e., in adolescence. With complete temporal balance and harmony between the various lines, the result could not fail to be a completely harmonious, well-balanced personality.

We know, of course, that such states of ideal normality do not exist except in our imagination and that what happens in reality is different. In fact, progress on any line is subject to influence from three sides: the variation in innate givens, which provide the raw material out of which id and ego are differentiated; the environmental conditions and influences, which only too often differ widely from what is appropriate and favorable for normal growth; the interactions between internal and external forces, which constitute the individual experience of each child. According to the impact of each of these, progress on any one line may be slow and obstructed, while being fast and unhindered on another. There may be slow forward movement on all lines, i.e., generally reduced but fairly balanced growth. There may be slight or grave temporal unbalance or, at worst, multiple failure on several of the most vital lines.

In any case, whatever happens in the individual picture, we are left with the impression that it is this variety of progress on the lines, i.e., developmental failures and successes, which can be held responsible for the innumerable variations in human characters and personalities.

TWO TYPES OF EARLY PSYCHOPATHOLOGY

We are, by now, alerted to the contributions made by what happens on the developmental lines to childhood psychopathology. What we have been most familiar with in the analytic literature so far are the abnormalities caused by the incidence of trauma, and of conflict between the internal agencies followed by anxiety, defense, and compromise formation. What have received much less attention[1] and are added here are the defects in the personality structure itself which are caused by the aformentioned developmental irregularities and failures. We can thus differentiate between two types of infantile psychopathology. The one based on conflict is responsible for the anxiety states and the phobic, hysterical, and obsessional manifestations, i.e., the infantile neuroses; the one based on developmental defects, for the psychosomatic symptomatology, the backwardness, the atypical and borderline states.

It would be convenient to take the point of view that success or failure on the developmental lines primarily shapes the personalities which secondarily become involved in internal conflict. But any statement of this kind would be a gross falsification once the infant ceases to be an undifferentiated, unstructured being. It would ignore the temporal relations between the two processes which occur simultaneously, not subsequent to each other. Progress on the lines is interfered with constantly by conflict, repression, and consequent regression, while the conflicts themselves and quite especially the methods available for their solution are wholly dependent on the shape and level of personal development which has been reached.

However different in origin the two types of psycho-

---

[1] Exceptions to be mentioned are Augusta Alpert and Peter Neubauer in the U.S., and Michael Balint in England, who has introduced the concept of "basic faults."

pathology are, in the clinical picture they are totally inter-
twined, a fact which accounts for their usually being
treated as one.

IMPLICATIONS

If, by the foregoing, I have encouraged colleagues to tackle
the difficult task of disentangling the two pathogenic processes from each other, I have done so because of its relevance for every analyst's diagnostic, technical, and theoretical concerns.

So far as the *assessment of cases* before, during, and
after therapy is in question, lack of distinction between developmental and conflictual pathology leads to errors
which are only too common at the present time: neurotic
symptoms in either children or adults are linked directly
with the earliest events in the infant's first year of life, an
assumption which, in my view, constitutes a serious shortcut. What actually happens at this early date, owing to the
interplay between infant and mother, is the laying of the
groundwork for personality building, i.e., the more or less
successful starting off of a number of developmental lines.
Whatever clashes occur at that time proceed externally between the infant and his environment, not internally within
a not yet existing structure. Where deprivation and frustration are excessive, this leads not to symptom formation but
to developmental setbacks. It is only in the later course of
differentiation and structuralization that the resultant
deviations from normal growth become involved in the
phase-adequate internal conflicts as they are known to us.

With regard to the *technique* of child analysis, we come

up against some unexpected questions. If we accept the view that childhood psychopathology has a twofold causation, one rooted in the conflicts, defense, and compromise formations, the other in the developmental processes, we have no reason to believe that the same therapeutic measures will be equally effective for both. We are on familiar analytic ground with the conflictual-neurotic pathology where interpretation lifts repressed or otherwise defended material into consciousness and helps the child's ego to find solutions for his internal struggles, which are no longer based on anxiety, panic, and infantile misapprehensions of reality. We also realize that, so far as the pathologies are interlocked, the analytic work will undo regressions and lift crippling conflicts off the developmental lines. But so far as the developmental progress itself is defective or unbalanced due either to innate or to environmental conditions, we cannot expect interpretation to undo the damage, even if it clarifies the past and may help the child toward better ways of facing and coping with its consequences. If, in spite of that, children also profit from analysis in this respect, such success may be due not to the truly analytic work but to admixtures to the technique such as new positive object attachment, new superego identification, suggestive influence, or even corrective emotional experience which with the very young can set arrested developmental lines going again.

So far as the *theoretical* thinking of the analyst is concerned, a closer look at the lines of development may help toward answering three open questions.

For one, we have always wondered what determines the *pathogenic impact* of an event. To mention examples: for some children, the birth of a sibling becomes a turning point in development to which all later pathology can be connected; others take this in their stride. Moving to another home can be traumatic for some and a pleasurable experience for others. Bodily illness, separation from a playmate, death of a parent have very different consequences for different individuals and different ages. We arrive at a better understanding of this if we connect the event with the particular point on the particular developmental line which is affected by it. We realize then that the arrival of a sibling has different meaning before or after the stages of object constancy or of ambivalence have been reached on the line toward emotional independence; that the impact of bodily illness depends not only on the age adequateness of castration fear but also on the station reached on the line toward independent body ownership and management; that loss of a parent changes its meaning altogether according to the time of occurrence and has different pathogenic value at the stages of biological unity, of infantile ambivalence, of need for oedipal involvement, or in adolescence when withdrawal from the parent is a developmental task which does not bear to be interfered with by the actual removal of the object. Moving house, even though all the human objects remain present, may prove traumatic in cases where the young child has deviated too far on the line away from human to material objects.

Secondly, the same reasoning, if applied to the *defense mechanisms,* may shed some light on the question of their chronology. We know, of course, that repression cannot come into action before division of the undifferentiated personality into id and ego has taken place; or that projection and introjection in their defensive use depend similarly on the ego's capacity to distinguish between self and nonself. We can now add that somatization and its later use in conversion (somatic compliance) become more understandable when we see them as predominantly based on the line from physical to mental discharge, in fact, caused by the arrests and regressions which occur on it. Regression as a defense is resorted to most readily by individuals whose entire progression on the lines has been halting and shaky. The obsessional mechanisms cannot come into use before two of the developmental lines have reached their climax, i.e., the line from physical to mental discharge as well as the line from irresponsibility to moral guilt.

Finally, we may hope that the further study of these connections will also provide some hints toward answering a question which has troubled workers in the field since the beginnings of psychoanalysis, namely, the *choice of neurosis*. What we can make out so far is that the type of pathology which an individual child presents is as closely tied up with the intricacies of his developmental processes as are his character and personality.

5

Beyond the
Infantile Neurosis
[1974]

As psychoanalysts engaged in therapy, we have always felt most comfortable and confident in the area of work for which we had been trained originally, i.e., when dealing with the adult conversion and anxiety hysterias, phobias, and obsessional neuroses. What were counted on as indispensable prerequisites for these treatments were the presence of a fully structured personality plagued by conflicts between the agencies within the structure, the patients' insight into the damaging nature of their symptomatology, their feeling of suffering, their wish to be cured, and, resulting from the latter, their cooperation with the analytic effort.

This paper is published here for the first time. German translation: Jenseits der infantilen Neurose. *Die Schriften der Anna Freud,* Volume 10. Munich: Kindler Verlag, 1980.

In due course, i.e., when turning from the symptom to the character neuroses, we learned to cope with a much diminished treatment alliance since we found ourselves interfering with elements ingrained in the individual's personal picture of himself, elements which, though neurotic, were nevertheless ego-syntonic and as such valued by the patient. When pressing further with our therapeutic ventures, we learned to do without the patients' insight when dealing with borderline psychotics; without their wish to be cured in cases of perversion, addiction, and delinquency; without the patients' recognition of suffering and inner damage when turning from the adult to the infantile neuroses. What confronted the analyst in this last instance was not only the children's much lessened understanding for the necessity of treatment but their actual, age-related inability to fulfill the analytic requirements for self-observation, sincerity, free association, and restriction to verbal expression.

However, none of the difficulties mentioned equals the situation which confronts the analyst who steps out of the realm of psychopathology caused by conflict and enters the area of abnormalities caused by defects in the structure and in the personality. This happens to the analyst of adults who ventures beyond the border between neurosis and psychosis and accepts patients whose inner structure is damaged, temporarily or permanently, beyond the point where id, ego, and superego are recognizable and functioning as distinct entities, separate but in contact with each other. It happens likewise to the child analyst who turns from private practice with neurotic problem children to clinic or hospital practice where he is expected to treat a wide variety of disturbances beyond those caused by the infantile neuroses. The diagnostic assessments of these children cover a wide range. Their defects are considered either as inborn and organic or as acquired due to early emotional deprivation. The diagnostic labels used for them differ from slow or irregular developer to serious backwardness, borderline, autistic, and psychotic states. What they have in common are severe failures of development, i.e., an immaturity of personality which is not age-adequate and subsequently outgrown, but threatens to be permanent and leave them incomplete as human personalities.

In our analytic work with the transference neuroses, we have learned that hysterical, obsessional, and other neurotic symptoms are compromise formations derived from interaction between the internal agencies, id, ego, and superego, the superego embodying within itself the demands and prohibitions, ideas and ideals of the external world. In our present concern with problems of development, we may learn to regard the child's progressive achievements in a similar way, namely, as compromises due to interaction between internal and external influences. The difference between the two processes, however, has to be seen in the difference of motive force behind them: while neurotic symptom formation is resorted to by the individual under the pressure of danger, anxiety, and guilt, the child's progressive moves forward proceed under the impact of positive maturational influences and, in Edward Bibring's (1936) sense, an inborn beneficial urge "to complete development."

Due to the results of child analysis and direct child observation, it has become possible to trace in detail some of the moves which lead from the infant's state of complete immaturity to the age-adequate functioning of the later ages. I refer here to René Spitz's (1965) description of the infant's advance *from self to object* during the first year of life, due to a series of minute but constant interactions between his id impulses, his maturing ego functions, and the mother's unceasing ministrations and responses; to Margaret Mahler's (1968) plotting of the path *from primary narcissism, autism, and symbiosis to individuation;* or to the series of *developmental lines* described by me (1965), which lead up to emotional self-reliance, responsibility in body management, control of body functions, peer relationships, capacity to work, etc.

What characterizes all these instances of developmental progression is their utter dependence on the quality of the contributions made on the one hand by the child's impulses, ego functions, superego precursors, and on the other hand by the influences, pressures, responses, and opportunities offered by the environment. Just as the shape and durability of a neurotic symptom depend on the quantitative and qualitative contributions from id, ego, and superego, so do the efficiency and adaptive value of a developmental achievement depend on the quality of the contributions made to it by the inner and outer world, i.e., on the one hand by endowment, maturation, and structuralization, on the other hand by environmental response, stimulation, and opportunity. To achieve normal, i.e., age-adequate, developmental results, the contributions from both sides need to remain within an average expectable norm. If either side, or both, depart from this in a more or less massive way, the outcome will be developmental irregularities, or delays, or complete arrests. For the resulting overt picture of abnormality it matters little whether the blame for the specific developmental failure is attributable to the organic, psychological, or environmental elements.

I cite in what follows some relevant examples. The developmental step on the line from need-satisfying object relations to object constancy is only made by children for whom the environment provides stable adult figures who act as their parents in the psychological sense of the word. Object constancy, once reached, is maintained only if there is reciprocity from the environment, not in cases where the parental figures are unsuitable or unreliable recipients for the child's affections. Even the powerful phallic-oedipal urges do not culminate in phase dominance of the oedipal stage if there is no libidinal interest or response from father or mother. The urge for individuation on the child's side needs to be complemented by the mother's positive attitude to his growing independence. The child's advance toward physical control and responsibility needs to be matched by the gradual withdrawal of the mother's narcissistic cathexis of her child's body, etc.

I want to correct any impression, conveyed perhaps by the foregoing, that, by now, our knowledge of child development is sufficient to identify and trace to their source most, or at least the most important, developmental failures. This is not so, unfortunately. Much is still left unanswered, concerning not only the failures but even the successful achievements of development.

Structuralization of the personality into separate id, ego, and superego agencies is a case in point. Regarding the advance to superego formation, we are well informed and can trace any gaps, lacks, or irregularities of function either to defects in the child's libidinal relationships or to defects in the availability and responsiveness of his objects. We can apportion blame for failure correctly since we know what both sides need to contribute to set the prerequisite processes of imitation, identification, and internalization in motion. However, our position is very different where the even more important advance toward id-ego separation is concerned. In analytic theory this is covered by the phrase that the ego develops out of the id, or separates off from the id-ego matrix, "under the influence of the external world." This leaves it wide open what precisely this influence or these influences are; whether they consist of libidinal or perceptual stimulation; whether it is, in fact, the presence or absence of these (i.e., mothering) which decide the issue; whether it is the infant's capacity or incapacity to respond to mothering (i.e., endowment); whether orientation in and improved adaptation to the environment proceed under the pressure of the urge for self-preservation; or whether, perhaps on an undefined sliding scale, a mixture of the contributions from all sides has to be held responsible.

There are similar uncertainties regarding the vital developmental step of division between physical and mental experience and discharge. We know that, roughly, after the first year of life, an entirely psychosomatic regime ceases to exist, with the exception of some remnants embodied in persistent psychosomatic symptomatology. With advancing age and ego development, new psychological pathways are opened up for the discharge of mental stimulation.

However, we have so far not learned to identify either the stations on this way or the influences which determine success or failure of advance. It remains an open question whether this is wholly a maturational matter or whether here, too, environmental influences of whatever kind play their part. We know from clinical experience the highly abnormal pictures of children in whom this advance has failed to occur and who, accordingly, attack their bodies to get rid of mental pain or produce hate reactions when in physical discomfort.

That we also are in the dark where the advance from primary to secondary process thinking is concerned hardly needs a mention. Where this fails, we look on the child's side for defects either in the libidinal or in the intellectual area. We do not know what part, if any, to attribute to environmental influence. It seems that only "experiments of fate" will be able to show whether a child living in a primary process environment can develop secondary process functioning.

It takes more than the child analyst's usual courage and therapeutic optimism to approach cases whose development is incomplete in one or the other essential direction, i.e., children who have failed to outgrow the stage of need satisfaction; who have not established dominance on any libidinal phase; whose ego has not separated off from their id, nor superego from ego; who have not learned to differentiate between body and mind; or have not set up sufficiently stable ego boundaries to distinguish between self and object. On the other hand, only the therapeutic attempts made by such analytic pioneers hold out the promise that we may learn to fill the gaps in our present insight into developmental problems.

6

Psychopathology Seen Against the Background of Normal Development

(1976 [1975])

When choosing a title for this paper, I hesitated between two possible ones, the one above which I finally selected, and another, termed "Links between Adult Psychiatry and Child Psychiatry." Although in wording they seem different enough from each other, I hope to show in what follows where the two subject matters meet.

Delivered as the 49th Maudsley Lecture before the Royal College of Psychiatrists, November 21, 1975. First published in *British Journal of Psychiatry*, 129:401–406, 1976. French translation: La Psychopathologie envisagée à partir du développement normal. *Revue Française Psychanalyse*, 41:429–438, 1977. Italian translation: La psicopatologia considerata sullo sfondo dello sviluppo normale. *Opere*, 3:1153–1154. Turin: Paolo Boringhieri, 1979. German translation: Die Beziehungen zwischen Psychopathologie und Normalentwicklung. *Die Schriften der Anna Freud,* Volume 10. Munich: Kindler Verlag, 1980.

THE FIRST OBJECT OF
PSYCHOANALYTIC INVESTIGATION

To begin with a look at the history of psychoanalysis. The first object of psychoanalytic study was the neuroses. This was due not to any predilection of the originator of the new discipline but to the exigencies of his private practice. Nevertheless, the nature of the matter under investigation proved decisive for many characteristics of the evolving theory. Since the neurotic manifestations emanate from the depth, psychoanalysis embarked on the study of the unconscious. Since they are due to conflict between internal forces, it became a dynamic psychology. Since conflicts are solved according to the relative strength of these forces, the economic viewpoint was developed. Since the roots of every neurosis reach back to the early years of the individual's life, the genetic aspects of the theory played a paramount part. Incidentally, this last-mentioned point also represented the first opportunity for bringing infantile psychopathology within the oribit of the therapist of adults.

THE WIDENING SCOPE OF PSYCHOANALYSIS

All this, of course, was only the beginning of the story. It did not take long for psychoanalytic exploration to widen its scope, with therapeutic efforts always in its wake. Its path went from the neuroses to the psychoses; from sexual inhibitions to the perversions; from character disorders to the delinquencies; from adult psychopathology to adolescence; from adolescence to childhood. As early as 1925, Freud can be read to say: "children have become the main subject of psycho-analytic research and have thus replaced in importance the neurotics on whom its studies began" (1925d, p. 273). Although at the date when it was written, this statement may have been prophetic rather than factual, child analysts today will be glad to claim it as the motivation and justification governing their work. In fact, it is less the increasing dissection of the adult's personality and more child analysis and the analytic observation of young children which are responsible for two important results: (1) for a chart of normal personality development; (2) for pointing out the relevance of its details for the assessment of adult psychopathology.

RECONSTRUCTION VERSUS THE DIRECT VIEW

As regards the developmental chart, it would be unjustified, of course, if child analysts claimed major credit for its setting up. It was reconstruction from the analyses of adults and not the direct analytic study of the child which established the fact of an infantile sex life with its sequence of libidinal phases; the existence of the oedipus and castration complexes; the developmental line of anxiety from separation anxiety, fear of object loss, fear of loss of love, castration anxiety to guilt; the division of the personality into id, ego, and superego, each inner agency pursuing its own purposes; the advance from primary process to secondary process functioning; the gradual building up of a defense organization. What was left to the child analysts was to make amendments wherever the direct contact with infantile functioning did not seem to confirm what had been glimpsed from the distance. There was the point, for instance, that in reconstruction no early developmental stage ever appears in its true colors, since it invariably is overlaid by characteristics which belong to later phases, even where regression in the transference has taken place; or that what appears in later analysis as a one-time traumatic event may in reality have been a series of such happenings, telescoped into one in the individual's memory. But besides and beyond these minor corrections, one major assumption emerged, namely, that reconstruction from adult analysis inevitably is weighted toward pathology to the neglect of normal developmental happenings; that it is always the conflictual and unsolved which does not come to rest in the individual's mind, which welcomes the opportunity to reestablish itself in the transference situation and thus captures and monopolizes the analyst's attention. In contrast, the satisfied impulses, the successful adaptive conflict solutions disappear from view by entering the fabric of the personality. They are outgrown with little incentive left for revival at a later date.

Thus, while the analysts of adults become expert in tracing psychopathology back to its early roots, only the child analysts appear to hold the key to the description of the course taken by normal infantile development.

THE CHILD ANALYST'S PICTURE OF NORMAL DEVELOPMENT

The "Abnormal" Aspects of the Norm

It may be necessary to stress that normal growth and development, as seen by the child analyst, do not appear as a smooth, unbroken line leading from early infancy via the latency period, preadolescence, and adolescence to a healthy adulthood. On the contrary, every single developmental phase as well as every single forward move can be shown to contain disturbing concomitants which are characteristic for them.

To take the first year of the child as an example. What belongs to this period of life are the diffuse distress states to which all infants are subject. We regard them as the normal forerunners of later anxiety and as such inevitable. Nevertheless, unlike the affect of anxiety which is psychologically caused and felt, they can be aroused and experienced on the physical as well as on the mental side, and they demand from the mothering person the utmost in care, comfort, and attention to the infant's body and mind. They are thus an instructive illustration of the double regime which governs functioning at this early date when the individual's body and mind interact freely: physical excitation such as pain or discomfort can be discharged via mental upset, while mental excitation such as frustration, impatience, or longing can find its outlet via the body, in disturbances of sleep, food intake, or elimination. This double source and experience of distress is disturbing to infant and environment alike. But nothing can prevent it from existing until developmental growth itself alters the situation by creating new mental pathways for the discharge of mental stimuli via the maturing ego (thought, speech, etc.).

On the other hand, these new developments, beneficial as they are in one respect, contain their own hazards in another. Evidence for this is the sleeping disorders which appear frequently at the border between the first and second year and cause distress to both infant and mother, usually in the form of inability to fall asleep. As analytic observers we ascribe these upsets to the child's reluctance to renounce recently acquired functions such as his emotional hold on the object world and his ego interest in his surroundings. Both militate against the body's need for rest and interfere with the return to narcissistic withdrawal and to renunciation of ego interests which are the preconditions for sleep.

There are other examples of difficulties which arise due to developmental progress. Motor skills advance in leaps and bounds at the toddler stage but are not equaled on the ego side by similar advances in motor control and/or appreciation of danger from heights, water, fire, traffic, etc. Consequently, the young child becomes accident-prone, a developmental occurrence which makes formidable demands on environmental protection. Simultaneously, the increasing complexities in the infant-mother relationship affect food intake. Since food and mother are still equated by the child, every hostile or ambivalent feeling toward her leads to food refusal and further to the endless and developmentally harmful battles at mealtimes. Other "normal" developmental manifestations are the upsetting temper tantrums which, before the acquisition of speech, are the growing toddler's typical mode of discharge for anger, frustration, and rage, with major involvement of the motor apparatus. There also is the excessive and distressing clinging which accompanies the fading out of the biological unity between child and mother, i.e., the upsets within the separation-individuation phase as described by

Margaret Mahler (1968).

The upsetting upheavals of the next phases are even more familiar in their characteristics. Obviously, the child in the anal-sadistic stage cannot be expected to deal with his instinctual tendencies on the one hand and environmental demands on the other without experiencing conflict, extreme distress, and emotional turmoil, resulting in occasional regression with accompanying loss of acquired functions or with sullenness, rebelliousness, obstinacy, or with phase-bound obsessional characteristics such as insistence on sameness and routine, and anxiety outbreaks whenever the self-imposed order and regularity are infringed by the environment.

As regards the phallic-oedipal development, we do not expect the child to cope with the accompanying emotional complications and anxiety increases without pathological by-products. Long before the advent of child analysis, it was one of the accepted psychoanalytic tenets that this is the time when the whole turmoil of anxieties, affects, and conflicts is organized into the clinical picture of one of the infantile neuroses. Whatever the fate of the latter, whether transitory or permanent in its impact on developmental progress, it represents the individual child's crowning achievement in his struggle for simultaneous adaptation to the inner and outer world.

Relevance of This Developmental Chart for Adult Psychopathology

There are several items in this chart of normal growth which therapists in the adult field may find relevant for their assessments of symptomatology.

The psychosomatic illnesses in adult life, for instance, may be easier to understand when seen as the survival of the psychosomatic regime which is legitimate in infancy. Although the communicating doors between body and mind are never completely closed for anybody, as evidenced by headaches after mental upset, the physical accompaniments of anxiety, etc., they are more open in some individuals than in others, and this becomes responsible for the mental contributions to such severe afflictions as migraine, asthma, high blood pressure, and stomach ulcers.

Furthermore, the pattern of some sleep disorders in adult life has something in common with those described for early childhood. Even though the sleepless adult's depressed or agitated state of mind differs in its content from the child's, what is identical in both instances is the painful struggle between a tired body longing for relaxation and a restless mind unable to rid itself of excitation.

There are some other characteristics of normal child development which serve as patterns for later pathology. One is the forerunner of object love proper, i.e., the infant's tie to the mother which is based on the satisfactions received from her. Certain disturbances of adult love life, such as shallowness and promiscuity, are understood better when seen as residues of this early stage of which too large a proportion has remained.

Similarly, the anxiety attacks of hysterical patients can be likened to the panic states of young children before the ego has acquired the mental mechanisms which defend against anxiety and reduce debilitating panic to the adaptive form of signal anxiety.

THE PREREQUISITES OF NORMAL DEVELOPMENT

Describing the chain of events leading from the infant's complete immaturity to the comparative maturity of the mental apparatus at latency age, I stressed the fact that progress — even if normal — is interspersed with conflicts, emotional upsets, and distress states; that it is also interrupted by regressive setbacks and halted by temporary arrests; in short, that it is neither smooth, nor unimpeded, nor effortless, nor painless. What has not been emphasized sufficiently so far is the experience that even this checkered advance is extremely vulnerable and open to a variety of threats. We see the developmental process as dependent on the interaction of three factors: endowment; environment; rate of structuralization and maturation within the personality. Provided that all three are within the expectable norm, the child will arrive in every crucial developmental phase with the right inner equipment and meet the right environmental response, i.e., have a chance of normal growth. If, however, any of the three deviates too far from the average, the developmental result will become distorted in one direction or another.

Examples of Normal Developmental Advance

That developmental achievements are not due to single factors but are multiply based is illustrated for certain instances in the child analytic literature. René Spitz (1965) traced in detail the origins of the infant's first tie to the mother and pinpointed three prerequisites for it: an adequate advance in the infant's libidinal capacity; normal maturation of the perceptive apparatus, which enables interest to be turned from the infant's own body to the environment; the mother's sufficient libidinal involvement with the child, expressed in comforting and satisfying handling. Provided that in the life of a normally born infant these various influences are at work and interact, the first step on the ladder toward mature object love will be taken.

Similarly, Margaret Mahler (1968), exploring the complexities of the separation-individuation phase in the second year of life, makes us realize how many elements are needed for its successful negotiation: sufficient maturation of motility to enable the child to run away from the mother as well as toward her; in the ego, the unfolding of inquisitiveness and curiosity; on the libidinal side, some advance toward object constancy and "basic trust" to allow for temporary separation without distress; on the mother's side, her readiness to release the child from the close union with her own person, to accept and even enjoy his status as a separate person.

Similar combinations of forces can be seen at work behind any further developmental advance, whether from one of the major libidinal stages to the next, or from one small step to the next on one of the long developmental lines leading toward mature object love; to companionship with peers; to independent body management; to the ability to work. Even to achieve reliable sphincter control, beyond mere reflex action, depends on a multiplicity of intact factors, such as: maturation of the muscular apparatus; adequately timed and exerted maternal intervention; the child's compliance due to his object tie; the process of identification with the environmental demand leading finally to the individual's own, so-called sphincter morality.

Examples of Developmental Deviations

None of these positive developmental results can be expected if either endowment, or environmental conditions, or the rate of personality structuralization depart too far from the average.

First, as regards *endowment,* our child analytic studies of the blind, deaf, and mentally deficient show that any single defect in the individual's inborn equipment suffices to throw the entire developmental course into disarray, far beyond the sphere where the damage itself is located. With the blind, attachment to the object world is delayed; once formed, it remains longer on primitive levels; motility matures later than normal and remains restricted; prolonged dependence interferes with the unfolding of aggression; verbalization suffers from a gap between words and their meaning; superego formation bears the mark of the initial differences in object relationship (Burlingham, 1972, 1979). With the deaf, the absence of acoustic elements affects the thought processes and the important step from primary to secondary process functioning. The mentally deficient miss out, not only as regards understanding of the environment, i.e., intellectually, but vitally as regards the ego's defense organization, i.e., impulse and anxiety control.

Secondly, concerning abnormal *environmental conditions,* their harmful impact on development has always been recognized, even without the added evidence from child analyses. What needs emphasis, though, is the fact that there is no one-to-one, invariable relationship between the fact of parents being absent, neglecting, indifferent, punitive, cruel, seductive, overprotective, delinquent, or psychotic and the resultant distortions in the personality picture of the child. Cruel treatment can produce either an aggressive, violent, or a timid, crushed, passive being; parental seduction can result either in complete inability to control sexual impulses ever after, or in severe inhibition and abhorrence of any form of sexuality. In short, the developmental outcome is determined not by the environmental interference per se, but by its interaction with the inborn and acquired resources of the child.

The third important influence on personality building, namely, the *rate of internal structuralization,* has received comparatively little attention so far. The facts are that individual children differ considerably with regard to the timing when their ego emerges from the undifferentiated ego-id matrix, or when their superego emerges from the ego; when they advance from the primary process to secondary process functioning; when the borders between unconscious and conscious are set up; when signal anxiety replaces panic attacks; when defenses change from the primitive to the sophisticated. Normally, this sequence of achievements matches the sequence of internal instinctual and external parental pressures and enables the child to find more or less adaptive solutions for the arising conflicts. However, when ripening of the mental apparatus is either delayed or accelerated, there is no such match between conflict situations and the appropriate means for coping with them.

Child analytic studies yield various examples of the developmental confusion which ensues.

For instance, during the boy's phallic stage, there occurs an age-adequate conflict between active and passive strivings. This is dealt with by repression of passivity, compensating masculine fantasies, heroic daydreams, and so forth, provided that the mental structure is up to date. But in cases where the latter is delayed in its unfolding, no such sophisticated mechanisms are available and their place is taken by muscular action (as in the infantile tantrums) resulting in aggressive outbursts, self-injury, atypical or borderline manifestations.

In the girl's age-adequate emotional move toward the oedipal father, there occurs the need to free herself by whatever means from her ties to the mother. This healthy advance is interfered with where the superego precociously upholds moral demands which forbid rivalry, hostility, death wishes, etc.

Precocious understanding of the difference between the sexes may involve a little girl in the throes of penis envy before there are adequate means at her disposal for defense against massive unpleasure.

RELEVANCE FOR ADULT PSYCHOPATHOLOGY

Knowledge of these developmental complications is relevant for the psychotherapist of adults so far as they affect the therapeutic possibilities.

Analytic and analytically oriented therapy is directed toward the patient's ego and attempts to widen its controlling powers. It is a radical therapy so far as it deals with damage which the ego has inflicted on itself by excessive repression which limits its sphere of influence; by unsuitable other defense mechanisms which distort it; by regressions which lower its functioning; by arrests which prevent further unfolding. However, with regard to harm inflicted on the ego by endowment, environment, and vagaries of internal maturation, i.e., by influences beyond its control, it is no more than an alleviating therapy, dealing not with causes but with their aftereffects and working toward better integration of the latter. A distinction of this kind may help to explain some of the therapeutic limitations which patients as well as analysts deplore.

SUMMARY

It was the object of this paper to pursue some links between mental health and illness, immaturity and maturity. It was its further aim to convince psychiatrists of adults that there is much to be learned from child psychiatry, and to convince child psychiatrists that infantile psychopathology should be assessed against the background knowledge of normal development.

7

The Principal Task
of Child Analysis

(1978 [1977])

THE TASKS OF PSYCHOANALYSIS

Even the most inveterate child analysts do not contemplate
the problems of their work except in comparison with
those in the mainstream of psychoanalysis of which, after
all, their discipline is no more than a subspecialty. It is for
this reason that child analysis always tended to stay near to
what is commonly called the classical model and to keep
every modification of it at a minimum. It may also be the
reason why I, today, find it difficult to discuss what I sug-

Presented on the occasion of the Tenth Anniversary Celebrations of
the Cleveland Center for Research in Child Development, on May 4,
1977. First published in the *Bulletin of the Hampstead Clinic*, 1:11–16,
1978. German translation: Die Hauptaufgaben der Kinderanalyse. *Die
Schriften der Anna Freud,* Volume 10. Munich: Kindler Verlag, 1980.

gest as a principal task for child analysis without referring back to the parallel concerns of psychoanalysis in general.

Obviously, the tasks facing psychoanalysts from the beginning were multiple, no single one standing out as principal: to devise and constantly improve a technique of therapy for the neuroses; to modify it for the purpose of widening its scope; to extract from it a general theory of mental functioning; to apply the latter to a large number of disciplines concerned with human beings. Except for a few individuals who tried and were able to cultivate all these aspects, the various members and institutions of the psychoanalytic movement made their own selection among them. Training institutes gave precedence to the teaching of technique; qualified analysts, while treating the neuroses, reached out toward the therapy of the more severe mental afflictions; training analysts built their professional reputation on the quality of theoretical publications. The technical, clinical, and theoretical contributions flourished in this manner in the various quarters. Only application of psychoanalysis to the humanities found a diminishing number of representatives and decreased gradually, at least within the teaching programs.

As we all know, child analysis, despite far-reaching differences in governing conditions and in the human material to be dealt with, followed faithfully in most of these directions. As in the training for adult analysis, the subject of technique had first place in the programs for child analysis as well. As the practicing analysts of adults had begun to treat perversions, addictions, delinquencies, and insanities, so did the child analysts turn from the infantile neurosis to the infantilisms, the autisms, the childhood psychoses. With regard to theory, what psychoanalysis had already established, child analytical work tried to confirm, extend, or disprove. There was only one area where the fate of child analysis differed markedly from its adult counterpart. The application of psychoanalytic findings to art, literature, religion, and anthropology had met only too frequently with reluctance or suspicion from the experts in the field. The reception of findings with regard to children was of a different kind. After the general public's initial indignation about the discovery of infantile sexuality had passed, progressively minded parents, educators, and teachers were, if anything, overeager to turn what they could learn from child analysis into new and revolutionary pedagogical principles.

Since, as in the adult field, all sides of the work clamored for attention, it was not easy for the child analysts to keep priorities straight. For a period, the need to adapt and fashion technique seemed the imperative one, in the face of obstacles caused by the patients' immaturity of personality, their different modes of expression, their lack of insight and reliable treatment alliance, of sincerity, of free association, of changes in the transference situation, of the inevitable inclusion and/or interference of the parents. Extension of treatment to the borderline cases engaged a (perhaps unwarranted) amount of effort and interest, since therapy was bound to prove frustrating prior to a more thorough investigation of their etiology (organic, chemical, innate, environmental, psychological). Simultaneously, theory as to the causation of pathology was a main concern, as it veered, rather wildly, from the oedipal period as the responsible constellation to the mother-infant relationship at the beginning of life; to the separation-individuation phase in the second year (Margaret Mahler); to the disturbances of narcissism (Kohut); to the developmental frustrations and interferences (Nagera). There was even the temptation for some to devote work more or less exclusively to the applied field, to correct errors made by the imprecise and piecemeal use of analytic knowledge, and thus to benefit the causes of upbringing, teaching, and prevention of pathology.

DEVELOPMENT AS A FIELD OF EXPLORATION FOR THE CHILD ANALYST

I believe that it was this quandary of conflicting pressures which let child analysts not notice that there is still another, if somewhat different field, one which may be exclusively theirs. While dissection of psychic material and reconstruction of past events are the hallmark of classical psychoanalysis, child analysis, based on its direct contact with the very young, may well add a pursuit in the opposite direction, i.e., may make the vicissitudes of forward development and exploration of the ego's synthetic function its specific aims. Obviously, the child analytic therapists have unique opportunities to do so. While treating and/or observing their patients, they are able to watch early mental functioning while it is ongoing, to witness maturation, growth, developmental change, and follow their interaction up to the final metamorphoses which qualify infantile elements for becoming integral parts of an adult's character and personality. To engage in all this may be a preferable way for child analysis to emulate classical psychoanalysis. As the latter has produced metapsychological theory as its crowning achievement, the former can add to this a new, developmentally oriented psychoanalytic theory of child psychology.

THE CONCEPT OF DEVELOPMENTAL LINES

In the early era of psychoanalysis, intactness of the sexual function and of the ability to work used to be quoted as signs of an adult's normality. There was no mention then of a multitude of other capacities, which we now recognize as equally characteristic of adulthood, perhaps because their completion was expected long before maturity is reached, or perhaps because damage to them is less obviously connected with the etiology of the neuroses, at that time the investigator's main concern. Since these functions are perfected very gradually throughout the whole long-drawn-out process of child development, their study and detailed description become a stimulating challenge for the child analyst. I have previously discussed them under the title of Developmental Lines and have attempted to show how they lead via well-marked stages from immaturity at birth to mature personality formation; also, how failure or success on them affects a person's performance in all respects.

The analyst of adults meets predominantly the end products of these processes. His patients, though mentally disturbed in one or the other respect, have, as a rule, achieved a certain amount of potential self-reliance and stability; they are in control of the body, its motility, of the processes of intake and elimination; they can look after its safety; they can discharge excitation via thought and speech, not only through physical pathways and psychosomatic involvement. Apart from the circumscribed areas of symptomatology, they have outgrown the exclusive domination of the pleasure principle and can function according to the reality principle. They regard the world no longer from a purely egocentric point of view and have learned to see external happenings objectively. Except for the anxiety hysterics, they have advanced from unproductive panic states to signal anxiety and the organization of an elaborate system of defense mechanisms. They have established positive or negative relationships with peers. Prestages of these very gradually acquired attitudes can be reconstructed during analytic treatment, of course, but usually this happens only so far as they have etiological significance. So far as they have become an uncontested part of the patient's normal personality, there is little or no reason for them to reappear, either in memory, or in free association, or in the transference manifestations.

DEVELOPMENTAL LINES AS THE CHILD ANALYST'S DOMAIN

I suggest that there is a realm here which child analysts can claim as their very own. Developmental steps and the intermediary stations on the developmental lines can be identified, described, and investigated as to their origin, not only with regard to their possible involvement in pathology and especially in neurosis at a later date, but also with a view to their role as factors responsible for the adult individual's characteristics as either reasonable or unreasonable, effec-

tive or ineffective, adapted or maladjusted, social, dissocial, or totally asocial.

To carry out such studies, we borrow concepts from the
theory of the neuroses such as multiple determination,
conflict, synthesis, compromise formation, and apply them
to the problems of development.

MULTIPLE DETERMINATION OF DEVELOPMENT

We are familiar with the idea that, beginning with the departure from the undifferentiated state, i.e., the id-ego matrix,
life proceeds under the impact of every part of the emerging
personality structure differing from every other part with
regard to mode of functioning and aim: primary process
functioning and search for drive satisfaction in the id;
secondary process and regard for reality in the ego; commands and prohibitions issued by the superego, the latter in
deference to and identification with external authority. In
terms of neurotic psychopathology, this explains why from
the beginning of structuralization onward, no individual
can feel a unified being and why conflicts, internal and external, are unavoidable and ubiquitous. Translated into terms
of development, it explains why mental growth is so
different from growth on the physical side, where bones,
tissue, and whole organ systems mature and unfold in a
more or less straightforward line. Forward moves on the
mental side cannot be simple and uncomplicated since they
owe their impetus not to a single determinant but to a variety
of them, all of them different from each other. It is not
difficult to demonstrate this, using as examples any of the
developmental achievements mentioned above.

The familiar line *from infantile to adult sex life,* for instance, has been shown to depend on the step-by-step interaction between four disparate influences: drive maturation which decides on the location of erotogenic zones (oral, anal, phallic, genital), supplying also the energetic (aggressive) impulse toward seeking gratification; maturing of ego functions which allows for recognition of the object of the drives and shapes the different modes of attachment to it; environmental influence which provides stimulation and response; superego action which adds checks and controls on the various levels.

We find a similar array of factors active on the line *from play to work.* As regards the consecutive forms of play (on the mother's body, with soft toys, with sand and water, with filling and emptying, with constructive toys, role play, games, hobbies), the id determinants concerning these are skin erotism, object attachment, cathexis of intake and elimination, constructive and destructive tendencies, phallic urges. The ego contributes curiosity, investigative spirit, manual skills, imagination; the environment contributes material opportunities as well as patterns for imitation and identification. Finally, when drive pressure lessens and the ego outgrows the need for immediate pleasure gain, its newly acquired way of functioning according to the reality principle changes the infantile activity of play into the all-important mature capacity to work.

Additional examples can be quoted, taken from the many other developmental lines, as for instance from the one *toward independent body management.* It leads from wetting and soiling to cleanliness; from being tied to the mother who owns the infant's body to free movement and self-determination; from endangering the body to safe-guarding its integrity and health. Here, too, a similar mixture of determining factors is at work. On the physical side: increasing muscular strength, sphincter control, motor ability and skill. On the id side, factors such as the biological union with the mother and the outgrowing of it; deference to her wishes and revolt against them; autoerotic urges. On the ego side, increasing orientation in the outside world, rational appraisal of dangers, love of adventure. On the side of the environment, the mother's skillful or unimaginative handling of toilet training and her response to the infant's wish for separation from her and for self-determination.

The line *toward peer relationships,* in its turn, depends on the decrease of primary narcissism, selfishness, and ego-centricity; on extending libidinal cathexes from their exclusive concentration on the mother to the inclusion of other objects; on the increasing ego need for companionship with playmates; and, finally, on acquiring the capacities for empathy, equality, consideration, and reciprocity which are essential for the formation of friendships.

NORMAL, TYPICAL VERSUS ABNORMAL, ATYPICAL DEVELOPMENT

Multiple determination as such does not necessarily imply hazard for mental growth. It is well known from neurotic symptom formation that the ego's synthetic function can deal with disparate and even with conflicting elements, and that it can devise compromises between them which, although pathological in nature, go far to meet at one and the same time the demands made by all the internal and external agencies in question.

What happens in this manner in psychopathology can be shown to happen, though with more adaptive results, in the area of normal growth. Here, too, the child's ego relies on its synthetic function. This integrates at every stage of a developmental line the various determining factors which are active on it. It forms compromises between them which result in the construction of the respective intermediary stations. The latter are normal, and the compromise formations adaptive, provided the responsible, determining elements are normal and typical. Provided innate endowment, drives, sensory equipment, personality structuralization, and external circumstances (id, ego, superego, parental environment) remain within the limits of the expectable, the child's development will be progressive, positive, more or less typical, i.e., normal.

On the other hand, aberrant features in all of the above respects are so frequent that they are almost the order of the day. Often enough, inborn drives are either excessively strong or unusually weak. There can be overemphasis on sex, or on aggression, or on any of the pregenital levels. There may be sensory defects, physical or intellectual handicaps. Superegos may be too lenient, or too inflexible, or too compliant, or too harsh. While some parents are overprotective or overpossessive, others lack in love, care, stimulation, constancy, guidance, and control. In fact, normality of all the determining agents is an ideal of which reality frequently falls short.

Since even under these unfavorable conditions synthesis continues to function, it inevitably incorporates elements which are detrimental to development. This implies that some developmental lines will be halted before their peak achievement is reached. Genitality may never be accomplished, with resulting impotence or frigidity. Work efficiency may be impaired if the individual does not move forward from the stage of play. Egocentricity and lack of objectivity may remain fixed, which prevents peer relationship to advance from infantile levels to mature friendship. In short, the developmental compromise formations will no longer be positive and adaptive. Instead they will turn out deviant, unsatisfactory, and maladaptive.

TIME FACTORS AS THE CAUSE OF DEVELOPMENTAL DISTURBANCE

Changes in the quality of determining elements, as they are described above, are not the only reason for developmental malformation and disorder. Another, equally important cause is a time factor, i.e., a different rate of growth of the different parts of a child's personality structure and badly timed environmental interference with the child's concerns.

Normally, we expect internal and external events to occur according to something like a preordained timetable. Cannibalistic oral impulses have their heyday before there is an organized ego, and certainly before there is a superego to object to them. Archaic fears occur at a time of life when it is legitimate to expect comfort and protection from the side of the mother. A certain amount of anal pleasure can be indulged in by the child, provided toilet training is not introduced prematurely. Unless seduction has occurred and interfered with the order of the libidinal stages, the anxieties of the oedipus and castration complexes do not set in before the ego has had time to construct adequate defense mechanisms to deal with them. In short, there is some balance and harmony between growth on the side of the drives and of the ego, and between them and their relations with the outside world. While it prevails, advance occurs on the various developmental lines.

It is this balance and harmony which is disturbed whenever drives and ego and superego progress at different rates, or when environmental interference is untimely. Precocious ego and superego development results in age-inadequate confrontation with the drives, i.e., untimely conflict. Precocious drive development presents insoluble problems for a helpless ego. Mental retardation delays or prevents the building up of age-adequate defenses against anxiety. Progress on the line from infantile dependence to the separation-individuation phase cannot proceed satisfactorily unless the mother's willingness to separate from the child coincides in time (i.e., neither precedes nor lags behind) with the child's wish for growing independence. Advance on the line from wetting and soiling to cleanliness runs into difficulties if toilet training is introduced at the height of urethral and anal involvement instead of postponed until its decrease.

DEVELOPMENTAL VERSUS NEUROTIC PATHOLOGY

There is a point here where the student of development and the analyst of neurotic patients meet, both facing disorders which are hardly to be distinguished from each other on the manifest surface, and which, in any case, intermingle with each other. In both instances, the pathological manifestations are based on disharmony, i.e., clashes between drive expression, ego functioning, and external or internalized interference. In both instances compromises are formed which attempt solutions. Nevertheless, the causation of the two is of a different order. Neurotic symptom formation, as we know it, begins with frustration on a higher developmental level, which forces the search for drive satisfaction to return to an earlier or even the earliest fixation point. Since the ego and superego stand firm and uphold their interdiction against such primitive gratification, the situation threatens danger, anxiety arises, defense is employed, and, as a result, symptoms are formed. Nothing of this happens where developmental pathology is concerned. It is a primary disturbance, due quite simply to imbalance in the unfolding of development itself.

As regards regression, this does not imply, of course, that it is absent from the developmental processes; only that, there, it need not play the role of initiator of pathology. All development consists of the alternation of forward and backward moves and, under normal conditions, the latter are no more than transitory.

CONCLUSION

The study of purely developmental aspects has not been taken up very seriously in child analysis so far. At least, it is still waiting to advance from the realm of mere observation and description of facts to their application to the technique of treatment. We have not yet learned how to deal with developmental deficiencies, although many of them underlie the infantile neuroses and, as mentioned above, are often inextricably bound up with them. Developmental disharmonies are a fertile breeding ground for almost every type of infantile neurosis.

As child analysts, we put our trust in the efficiency of the analytic method, as it has been modified to fit the child. We are right to do so when treating the infantile neuroses and the many disturbances of behavior and social adaptation which are based on them. The uncovering of unconscious motivation, reconstruction of past events (traumatic or otherwise), interpretation of transference feelings and behavior serve well for combating wrong conflict solutions and inadequately primitive defense, and above all for undoing the regressions which have initiated the whole neurotic process. However, they are apt to fail us when we are faced with the task of going beyond neurotic, conflictual pathology and arrive at the more primitive pathological manifestations which are due to the developmental deficiencies. Here, too, the analytic method is essential for clarifying the clinical picture and for revealing causation. Nevertheless, by itself, it is unable to undo the damage.

To the extent to which developmental harm can be undone belatedly, child analysis may accept it as its next duty to devise methods for the task. In the interim, the best that can be done is to identify developmental defects wherever they are located and to pinpoint their differences from neurotic symptomatology. If we help the child patient at least to cope with their consequences, this may be the first step toward a more basic therapy.

8

Mental Health and Illness in Terms of Internal Harmony and Disharmony

[1979]

We have learned from the study of the neuroses and psychoses of adult life that pathology arises if a person's urge for drive satisfaction returns from an age-appropriate mode of gratification to a formerly outgrown infantile one. Whenever and for whatever reason this happens, the revived infantile urges clash with those parts of the personality which have maintained their former mature level, and internal conflict arises. This, in turn, is followed by symptom formation, that is, by one of the ego's manifold

Contribution to a forthcoming publication by Clifford Yorke, Thomas Freeman, and S. Wiseberg. It is here published for the first time. German translation: Psychische Gesundheit und Krankheit als Folge innerer Harmonie und Disharmonie. *Die Schriften der Anna Freud,* Volume 10. Munich: Kindler Verlag, 1980.

attempts to restore inner peace by forging compromises between the unacceptable drive representative and the opposing ego and superego agencies.

Vice versa, it may be the ego organization which regresses due to psychological or organic causes or which may even be threatened by complete dissolution. This affects all or many of the vital ego functions, which then reassume modes characteristic for early childhood before secondary process thinking and impulse control were established. In these instances, symptom formation also can be shown to follow the disturbance of internal balance between drive and ego activity.

Seen from this point of view, mental health in an internally structured personality can be understood as the harmonious interaction between inner agencies which have reached and are maintaining the same level, and symptoms of mental illness as the result of the ego's striving to reconcile with each other what are in essence mutually contradictory impulses and aims.

MENTAL EQUILIBRIUM IN CHILDHOOD

To achieve the degree of inner equilibrium which is compatible with normality is even harder in the early years when the forces determining the child's development are external as well as internal. What needs to be integrated with each other at this time are the potentialities inherent in the inherited constitution; the vicissitudes connected with the gradual structuralization of the personality; and the influences emanating from the parental environment which is responsible for the atmosphere in which development proceeds. While the task of attuning these influences to each other is difficult under any circumstances, it remains manageable provided that all or most of the responsible factors are within a normal range so far as their momentum and quality are concerned, and differ not too much from each other with regard to onset and rate of advance. However, with inborn dispositions, individual patterns of growth, and family backgrounds as divergent as they are, this is by no means always the case.

DISTURBANCES OF EQUILIBRIUM DUE TO QUANTITATIVE AND QUALITATIVE DEVIATIONS FROM THE NORM

So far as quantity and quality are concerned, each of the factors named can depart considerably from what is typical and normal. The consequences of this for healthy personality development are always adverse and, at times, disastrous.

Constitutionally Determined Deviations

The innate givens, for example, which underlie an individual's instinctual development can distort this in more than one direction. Most frequently they do so by lending undue weight to one of the early pregenital stages, usually either the oral or the anal one. As a consequence, the drive representatives of this particular phase dominate the child's sex life and prevent him from reaching primacy on either the phallic or, later, the genital level. This also creates a point of almost irresistible attraction (a fixation point) to which the individual's wishes for drive satisfaction return whenever frustration is met in later life; that is, it encourages the very drive regression which psychoanalysis has found responsible for initiating neurotic symptom formation.

Apart from these interferences with the normal course of developmental progress, sexual or aggressive endowment as such may be deficient in quantity, as a consequence of which the individual's efficiency in adult love life and adult work is lowered or, in contrast, it may be excessive, so that it becomes exceedingly difficult to accommodate the resulting urgency of the drives within the framework of an otherwise normally equipped personality.

Deviant Modes of Structuralization

Individuals differ no less where structuralization of the personality is concerned, that is, its division into separate id, ego, and superego agencies. The original emergence of the ego out of the undifferentiated id-ego matrix may be incomplete and unstable. In this case, id and ego retain a tendency readily to merge again, and the child is apt to respond according to the primary process which favors drive satisfaction at ages when his ego should already be able to keep its independent status, to continue to think and act according to the secondary process, and to maintain drive control. However, the division between the two agencies also may err on the side of being too final and too immovable. This deprives the ego of the normal possibility of acting on many occasions in accordance with, and as a helpmate to, the drives, and it establishes within itself what is frequently described as its basic hostility toward them. Likewise, the later emergence of the superego out of the ego can be either too complete or too incomplete, too stable or too unstable, for normal functioning. Where ego and superego are never in full agreement with each other and can never act as one, unjustified guilt feelings prevail at the slightest opportunity and interfere with the child's enjoyment of developmental achievements and advances. Where, in contrast, the monitoring and critical function of the superego hardly rises above the level of that of the ego or is easily corrupted to fall in with the latter's wishes, character development is in danger of taking a turn toward the egocentric and dissocial.

Beyond and above the foregoing, it is almost self-evident that within the personality structure the quantitative factor as such is decisive for the maintenance of peaceful growth. The three inner agencies need to be matched with each other in their relative strength to avoid either compulsive or impulsive excesses of development. Alterations of intensity in any of them, as they occur during the transitions from one pregenital stage to the next or, inevitably, with the onset of adolescence, cause internal upheaval and are responsible for much of the diffuse pathology of the formative years.

Deviant Environmental Factors

That parental involvement with a child's developmental progress can err both on the side of too much and on the side of too little is a well-known fact which hardly needs stressing. Where care, comfort, stimulation, support, and guidance are deficient, developmental advance suffers in all areas, with regard to the emotions, the intellect, moral functions, social adaptation, and so forth. Where, in contrast, a child is overprotected, overstimulated, and too restrained, the prospects for building up his sense of identity and for becoming an independent personality in his own right are stunted from the start.

DISTURBANCES OF DEVELOPMENT DUE TO BREAKDOWN OF SYNCHRONIZATION

When we observe a young child's normal development, we receive the impression of preordained synchronization between the unfolding of the drives, of the ego functions, of the superego, and of the environmental interventions. This picture is disturbed when timing goes wrong on any of the four sides.

The *cannibalistic* impulses and fantasies, for example, which are the legitimate mental representatives of the infant's oral stage, are destined to appear before any organized ego activity exists with which they might conflict. Normally, therefore, they are unopposed and do not form a source of disturbance. However, this situation alters when they persist beyond their time; or when a critical ego activity sets in too early; or when, as in later life, they have regressed to and are revived at a period when they come into conflict with all the moral and aesthetic principles of a mature superego.

The *archaic fears* of darkness, loneliness, loud noises are normally at their height at a period when the infant can count on maximum support, comfort, and reassurance from the adults who take care of him and act as his auxiliary ego; or when his own ego's awakening reality sense can help to dispel panic. They become a serious threat to peaceful development only either if environmental care is withdrawn too early, as happens to neglected children, or if ego functioning matures too late, as is the rule with the mentally deficient.

The *separation-individuation phase* of the second year of life is negotiated successfully only in cases where there is perfect synchronization between three factors: motor development which provides the means for the infant's physical departure from the mother and for his rejoining her; the ego's awakening wish for exploration and adventure; the mother's readiness to grant the child a measure of independence. If any of these influences comes in too early, or lags behind the others, development is interfered with and the infant, instead of advancing, misses out on an important step.

Even more than in the other instances, the fate of the *anal-sadistic impulses* is connected with timing. Normally, there should be at least a short period in which the infant can indulge these drive representatives without meeting either external or internal opposition. As a rule, though, this is not the case. All too frequently, environmental pressure toward toilet training and condemnation of aggressions set in while the anal-sadistic phase is still at its peak. The infant may concur or identify with both these attitudes, which puts an end to any possible enjoyment of dirty matter or of the urge to attack and hurt people who are at the same time his most important love objects. The child's efforts to come to terms with the offending part within himself then lead to the precocious employment of defenses such as repression, reaction formation, and turning aggression against the self. Following this, there appear such manifestations as disgust with dirty hands, excessive tendencies toward orderliness, and repetitive behavior. These are extremely similar to the later obsessional symptoms, although they are diffuse and lack the coherence and organization of a full-blown obsessional neurosis. Furthermore, while the obsessional neurosis and obsessional character are fixed structures, difficult to dissolve even in psychoanalytic therapy, this early, developmentally caused symptomatology is transient. It disappears again when drive development advances beyond the anal stage, that is, when its representatives lose their intensity and, in their weakened form, pose no further threat either to external or to internal authority.

For dealing with the problems of the *oedipal stage,* it is essential that the ego's defense organization is in tune timewise with the advance in drive activity. Children who meet the castration fears, or penis envy, the rivalrous jealousies and the death wishes against the parent of the same sex while they are equipped only with the most primitive defense mechanisms develop pathology beyond the range of the common infantile neuroses.

DEVELOPMENTAL VERSUS NEUROTIC AND PSYCHOTIC PATHOLOGY

Although important as a background for adult psychopathology, the irregularities of infantile development easily escape notice. Once they are overlaid by the later neuroses and psychoses, the symptoms produced by either of them intermingle and become more or less indistinguishable from each other. The confrontations between drive and ego activity, which in the immature being are primarily due to the quantitative, qualitative, or temporal developmental deviations described above, are matched in the structured personality by the internal conflicts due to secondary drive regression.

However, so far as therapy is concerned, the two types of pathology need to be thought of as different. The pathogenic sequence of frustration, regression, internal incompatibility, anxiety, defense by repression, return of the repressed, and compromise formation — the sequence which is characteristic for the neuroses — is relieved by analytic work which lifts all partners in the process to the same level of consciousness and thereby enables the patient to find different, healthier, and adaptive solutions for his conflicts. Developmental pathology, on the other hand, does not respond to interpretation. Even if confronted with the details of their aberrant development and the reasons for it, children or adult patients remain quite unable to alter what has happened and what is, after all, the very basis for their personality structure. If anything, supportive intervention in the earliest years may help to correct some of the most glaring developmental discrepancies.

9

Child Analysis As the Study of Mental Growth, Normal and Abnormal

[1979]

The contributions of psychoanalysis to the understanding of human development and its many deviations from the norm have been manifold from its beginnings. They have become all the more significant with the advent of child analysis when the reconstructed picture of early mental growth was deepened and extended by direct analytic ex-

First presented as a videotape at a symposium of the San Francisco Psychoanalytic Institute on April 21, 1979. This paper is published here for the first time. It will also appear in a forthcoming publication, *The Course of Life: Psychoanalytic Contributions Toward Personality Development,* edited by George H. Pollock and Stanley I. Greenspan. Washington, D.C.: National Institute of Mental Health. German translation: Die Kinderanalyse als Untersuchung der psychischen Entwicklung: Normal und abnorm. *Die Schriften der Anna Freud,* Volume 10. Munich: Kindler Verlag, 1980.

ploration of the hidden mental processes in the very young as well as by the analytically guided direct observation of their manifest reactions and types of behavior.

TRENDS IN CHILD ANALYTIC WORK

It is well known to workers in the field that the gradual spread and intensification of child analysis produced a variety of trends, consecutive or simultaneous, permanent or transitory, with lasting or evanescent results, each direction of interest upheld by prominent representatives and also, in some instances, disappearing from the field with them.

The Infantile Neurosis and Its Prevention

The most familiar of these is the early era devoted to the study of the infantile neurosis and its prevention, initiated by Freud's case history of Little Hans and followed on the one hand by the first child analytic treatments in Vienna, Berlin, and London, and on the other hand by the first analytic-educational experiments in Vienna, London, and Moscow.

The Technique of Child Analysis

There followed as a permanent, still ongoing trend, the struggle for the creation of a child analytic technique, whether dependent or independent of the classical technique for adult analysis. Such a method was meant to mitigate the effects of the child's unwillingness or inability to embark on free association, his reduced insight and sincerity, his different transference reactions, and his unreliable therapeutic alliance due to the heightened pressure for immediate wish fulfillment and resulting diminished tolerance for frustration and anxiety.

The Widening Scope of Therapeutic Effort

Intermittently, as in the mainstream of psychoanalysis, the ambition to widen the scope of therapeutic application dominated the scene and led to the experimental treatment of disorders beyond the limits of the infantile neuroses, namely, to the inclusion of borderline cases, autisms, infantile psychoses, and mental deficiencies.

Child Analysis versus Adult Analysis

At times, the interrelations between child analysis and adult analysis were pushed into the foreground with questions posed and answered such as the following: whether the child analyst's findings confirm, refute, or amend what adult analysis had gleaned about the individual's early history; whether, beyond this, child analytic work can break new ground; and, more recently, whether the added developmental information gained in child analysis has repercussions for the technical approach to adult patients and helps in the understanding of some of their more obscure deficiencies and abnormalities.

The Search for the Onset of Pathology

Finally, in our times, these various efforts culminated in

one overriding concern, namely, in a determined search for the starting point of pathological involvement as such, whether this manifested itself as neurotic or psychotic symptomatology, as ego distortion, as character malformation, or as social casualties of every description and severity. As the studies proceeded, pathogenic processes which were originally ascribed to the phallic-oedipal phase were traced further and further back to the very beginning of mental or even of physical life.

Specialization of Theoretical Interest

It is this last-mentioned concern which caused many child analytic authors to move toward a specialization of interest, i.e., to select as their particular subject of study the one period of life which to them seemed outstanding in its significance for determining the future difference between function and malfunction, efficiency and deficiency, adaptation and maladaptation, in short, between normality and pathology in human growth. Some authors fasten onto the birth process itself, hold its accumulation of distress responsible for creating an imbalance within the pleasure-pain series and for reducing the individual child's later frustration tolerance. Others choose as the vital era the first year of life with the transition from primary narcissism to object-directed libidinal interests, the whole process monitored by a successful or stunted by a deficient mother-infant relationship. Following Margaret Mahler's lead, still others select the fascinating period of separation-individuation in the second year of life as the crucial one for deciding about the individual's further healthy independence and intact sense of identity. The oral, anal, and phallic levels have each found their own protagonists, with links being forced between the happenings of them and specific pathological manifestations. If less pathogenic significance is attributed to the latency period (the normality or disruption of which is seen in itself as a function of the preceding developmental processes), this is offset again by a concentration of interest and accumulation of publications on the adolescent years which, after all, have the final say about the young person's adult sexuality and social adaptation.

The relevant child analytic literature thus presents to its readers a multitude of phase-centered studies, basically independent of each other but almost identical in their orientation toward the elucidation of pathology as the derivative of one or the other specific developmental stage.

THE CONCEPT OF DEVELOPMENTAL LINES

What the child analytic literature does not offer, so far, are consecutive longitudinal lines of development which, irrespective of health or illness, are concerned with all the characteristics which distinguish the mature from the immature human individual.

Three Examples of Developmental Lines in Psychoanalytic Theory

Not that, in the main body of psychoanalytic theory, we are left without prototypes for such lines. Concerning the development of the sexual drive, this is offered by the step-for-step advance from one level to another, the oral, anal, and phallic organizations following each other in a sequence determined on the physical side by the prominence of certain relevant body zones, on the libidinal side by the moves from anaclitic to constant, from ambivalent to post-ambivalent relationships, both series of progress heavily influenced by the environmental responses of the human objects toward whom the child's urges are directed.

Concerning the ego's mechanisms of defense against danger, anxiety, and unpleasure of all types, we have been given a distinctive line of defense leading from flight and denial (against external dangers) to projection and introjection (against internal ones) and from these primitive methods to the highly important sophisticated devices of repression, reaction formation, and sublimation.

As regards the phenomenon of anxiety and the reasons for its arousal, a line has been traced, leading from the archaic fears of darkness, noise, and loneliness (caused by the ego's weakness and immaturity) to the fears of abandonment, object loss, and loss of love (caused by the child's libidinal dependence), and finally to fear of the superego's disapproval, i.e., guilt (caused by the internalization of parental demands).

Some Child Analytic Work on Further Lines

What concerns us today, however, are the many other characteristics expected from the average adult which, on the basis of analytic work with adults, are described as to their end products, but for which no developmental pre-stages are itemized. This omission not only leaves a gap in developmental theory, it also creates the false impression that such achievements are come by easily, in fact, that they are simply the result of smooth, undisputed, nonconflictual maturation.

By now, there are a number of instances where child analytic work has been able to correct this error. Developmental lines have been traced, and implemented in detail, from libidinal dependence to self-reliance; from egocentricity to peer relationships; from inability to manage the body and its functions to the child's control of them; from play to work. Apart from the steps which lead up to the final achievement in each instance, three important characteristics of such advances have been elicited:

— that they are, without exception, determined by a multiplicity of influences;
— that, not unlike neurotic symptoms, their various stages are compromise formations, constructed to comply at one and the same time with all of these disparate determinants;
— that they are the result of the ego's synthetic function, of the working of which they give important evidence.

Developmental Moves under Multiple Determination

As reported above for the line of sex development, the unfolding of all the other adult characteristics also proceeds under the combined influences, stemming on the one hand from the agencies within the personality structure, on the other hand from the environment. To name a few examples only:

For the step from anaclitic (need-satisfying) relationships to object constancy, the *id's* urgency for gratification needs to decrease; the *ego* needs to acquire the ability to retain memory traces of objects, regardless of their absence; the human *objects* of the child's libido need to be constantly and reliably available in the external world.

The separation-individuation process is completed under three determinants: on the *physical side,* the attainment of independent motility; on the *libidinal side,* a lessening of utter dependence; on the *environmental side,* the mother's acquiescence with her child's growing independence.

Control of elimination proceeds under the combined influence of the *physical* maturing of the sphincters; of the *environmental* routine imposed by the mothering adult; by the *ego's* tendency to comply to avoid loss of the latter's love.

The various steps on the complex line from play to work depend on the child's need for direct (or sublimated) *drive* satisfaction; on his awakening *ego* interests; on *environmental* provision of toys and opportunities; finally on the ego's maturing ability to maintain aim-directed activities *regardless of immediate pleasure gain.*

Developmental Moves As Compromises in Two Types of Conflict

To render the described developmental advances nonconflictual would presuppose that the multiple influences on them are basically united as to their purposes and essentially coordinated as to the timing of their maturation. Since neither is the case, conflicts are inevitable. As described in the theory of the neuroses, each agency within the personality structure pursues its own aims, while the environmental forces insist firmly on theirs. Thus, each step on each developmental line also needs to be a compromise and respond at least partially to each determinant. For example, while acquiring sphincter control to satisfy external authority, the child manages to salvage at least some pride and interest in his anal products and to satisfy these in indirect, displaced ways. While adopting the reality principle, he develops a whole secret domain of imagination and fantasy, free of interference by external demands. While learning to work in obedience to ego and environmental pressure, he invents the hobbies to replace the pleasures formerly gained from play.

Compromises of this kind are adaptive and stabilizing for development. Uncompromising advances, which exclusively serve either external or a single internal agency, prove intolerable for the individual in the long run and are apt to lead to breakdowns.

There is a second source of conflicts which impede progress and need to be resolved. The four interacting forces are frequently in disharmony with each other as regards the time factor. Ego and superego development may reach a level of maturity which is far in advance of the maturing of the drives. Vice versa, progress on the side of drive development may outstrip a delayed ego-superego growth. External intervention may be either too early or too late. Such different rates of progress in the various parts of the personality structure as well as wrongly timed environmental action throw development into confusion. The examples of this are manifold. For instance, the *archaic fears* (of darkness, noise) do not fade out and give way to the next type of anxiety at the appropriate time in cases where ego growth is delayed due to mental deficiency. The *oral-cannibalistic* fantasies, which normally arise before the ego's critical function is in action, become unacceptable, i.e., a source of conflict, in cases where ego functions are precocious. *Individuation* is hindered where the child's readiness to separate does not coincide in time with the mother's readiness to detach herself from symbiosis with him. *Anal satisfactions* are defended against too energetically and cause obsessive manifestations in cases where the superego is premature. In short, temporal disharmony, within the structure and/or with the environment, disrupts the order of developmental lines with pathological results on all levels.

Development As the Result of Synthesis

During our therapeutic activities, we are confronted routinely by the psychological formations which, as the result of introjection, identification, and integration, make up the personality. Firmly embedded as they are in the adult, they put our analytic efforts to dissect and dissolve them to a severe test. It is only during our work with children that we are offered the opportunity to meet psychic structure in the making and watch the ego's synthetic function while it is at work.

Integration serves healthy growth provided the elements synthesized by it—namely, the constitutional givens, the rate of structuralization, and parental influence—remain within the limits of an expectable norm. As frequently as not, this is not the case. Constitutional handicaps often affect the ego-id substratum. Structure building often is uneven, with defects on the id, ego, or superego side. Parents often happen to be indifferent, absent, rejecting, punitive, insensitive, or, contrariwise, overprotective, possessive, and seductive. Whatever the elements for personality building which thus are offered to the immature being, integration will take hold of them and forge them into a whole. It is the hallmark of the synthetic function that, while doing its work, it does not distinguish between what is suitable or unsuitable, helpful or harmful for the resulting picture. Thus, every step on a developmental line, besides being a compromise between conflicting forces, also represents an amalgamate of beneficial with malignant ingredients. The various mixtures which thereby are produced can be held responsible for the numerous variations, deviations, quirks, and eccentricities displayed in the final personalities.

SUGGESTIONS FOR FURTHER WORK

The Range of Developmental Lines

The samples of developmental lines named above must not, by any means, be mistaken for a complete enumeration. The list of adult characteristics is vast, and none of them is exempt from step-by-step, gradual evolvement.

Secondary process functioning, for example, is attained very slowly, linked with speech development, but with many, so far uncharted, halts and relapses which occur whenever the urge for immediate drive gratification reinstates direct primary process action.

Distinguishing between the *inner* and *outer world* has many—not yet described—prestages before it reaches its final form as the adult's *reality sense*.

On the line toward *discharging mental excitation* via mental (not somatic) pathways, there are all the notable (but not yet noted) holdups, breakdowns, and exemptions which occur whenever the road to conscious psychological expression is blocked by repression.

The line toward *impulse control* needs to be studied with a view toward degree and extent on the one hand and its constant alternation between success and failure on the other hand.

The development of a *time sense* in the adult is too much taken for granted, with too little attention paid to the pre-stages when time is measured exclusively by the id via the urgency of the drives, or to the period when environmentally imposed routine begins to prepare the child for the understanding of clock and calendar.

Likewise, the intermediate steps need to be characterized on the road from the child's *egocentric* to the adult's *objective* view of external events; on the road from childish *lack of insight* into internal processes to the adult's *acknowledgment* of them; as well as on the road to many other achievements.

The Respective Importance of Developmental Lines

That progression on the various developmental lines has different value for the final personality picture needs further elaboration. What can be stated now is only that some are vital, others of contributory relevance.

Obviously, the essential lines are those toward secondary process functioning, reality sense, objectivity, and insight (with some others to be added). No individual is deemed mature before all the steps on them have been taken, and before the end result is not only reached but made secure. This is different in the case of impulse control, mental discharge, peer relationships, even sex. In these respects, numerous individuals achieve no more than partial results, i.e., they stop at some intermediate station on the way which affects the qualitative performance of their personality while leaving their adult status unquestioned.

We know that, in *sex,* large numbers of people never reach the end point of the line, namely, true genitality, and, being otherwise adult, function sexually on a pregenital or prephallic level.

With regard to *impulse control* by the ego, many individuals cannot maintain this securely in the face of all conditions. They are adults, but their adult status in this respect is interrupted intermittently by temper outbursts or uncontrollable irritability when aggression reverts to the former state of being dominated by the id.

Where the line from *motor* to *verbal* expression of *aggression* remains uncompleted, it produces adults with violent characteristics.

The changeover from *somatic* to *mental* discharge of excitation is rarely carried to completion (except perhaps at the price of an obsessional neurosis); in many adults, affects such as anger, fear, impatience, and frustration still find outlet in headaches, sleep disturbances, stomach and digestive upsets.

Any study of the line toward *peer relationships* demonstrates how rarely, even in maturity, its final point is reached and how often the intermediate stages of rivalry, jealousy, and lack of empathy continue to be dominant.

The Interdependence of Developmental Lines

There are many open questions in this respect, beyond the obvious fact that certain lines of development cannot materialize without being preceded or at least supported by certain others.

Ego control of body functions and impulses depends on prior steps from dependence on objects to identification with them.

Secondary process functioning implies a simultaneous advance toward impulse control.

The reduction of *panic to signal anxiety* presupposes advances in the maturity of defense activity.

Any step from *play to work* needs a prior commitment to the reality principle.

More knowledge about these interrelations will benefit the upbringing as well as the treatment of children with manifest developmental difficulties. In the case of any particular trend failing to progress, it is important to determine whether the deficiency is rooted in that particular line itself or whether it is the secondary consequence of failure on another line.

It is wasted educational or therapeutic effort to try and urge a child toward advancing on the line of play materials if the real reason for backwardness in this developmental area is an arrest on the line of libido development (i.e.,

utter dependence on the mother which results in a preference for soft toys as transitional objects).

A solitary child will not develop better peer relationships
by being exposed to community life if his failure to progress on this line is due not to lack of opportunity, but to a
deficiency in the advance from narcissism and egocentricity
to object-libidinal relationships.

A Chronology of Developmental Lines

A chronology of development will always have to restrict
itself to general terms in view of the wide range of individual variation. What can be hypothesized at present is
no more than a rough division into three successive periods, each characterized by the number of forces interacting
within it and to some extent by the major lines of development which have their beginning in it.

The *first period,* which covers approximately the first
year of life, is simple in one respect, however important it
may be in others. Interaction is restricted to two agents,
the infant on the one hand, the mother on the other. The
infant supplies to the combination the needs and urges inherent in his id-ego matrix; the mother, her care in response to them.

Provided that constitutionally and environmentally the
ingredients from both sides are within the norm, three developmental lines take their departure from here: distinction between soma and psyche; between the child's own
and the mother's body; between self and object. However
modest these beginnings are, and how distant still from the
later mental discharge phenomena, from reality testing,

and from true object relationships, their occurrence is vital and their absence has disastrous results. A child who tries to rid himself of unacceptable thoughts by standing on his head to shake them out is definitely borderline. A child who does not acknowledge the extent and limits of his own body jeopardizes his later sense of identity. A child who maintains symbiosis with the mother fails to move toward the higher levels of libidinal relatedness.

The *second period* which, roughly, extends over the remainder of the preoedipal stages marks the interaction of three forces. Id and ego, after the onset of structuralization, act as two separate ones, with parental intervention making up the third.

The developments which are initiated, respectively continued, under these conditions are, among others, those toward the control of *motility* and other *physical functions,* toward *impulse control, secondary process* functioning, and object *constancy.* They are vital as a basis for further growth, and their failure or serious defect in them constitutes an ominous departure from mental health. They share at this stage the characteristic that forward and backward moves on the lines, progression and regression, alternate with each other. This is due to the state of the ego which, while immature, vascillates in its allegiance. When under pressure from the drives, it sides with the id in the interest of gratification. When under pressure from parental demands, it sides with the environment to avoid recrimination and loss of love.

Irregularity and interruption of advance in this second period are normal, provided the relapses are temporary. If, instead of being short-lived, they are prolonged or even permanent, they cause pathological manifestations which resemble neurotic symptoms but which, according to their structure, are not identical with them. They are pre-neurotic insofar as the conflicts which they are trying to solve are not yet truly internal but due in equal parts to disharmonies within the personality and with the external world. However, they represent a fertile breeding ground for the later infantile neuroses.

In the *third period,* after completed structuralization, all further steps toward maturity on all developmental lines take place under the combined and competing influence emanating from four sides: id, ego, superego, and environment. However, as the superego gains independence due to its introjections, it strengthens the ego in its attitudes on the one hand and, on the other hand, takes over much, or all, of the environment's role in shaping progress. Accordingly, advance becomes stabilized, and the disharmonies and conflicts involved in it change from the partly external to the truly intersystemic. Their solution, reached by compromise, may be adaptive, i.e., normal; or nonadaptive, i.e., truly neurotic.

CONCLUSION

On the basis of the foregoing argumentation, normality or pathology of development is seen to depend largely on four factors:

(i)   on the constitutional and experiential element in the life of an individual not departing too far from what is average and expectable;

(ii) on the internal agencies of the individual's personality maturing at approximately the same rate of speed, none of them being either delayed or precocious compared with the others;

(iii) on external intervention being well-timed, coming neither too early nor too late;

(iv) on the ego's mechanisms used to achieve the necessary compromises being age-adequate, i.e., neither too primitive nor too sophisticated.

To investigate the happenings on individual developmental lines from the aspect of these four points is recommended as a next rewarding trend for child analytic work.

10

Insight: Its Presence and Absence As a Factor in Normal Development

[1980]

SELF-KNOWLEDGE AS THE
COMMUNICATION BETWEEN ID AND EGO

The extent of an individual's knowledge of his own psychic processes is one of the foremost problems which confront the psychoanalyst. Most members of the profession are concerned with this above all as a phenomenon within the

---

Based on a paper presented at the Hampstead Clinic International Forum on The Significance of Insight in Psychoanalytic Theory and Practice, held in London, November 1979. This paper, written in 1980, is published here for the first time. It will also appear in *The Psychoanalytic Study of the Child,* Volume 36. New Haven & London: Yale University Press, 1981. German translation: Über Einsicht in das unbewusste Seelenleben. *Die Schriften der Anna Freud,* Volume 10. Munich: Kindler Verlag, 1980.

analytic treatment situation and significantly influenced by it. I maintain here that it is of no less significance as a factor within the ongoing developmental processes and of decisive influence on their positive or negative outcome.

The word used within the psychoanalytic terminology for this specific manifestation is "insight" (i.e., the English translation of the German *Einsicht*). Freud used the term *Einsicht* almost exclusively for a patient's acknowledgment of the presence and significance of his psychological troubles (*Krankheitseinsicht*), though it occasionally also occurs in his *Gesammelte Schriften* as denoting "knowledge" in general, and in one special instance as denoting "revelation." The German adjective *einsichtig,* which is derived from the noun, means "reasonable," "open to argument," "not stubborn," while its English form "insightful" means "knowledgeable." In fact, whenever we find the term "insight" used by English authors, it is always as a synonym for self-knowledge, i.e., for the links between consciousness and the unconscious, for understanding the reasons for one's moods and feelings, the relationships between past and present, the motivations for one's actions, one's predilections or their opposites.

TWO OPINIONS CONCERNING INSIGHT

Taking this wider connotation of the term as our starting point, we find in the psychoanalytic literature two contrasting opinions concerning it. There are many authors who maintain that it is the task of analysis to return to the patient the insight he has lost due to his neurosis, i.e., due to the crippling use of defenses employed against the upsurges from the id and embedded in his symptomatic compromise formations. There are others[1] who express the point of view that psychoanalytic treatment takes the patient much further regarding the capacity for insight than is achieved by the normal person who has never undergone psychoanalytic therapy. Personally, I incline strongly toward this second opinion. I believe that the psychoanalytic technique opens up for the analysand a possibility to view his inner life to an extent never reached under the normal conditions of life, thus not merely *restoring* but *creating* insight. I also believe that this fact is responsible for a complaint frequently heard from young individuals who have undergone successful analytic treatment. To their own astonishment, they find it quite difficult to communicate with those of their contemporaries who have not undergone the same experience. The new way of looking into and at themselves which they have acquired in analysis isolates them to a certain extent. Or, to put it in other words: they are now more insightful than their peers, a fact which makes them stand out among them.

TWO STANDARDS OF BEHAVIOR: TOWARD INSIDE AND OUTSIDE

As analysts, we take it for granted that the amount of insight possessed by an unanalyzed person is minimal, and that this is due to the protective barrier between id and ego, erected to shield the latter from any excessive awareness of mental discomfort, pain, anxiety, narcissistic hurt, etc.

[1] See in this connection Kennedy (1979) and Clifford Yorke (1965).

However, this explanation, although enlightening in one respect, leaves many questions unanswered in others. It fails to answer, for example, why the mental apparatus is so selective in its avoidances; why it can blind itself to unpleasure provided this arises from within, while there is no equivalent response to unpleasure which threatens from external reality. There is, after all, no lack of evidence from mountaineers, explorers, rescuers, firemen, political dissidents, and others that they are able to brave the adverse consequences of their actions and have no inclination to shut their eyes to them, as they might do in the case of internal danger. There are also the scientists who relentlessly pursue the truth in their physical fields, but accept at the same time the most shallow rationalizations with regard to their own psychological motives.

It needs additional explanation *how* human beings can, at one and the same time, be heroic and cowardly, truth-loving and victims of self-deception;[2] *when,* at which points of development, the different behavior toward inner and outer reality comes into being; *why* the defense mechanisms which ward off unpleasure work in one direction only, i.e., toward the inner hazards; *whether* the analytic techniques of free association, dream and transference interpretation are really the only means of widening the individual's awareness of the psychic processes within himself; or *where* in his progress toward maturity similar chances

[2] That the difference between the two attitudes cannot be explained simply by the presence or absence of fear is borne out by the remark of a little boy who was admonished by his mother not to be so fearful of the dark. "Imagine," said the mother, "what you would do if you were a soldier," to which the child replied very wisely: "Soldiers also are afraid. They just do not mind."

exist for increasing insight.

Even though it may at present be impossible to find answers to all these questions, the mere posing of them might prove a profitable exercise.

INSIGHT VERSUS ORIENTATION: A QUESTION OF TIMING

The described discrepancy between insight (into the psychic processes) and orientation (in the external world) seems to start with the maturation of ego functions in the first two years of life. It is these functions which, very gradually, turn the drive-dominated, almost animallike newborn into an acceptable social being. They humanize him in the sense that they make him susceptible to influence from the environment, promote his emotional attachment to the object world, strengthen his desire to comply with the parents' wishes, in short, serve his adaptation. However, at the same time, and especially in the second year of life when the infant becomes mobile, they also represent a danger. While the balance between the strength of id and ego forces is still a precarious one, there is the distinct possibility that whatever the ego learns may be drawn totally into the service of the id, in fact, help it to attain the fulfillment of drive derivatives which are unacceptable to the environment, bring with it the threat of punishment or loss of love, and, instead of serving adaptation, disturb it. This, then is the moment when defense sets in.

Defense activity, as understood in analytic theory, begins in the most primitive way with denial and externalization and advances from those to introjection and projection, repression and reaction formation, sublimation, etc. With their combined aim of blotting out, keeping off, deflecting, and mitigating the id derivatives, they represent the (partial) enmity of the ego toward the id, i.e., the need to protect the ego organization itself as well as the ego's relationship to the environment from the disruptive interference of the drives and the urgency with which they strive for fulfillment.

DEFENSE MECHANISMS AS
IMPAIRMENT OF EGO FUNCTION

However, the defense mechanisms of the ego do not only oppose and modify the id wishes. They do not only borrow some of the characteristics from the primary processes, as, for example, when turning a striving into its opposite, a process that makes use of the identity between opposites which exists in the unconscious; or when externalizing a wish, a process that is very similar to the easy displacement of strivings which occurs within primary process functioning. They also have another close and potentially damaging relationship to the ego functions which often escapes notice or, rather, becomes visible only during the earlier periods of development.

Attention, perception, memory, reason, reality testing, understanding of causality, secondary process thinking improve constantly during the whole course of early childhood. They help the child to orient himself and alert him to dangers, whether these arise from water, fire, heights, imprudent actions, or from evoking disapproval. The keener these functions are, the safer can the older child feel in his environment, in contrast to the less developed toddler who is in permanent need of adult protection. However, while threats from without are adequately dealt with in this manner, dangerous impulses from within do not respond to the same methods. They are more difficult for the child to combat when they are perceived, acknowledged, and remembered, and for that reason defense turns not only directly against the id derivatives themselves but tries simultaneously to put the relevant ego functions at least partially out of action. From then onward, perceptiveness of the external world takes precedence over perceptiveness of internal processes. Insight becomes doubly blunted, every defense against the drives damaging at the same time one or the other of the developing ego functions.

Denial (of internal unpleasure) sets in simultaneously with the child's progress toward correctly perceiving, apperceiving, and acknowledging facts in his surroundings. Thus, while his senses are sharpened in one direction, they are, by the use of this defense mechanism, at the same time blunted in another. Reality sense with regard to the outside world and denial with regard to internal processes are obviously at cross-purposes with each other. What suffers is insight.

Externalization is widely used by the young child to ascribe his own unwanted feelings, wishes, and impulses to some outside agency, whether human being or animal, and so to escape responsibility for them. *Projection* acts similarly, while *introjection* appropriates wanted items, qualities, attitudes from other people. This merging with the affairs of others happens while, at the same time, the child's differentiation from others and sense of his own identity are built up. There is no doubt that the two moves run counter to each other, the latter dominating the relations with the outer, the former the relations with the inner world.

Isolation, a much-used defense mechanism for the purpose of splitting feelings from factual experience, works simultaneously with the development of the all-important synthetic function whose purpose it is to create a whole out of the miscellaneous experiences of life. While the synthetic function binds the various parts of the personality together, thus creating the self, isolation, for its own defensive purposes, èstranges them from each other and keeps them apart.

Rationalization which deceives the individual about his motives for action runs counter to the important ego capacities for cognition, fact finding, and reality testing.

Denial in fantasy obscures and changes to the opposite what reason and logic try to present to the individual as unalterable facts.

Finally, and perhaps most importantly for the fate of insight, *repression* destroys the intactness of memory which, at this time, is in the process of being perfected as a function. With the withdrawal of conscious cathexis from dangerous, frightening, and upsetting items of psychic content, memory becomes incomplete and gaps and deletions interrupt its coherent sequence. It is especially these gaps which the widening of consciousness in analytic therapy attempts to fill.[3]

[3]There are certain clinical experiences which reveal that damage to memory by repression can go beyond the blotting out of inner experience and spread to the ordinary events of life. An example of this is

In case the developmental outline sketched above is at all correct, we have to picture the child as emerging from his early years with his ego well equipped for formal learning and doubly protected against inroads from within, on the one hand by the defense mechanisms which have been chosen and on the other hand by their dimming the very functions which otherwise stand him in such good stead for the exploration of the world. Whether this contrasting attitude toward within and without is totally explained by his individual needs, i.e., in ontogenetic terms, is an open question. It may go back to phylogenesis, when men had to maintain themselves in surroundings which were more hostile and more dangerous to them than any of their own instinctual drives.

THE CHANCES TO REGAIN INSIGHT

A Missed Chance in the Latency Period

Since, according to the foregoing, the individual's restriction of insight is based on the hazardous imbalance of id and ego forces in the under-five, the weakening of the id and strengthening of the ego in the latency period should alter the situation and enable the latency child to be less defensive. However, this is not what happens. On the contrary, latency children, and especially those with a strong superego, rely all the more on their existing defenses.

---

a boy patient who had developed such consistent "forgetting" for his wrongdoings that his memory also became unreliable for the purpose of learning, for totally permitted pursuits, etc. He had altogether turned himself into a generally "forgetful" person.

There is no spontaneous move toward dismantling the defenses and of taking a closer look at themselves. Even in analytic treatment, they display the most extraordinary resistances against this possibility. They get furious with the analyst's interpretations which they consider unfair. According to their own belief, they have done the right thing to deflect or close their eyes to their drive derivatives and even under the reassuring guidance of the analyst, they are reluctant to believe that a clearer view of internal happenings would increase, not lessen, the chances of moral control.

Adolescence As a Second Chance

Whoever works with adolescents, analytically or otherwise, is impressed with their extreme preoccupation with themselves. Whatever happens in them looms very much larger than any events in their everyday life. There is an unmistakable move toward and wish for insight, which, however, takes on a peculiar form. Thought, wishes, fantasies, fears, and judgments are translated into concern with cosmic, political, or philosophical matters. They are, thus, removed from the personal sphere as far as possible. Obviously, such adolescents hope to understand what happens in themselves in the less frightening terms of the world at large.

Nevertheless, this attempt to gain or regain insight also fails or, rather, remains abortive.

Chances for Insight in Adult Life

We do not expect any spontaneous changes in the capacity

for insight once development has ceased. Within the adult individual, the relations between id and ego are regulated by his own personal defense organization, and they remain permanent unless there are upsetting alterations in the relative strength of drive and ego forces, or unless frustration, regression, and intolerable conflicts lead to pathological, symptomatic compromise solutions. It is only in these instances that analytic therapy is called upon to widen the ego's view of what is happening in the unconscious and, with it, its area of effectiveness. Under all other circumstances, normal life can proceed however limited the amount of self-knowledge which is at the disposal of the individual.

There are, however, some exceptions to this common rule.

Poets are renowned for knowing almost as much of unconscious motivation as do analysts or successfully analyzed persons. Even though their insight is not always directed toward their own psychic processes, it is most impressive with regard to the figures they invent. One of the reasons for this may be that in the creative writer the unconscious and consciousness are not closed off from each other by the usual barriers. On the one hand, the phenomenon of "inspiration" gives evidence that elements from the id have no difficulty to reach the conscious surface; on the other hand, ego functions are not prevented in the usual way from penetrating the id.

There is also the other possibility that for the creative artist, the respective importance of inner and outer events is reversed. What is of real relevance for him are the psychic events, as they happen in him, or as he fashions them in his creations, while reality is comparatively negligible. Therefore, he can direct toward the inner world the same undiminished ego capacities which ordinary people use for orientation outside.

There are, finally, some rare individuals who, driven by the wish for discovery and regard for truth, succeed in transgressing the protective borders between their internal agencies. On their own, and open-eyed, they investigate what lies beyond consciousness, in the spirit of examining strange tribal customs in a dark continent. It may be interesting to remember that Freud thought of himself as an explorer of this kind.

Part II

Contributions to
Psychoanalytic Symposia

11

Comments on Aggression
(1972 [1971])

Psychoanalytic concepts from the areas of technique, clinical practice, or theory are occasionally elevated to a position where the scientific discussion of one of the International Psycho-Analytical Congresses centers around them. Whenever this happens, speculation invariably arises as to the reasons for their choice. What the Program Committee may have had in mind might have been the need to place an important but recently neglected subject, such as the *obsessional neurosis,* once more into the limelight of general interest; or to restore significance to an orig-

Closing Scientific Presentation on the Theme of Aggression, delivered at the 27th International Psycho-Analytical Congress, Vienna, July 1971. First published in the *International Journal of Psycho-Analysis,* 53:163-172, 1972. Italian translation: Commenti sull'aggressività. *Opere,* 3:1117-1136. Turin: Paolo Boringhieri, 1979. German translation: Bemerkungen zur Aggression. *Die Schriften der Anna Freud,* Volume 10. Munich: Kindler Verlag, 1980.

inally precise term such as *acting out,* which had lost meaning over the years due to overuse; or to create some order and, if possible, consensus of opinion with regard to a major issue in psychoanalytic thinking as — for this Congress — on the subject of *aggression.*

Whatever the results of earlier ventures, the last-named one did no more, obviously, than to demonstrate some of the limits of scientific group efforts of this nature. It yielded a useful survey of the relevant publications as provided by the psychoanalytic journals of the last thirty or forty years, partly in the form of reviews, for the greater part in the form of repetitions and reassertions of original opinions. What it failed to produce was the removal of uncertainties concerning the status of aggression in the theory of drives, or the clarification of some urgent problems such as the part played by aggression in normal infantile development; its involvement with the various agencies in the psychic structure; its role for character formation; its part in the pathogenesis of neurosis, psychosis, delinquency, the perversions, etc.

The failure met with in these respects is all the more conspicuous since, by virtue of their previous work, analysts seemed well equipped for the study of aggression. This was emphasized in the symposium by Martin Stein (see Lussier, 1972), who claimed the subject as a legitimate area for analytic investigation and marveled at the "clouded vision" displayed by authors when actually grappling with the problem of aggression.

However, a closer look at the situation leads to a different opinion, though this at first glance may appear paradoxical. What obscures the analyst's view when he approaches the subject of aggression may be his very experiences with the vicissitudes of the sexual drive. Such findings, when displaced from the area of their origin to a new set of circumstances, inevitably create expectations, whether warranted or not. In the latter case, they take on the role of preconceived ideas which handicap an investigation, i.e., hamper the kind of unbiased clinical-psychological examination of the problem which was demanded, even if not achieved, by many of the speakers at the Congress.

What I have in mind here are the notions which are firmly entrenched in the sexual theory of psychoanalysis: the discovery of the infantile levels and stages through which the drive has to pass before the end product is reached; the characterization of the drive from the aspects of source, aim, and object; finally, the inclusion of the drive in the framework of a dualistic theory of drives.

It seems worthwhile to examine these notions derived from the study of sex with regard to their applicability to aggression; to take note of similarity or difference of fit; and, in general, to determine whether there are points where, far from being assets, they have become straitjackets within which the study of aggression has remained confined.

THE CONCEPT OF STAGE DEVELOPMENT

In the unbiased investigation of the sexual drive which preceded the publication of the *Three Essays on the Theory of Sexuality* (1905), the notion of consecutive libidinal stages as precursors of adult genitality stands out as the most significant discovery. To pursue the adult patient's sex life to these infantile roots and to trace their residues in its distortions and perversities has always been one of the legitimate tasks in psychoanalytic therapy. Further, and long before the beginning of independent analytic studies of aggression, the aggressive nature of infantile sexuality was taken for granted, as evidenced by the cannibalistic tendencies and fantasies on the oral level; the sadistic, tormenting, possessive attitudes characteristic of the anal stage; and the domineering, thrusting qualities of phallic sexuality. Any doubt as to the essential role of aggressive admixtures to these early forms of sex life was removed by the analytic investigation of cases where, due to endowment or neurotic interference, aggression was absent, repressed, or inhibited, with the invariable result that oral, anal, and phallic pleasure was diminished or missing and none of the normal aims of the child's libidinal life could be achieved.

Experience with this close interrelation between sex and aggression in infantile life can be held responsible, therefore, for the analytic investigator's readiness to conceive of stages and levels in the development of human aggression as well. In fact, the terms of oral, anal, and phallic aggression are scattered profusely through the whole analytic literature, not only as shorthand descriptions for aggressive elements being fused with orality, anality, and phallic sexuality, but as if it were a proven fact that it is the aggressive drive itself which, similar to the sexual one, undergoes consecutive qualitative transformations. Before this can be asserted with any confidence, further developmental studies of the infantile drive mixture need to be undertaken, this time from the aspect of aggression.[1]

SOURCE, AIM, AND OBJECT

Other notions to be examined from the point of view of applicability are those of source, aim, and object. With regard to sex, dissection of its manifestations from these aspects has proved so useful that, in analytic thinking, they are applied almost automatically to any other instinctual striving.

The Source of Aggression

The source of aggressive phenomena has been discussed not only in the analytic world but, far beyond it, by ethologists, anthropologists, social scientists, and others. There is among the latter a wide variety of beliefs to be found, ranging from the conviction that "In the case of the human species aggressive behavior also has a phylogenetic basis" (Lorenz, 1963) to the equally firmly held theory of the environmentalists that aggression is a "learned response" with "no biological preformed basis," and "aggressive behavior [is] entirely determined by environmental forms such as cultural conditioning." "Electrical or chemical stimulation

[1] That such studies may lead to a far-reaching reappraisal of the libidinal phases themselves is suggested by K. R. Eissler (1971) in a paper written, though not presented, at the time of the symposium. On the basis of observations carried out on the licking and sucking movements of the newborn, Eissler claims the oral phase as predominantly representative of the aggressive drive since the "effect of the sucking reflex is the disappearance of the object at which it is aimed; this makes it easy, indeed unavoidable, to refer to it as the prototype of aggression" (p. 39). Only the lip and tongue sensations are left for the libidinal side.

of the brain," "basic neuronal structures," etc., are held responsible by others.[2]

What appears in the nonanalytic world in this manner as a revival of the nature-nurture controversy is mirrored among analytic authors by the dispute whether to allocate aggression to the ego or, with Freud, to the id. Accordingly, pronouncements range from the view of aggression as a "capacity," in addition to being an instinctual drive (Sandler, in Lussier, 1972), to its status predominantly as an "independent, primary, innate drive" (Loewenstein, in Lussier, 1972), the latter backed in clinical opinion by three observable manifestations: the unmistakable *impetus* which is inherent in any aggressive striving; the unmistakable *relief* which follows its discharge; the unmistakable *distress* and its pathological consequences when discharge is blocked.

Further argumentation centers around the question whether there are "aggressiogenic" zones, equivalent or at least comparable to the erotogenic ones. Several authors remark on their obvious absence (Brenner, 1971; Gillespie, 1971), as well as on the present lack of any evidence for links with physiological or endocrine phenomena (Brenner, 1971). Others regard the musculature as an aggressiogenic zone (Stone, 1971), a view emphatically opposed by Gillespie, who sees the motor apparatus not as the source but as the executive organ of aggression. There is also the opinion that "there are no purely erotogenic zones" and that all of them serve both libido and aggression (Eissler, 1971, p. 42).

Altogether, with the array of opinions as divergent as

[2]See a useful summary of these views in "Aggression: Instinct or Symptom," by Derek Freeman (1968).

described, listeners were left with the impression that the problem of the source of aggression is unsolved so far, i.e., that while with regard to sexual development "the physical links between stimulation and gratification can be mapped out with relative ease," the processes are not as well marked in the area of aggression (Eissler, p. 44).

A similar verdict of "nonproven" was expressed by Gillespie (1971), with the suggestion therefore to define aggression as "a fundamental, irreducible element in the human constitution" (p. 159). By leaving the nature as well as the source of this element an open question, the formulation obviously is designed to circumvent controversy and to build a bridge between differing assertions.

The Aim of Aggression

As is to be expected, the differences of opinion concerning the source of aggression extend to the topic of its aim. The various suggestions brought forward here also cover a wide area, ranging from aims such as discharge, avoidance of rising tension, removal of upset and displeasure, upkeep of homeostasis (Gillespie, 1971) to destruction for its own sake.

However, in this multitude of descriptions, to my mind, not enough notice is taken of a glaring difference between sex and aggression with regard to aim. The libidinal aims, whether biologically or physiologically prescribed, whether direct or sublimated, are always specific to the drive. In contrast, aggression can associate itself with aims and purposes of extraneous kinds, lending them their force. We are familiar with this, of course, from the study of infantile sexuality, where aggression fuses with the libido and helps to pursue and attain the latter's aims. But this is only one example among many. Aggression also comes to the aid, either constructively or destructively, of purposes such as, for instance, vengeance, war, honor, mercy, and mastery (Stone, 1971), i.e., in the service of aims which are dictated either by the ego or the superego.

There is in this respect even the suggestion of a developmental line of aims, positive and negative. Eissler (1971) describes an initial stage of "self-preservation intensely cathected with aggressive energy" and later stages of "narcissism and ambivalence serving as the steering-wheels for aggression, narcissism taking hold of aggression and using it for its own purposes."

The Object of Aggression

The danger of transferring expectations wholesale from one area of study to another is even more obvious when we proceed to the subject of object relations. It remains true, of course, that at the beginning of life the processes which underlie object attachment do not differ for the two drives. Both take the mother as their first target and cathect her anaclitically, i.e., on the basis of her satisfying and frustrating functions vis-à-vis the infant's needs. Nevertheless, the correspondence between the two processes does not continue and, after infancy, the developmental lines of sex and aggression become significantly different. For the libido, the anaclitic relationship, which is dominated by the urgency of body needs and therefore intermittent, is merely a transitory phase of comparatively short duration.

From it, development proceeds to an ever-increasing independence of needs and tensions and, with this, to object constancy. The highest level reached in this respect is the permanent, or at least semipermanent, loving attachments which, on the one hand, are rooted in the subject's total personality and, on the other hand, take account not only of the object's services and functions but of the totality of his personal characteristics and qualities.

This is different for the aggressive drive. Aggression, and with it the coordinated affects of hate, anger, resentment, etc., remains "anaclitic" much longer and more thoroughly, i.e., more closely tied to the pleasure-pain, satisfaction-frustration experiences. What is missing is the developmental step away from intermittent and toward permanent commitments. It may be correct to say that there is no object constancy for aggression as there is for the libido. There is an apparent clinical example of it in the fixed hate with which the paranoid patient is tied to his persecutor. But this, of course, is no more than a semblance since hate in the case of paranoia is a pathological vicissitude of the libido rather than a direct expression of the aggressive drive.

We call a "good lover" one who is faithful to his objects, i.e., constant in cathecting them. In contrast, the "good hater" is promiscuous, i.e., he has free aggression at his disposal and is ready to cathect with it on a nonpermanent basis any object who, either by his actions or his characteristics, offers adequate provocation.

THE TWIN ROLE OF SEX AND AGGRESSION IN PSYCHIC CONFLICT

While the foregoing findings alert us to the differences in

functioning between sex and aggression, an impression of their sameness remains, derived from the twin role played by the two drives in psychic conflict (Brenner, 1971).

Sex and aggression have in common that in their original form and strength they cannot be accommodated in the individual's life within a community and that because of this they have to be reduced in quantity and changed in quality. The pressures which their demands exert on the ego in the resulting intersystemic conflicts are equal in both cases. So is the anxiety aroused in the ego and the need to bring the ego's mechanisms of defense into action against them, i.e., to limit, modify, control, and bind them. There also is identity with regard to the compromises which are formed between the drives and the defending forces, i.e., the neurotic symptom formation which results. The most convincing clinical illustration of the identical roles played by the two drives in this respect is the obsessional neurosis with its symptomatology derived equally from the warding off of both the libidinal and the aggressive elements of the anal-sadistic stage.

However, even identical twins have their differences, though these tend to be overlooked in favor of their more striking similarities. The latter, in fact, is what happens to our view of the defense organization and its dealings with sex and aggression: we habitually stress similarities and ignore differences. What probably prejudices us in this respect is the fact that a considerable number of major defenses are equally effective in dealing with either drive. Those to be named as such are *denial, repression, reaction formation, projection, identification, turning from object to self, turning passive into active.*

But there also are others, though admittedly minor defenses, where differences are worth noting. The mechanism of *identification with the aggressor,* as a means of achieving the turn of passive into active, by implication deals not with the libido but with aggression (or rather masochism as its counterpart). The mechanism of *displacement of object* from the animate to the inanimate, or from humans to animals, does play some role in the conflicts with infantile sexuality but holds a much more significant place in the child's or adult's struggle with his aggression. *Undoing,* as it is known from the obsessional neurosis, is directed against aggression only. *Delegation* (Stone, 1971) is another defensive measure, effective in curbing the individual's aggression, and does so in two ways. One consists in attributing responsibility for the aggressive action or wish to another person or external influence; this happens normally in early childhood or, abnormally, in the paranoid reactions. The other is the familiar social phenomenon that the individual denies himself the fulfillment of aggressive wishes but concedes permission for it to some higher agency such as the state, the police, the military or legal authorities. This latter instance resembles somewhat the working of *altruism* on the libidinal side; the "altruistic" individual "delegates" to others the libidinal wishes which he denies to himself; i.e., he "externalizes" or "displaces" them, with the result that he can enjoy their fulfillment vicariously.

Change of Instrument as a Defensive Measure

If we look for defenses which are employed exclusively in the struggle with aggression and are, indeed, specific for it,

I suggest that we explore the consecutive change of tools or instruments by means of which aggression is expressed. It is no new concept, of course, that there are executive organs coordinated with a drive which serve its discharge (Freud, 1923a; Gillespie, 1971; Eissler, 1971). This is well known on the side of both libido and aggression, even though with some authors we find some blurring of the distinction between the creation of a craving in a specific organ and the same organ serving its discharge.

However, there are significant differences here between libido and aggression and these should be taken into account so far as the role, functioning, and fate of the executive organs are concerned. On the side of sex, the organs for discharge are increasingly suited to their task, the more the immature individual grows toward maturity. This is evidenced clearly by the advance from the pregenital to the genital sexual apparatus. This is different on the side of aggression where, with advancing age of the child, the organs for discharge are increasingly geared to the qualitative transformation and quantitative mitigation of the drive, i.e., to the defense against it.[3]

Owing to the interrelations between sex and aggression in early childhood, various tools for aggressive discharge are borrowed from one or the other of the libidinal stages; so, for example, the *teeth* during the later part of orality for the aggressive purpose of biting; *excrement* during anality for the aggressive purpose of dirtying, polluting; the *penis*

---

[3] If there is, in fact, a decrease of aggression during the process of growth (as assumed by Eissler), this may well be due not to a vicissitude of the drive itself but to an increase in the working of this particular defensive device, i.e., defense via change of instrument.

in the phallic phase for aggressive display.

However, these tools are not the only ones, by any means. Almost any part of the infant's or young child's body can serve the same aggressive purpose: the *voice* for screaming and crying to express anger, rage, fury; the *mouth* for aggressive spitting; the *feet* and *legs* for kicking; the *hands, fists, arms* for hitting; indeed, the *musculature* as a whole for aggressive attack.

In the upbringing of children, there was always some tacit understanding that one or the other of these tools of aggression is appropriate for a particular age while others are not. Thus, *screaming* is considered legitimate in the preverbal period, but taken as part of a temper tantrum when in use later. *Biting* as a method of attack is conceded to the toddler but not to the older child. *Feces* (which also play their part as a libidinal gift in infancy) are not supposed to be used aggressively after the anal stage, although some of this use survives until much later as an expression of contempt and derision in connection with criminality. *Kicking* and *hitting* are allocated to almost any stage, although after the toddler age they lose their random quality and become increasingly purposeful.

Concern for the object of aggression, whether animate or inanimate, also plays its part: with advancing age, the child is expected to view his aggressive expressions from the aspect of their harmful effects and to modify the tools used for them accordingly.[4]

---

[4] An instructive clinical illustration in this respect is the experience with a little girl of three, in the throes of a struggle with her rather wild, aggressive nature. She returned one day from nursery school, to report triumphantly on her "good" behavior in the group: "Not hit, not kick, not bit, only spit!"

Thus, with increasing ego development, secondary process functioning and verbalization, important changes take place in the pathways through which aggression is discharged. Nevertheless, it would be an error to assume that the move toward mitigation of aggression is a constant one. Not all the changes of instrument which occur serve the purpose of defense. There is a break in the process which occurs at some time, most likely at the border between early childhood and the latency period, when further aggressive development branches out in two different directions. One is toward mitigation and control of the drive by means of verbalization: words, from then onward, are expected to take the place of muscular action. Hence the older child's pleasure in swearwords, which simultaneously serve the defense against anality and aggression. ("Dirty words" instead of dirty actions; verbal abuse instead of physical attack.) The other branch leads in the opposite direction. There also is, in the child, growing discontent with the use of mere body parts as the executive organs of aggression and the wish to amplify them by the introduction of tools, toys in the beginning, real offensive weapons in later life: knives instead of the teeth; sticks and stones instead of fists and feet; guns, bombs, and poisons instead of emanations from the body, etc.

The significance of this split in development is important. If we accept the dictum that "the man who first flung a word of abuse at his enemy instead of a spear was the founder of civilization" (Freud, 1893, p. 36), then we might say that the individual who first supplemented the action of his fist by the power of a mechanical device was the inventor of war.

Some evidence for the role played by body parts as tools of aggression is found in the clinical material of adult analytic patients in whom faint, rudimentary physical accompaniments to affects such as anger, hate, rage can be discerned. Every aggressive reaction of this kind gives rise in them to sensations, for example, in the feet, coupled with a fantasy of stamping on the enemy; or in the hands, with a fantasy of strangling or squashing him; or as a gnashing of teeth as if biting the victim. Sensations such as these are specific for the individual and, in the analysis, can serve as pointers to the childhood phase when his aggression had been at its peak and before defense against it had been instituted.

CLINICAL STUDIES OF AGGRESSION

There was general agreement in the Congress symposium as to the urgent need for more detailed, unbiased clinical studies of aggression. However, contributions in this respect were more in the nature of impassioned pleas than of sober, practical recommendations. They left to the individual analyst how and where to look for his material.

My own suggestions in this respect are the following:

Aggression Studied during Analytic Therapy

If we accept the view that the defense activity employed in the *transference neuroses* is qualitatively the same as in normal development and merely quantitatively exaggerated, much additional information about the fate of the aggressive drive can be extrapolated from analytic treatments.

We can glimpse via the obsessional symptom resulting from *undoing,* for example, a picture of the young child's laudable efforts to "make good" what he has damaged or destroyed while behaving in an unruly manner; via the obsessional *rituals,* the young child's preference for sameness as a safety measure, meant to strengthen his ego for the battle with the drive; in the obsessional's *slowing up,* the child's advance from impulsive aggressive behavior to the ability of interpolating thought between impulse and action, i.e., of "counting to ten before giving way to anger."

When we analyze a child's school phobia, much can be learned about the ego's struggle with hostile wishes, especially with the death wish directed toward the mother, which seems to be the culminating point of infantile aggression. The school-phobic child deals with this by his inability to leave the mother, a symptom which exaggerates the desperate clinging to the mother at the toddler stage of heightened ambivalence, the latter defense against aggression being developmentally normal.

In fact, almost all the ego's normal ways of controlling the aggressive drive during development are represented in the transference neuroses as pathogenic elements and can be studied there at leisure during the analytic process. Familiar examples are the following:

> to cling to the object threatened by the subject's aggression, thereby assuring its safety;
> to avoid the object threatened by the subject's aggression, thereby assuring its safety;
> to deny or repress the aggressive side of an ambivalent relationship, while overemphasizing the libidinal one; etc.

Analytic treatments beyond the category of the transference neuroses can also be extremely profitable for the study of aggression. I refer here to the swings between *murder and suicide* within one and the same individual (Karl Menninger, 1938) which show aggression directed alternatively toward self and object. Or to the adolescent *self-mutilation* and suicide attempts (Friedman et al., 1972) which show aggression moving between the object world, the self, and the body as the source of all evil.[5]

It is, further, worthy of note in this connection that *child analysis,* not only of specific cases but as such, opens up possibilities for the clinical study of aggression which, so far, have not been utilized systematically.

There is no doubt that aggressive material abounds in child analysis. This may be due to the fact that motor action, one of the main tools of aggression, is not excluded as a medium of expression; or to the fact that the permissive atmosphere of the analytic session acts more effectively toward liberating the aggressive strivings than the sexual

[5] Although such states are rare in early childhood, one such case is presently under treatment in the Hampstead Clinic (analyzed by Mrs. S. L. Johnson). This boy of four and a half years, referred to the Clinic as a killer of animals, was suspected of an active impulse to strangle his baby brother. In analysis, it emerged that his aggressive impulses were under pressure from ego and superego and alternated with suicidal ones, leading to accidents and severe injuries. After aggressive transference behavior, for example, the child proposes almost regularly to kill himself, by jumping out of a third floor window, by throwing himself down the stairwell, etc.

We recognize it as the familiar "return of the repressed" that secondarily these suicide attempts also are used by the boy to frighten, threaten, and provoke his environment. In this concealed way, at least part of his aggression continues to reach its original goal, i.e., the object world (Eissler, 1971).

ones; or to the analyst's putting up more easily with aggressive attacks on his person than with sexual ones since too much license in the latter respect makes him appear seductive.

Whatever the correct explanation of the phenomenon may be, it is undeniable that, against previous expectation, aggression looms larger than sex in child analysis, dominates the child patient's acting out and transference behavior, and poses questions of technique, many of which are still unanswered.

When one deals with this state of affairs, many lessons about aggression can be learned, especially about the widely divergent motivations for and derivations of aggressive behavior, all of them represented perhaps by identical surface manifestations. Children in analysis may be angry, destructive, insulting, rejecting, attacking for a wide variety of reasons, only one of them being the direct discharge of genuinely aggressive fantasies or impulses. The rest is aggressive behavior in the service of the ego, i.e., for the purpose of defense:

as a reaction to anxiety and effective cover for it;
as an ego resistance against lowering defenses;
as a resistance against the verbalization of preconscious and unconscious material;
as a superego reaction against the conscious acknowledgment of id derivations, sexual or aggressive;
as a denial of any positive, libidinal tie to the analyst;
as a defense against passive-feminine strivings ("impotent rage").

There is, in meaning and import, a world of difference

between these aggressive phenomena and, for example, the aggressive attacks of the little animal-killer mentioned above, even though phenomenologically they are identical. To distinguish between genuine drive expression and aggressive behavior in the service of extraneous purposes is essential for child analysis since, among other things, it avoids the diagnostic confusion between aggressive, anxious, passive, and overdefended children. But the advantages of exploring this material go beyond that aim. The knowledge to be gained here may be useful for elucidating many of the problems concerning the vicissitudes of aggression in normal and abnormal development as well as in adult life.

Aggression Studied via Infant Observation

Valuable hints were offered during the symposium that mother-infant observations from birth onward provide important data as to the links between aggressive development and the incidence of maternal care or maternal deprivation (Solnit, in Kestemberg, 1972). Such studies confirm the assumption that the infant's experiences of pleasure promote libidinal growth, while the massive experience of unpleasure promotes aggression. To this I add a plea for setting up similar observations on infants who undergo severe physical illness and pain in early life and to explore whether such experiences, outside the infant-mother relationship, also promote aggressive at the expense of libidinal development.

This may also be the place to point back to previous studies of autoaggression in early childhood (Hoffer, 1950) which could be pursued further. There is a wide range here from transitory mild head banging that is near normal to persistent head banging resulting in injury, from harmless nail biting or hair pulling (also queried as masturbatory equivalents) to the severe and wholly unmanageable self-mutilation by biting as it occurs in defective and psychotic children. Links might be established here with the adolescent or adult tendencies toward self-mutilation which were mentioned above.

Aggression Studied in Play

Mothers and nursery school workers who watch young children at play have ample opportunity to realize the co-existence of constructive and destructive wishes. When a child builds with blocks, for example, to add one to the other until a high tower is achieved is as pleasurable for him as it is to throw over the structure and scatter the blocks. It would be an error to believe that only the former is done in a positive mood, the latter in anger, disappointment, frustration. On the contrary, the child feels gleeful when carrying out either activity, his mood betraying equal pride in achieving control and mastery of the medium.

We may be justified in assuming, I believe, that the child's pleasure in construction is libidinal, his pleasure in destruction aggressive. Both pleasures seem to exist side by side, simultaneously or in quick succession, without interfering with each other, each as the derivative of a primary id tendency.

Aggression Studied in Toddlers' Social Behavior

One of the most promising fields for the observation of

early aggression is an age group of toddlers, i.e., children in the second year of life, when their behavior is dominated alternately by primary and secondary process functioning and therefore more transparent than it will be at later stages of development. I refer in what follows to two different findings which may serve as examples.

1. Toddlers are not easy to control in groups since they are extremely aggressive toward each other. To take hold of a toy, food, sweets; to get attention; to remove an obstacle, whether human or material; or for no obvious reason at all—they will bite, scratch, pull hair, throw over, hit out, kick, etc. Nevertheless, what emerges is not a physical fight between two hostile partners as it would with older children. Instead, the victim of attack dissolves into tears, runs for protection, or stands helpless and needs to be rescued. What puzzles the observer is the fact that this attacked child may have been an aggressor himself a short time previously or may be so soon afterward, i.e., that he is by no means without aggression and its tools himself. He has both but is still unable to employ them in the service of defense.

To my mind, this observed item suggests that in the developmental line of aggression the ability to attack others precedes the ability to defend oneself. Or, to put it in other words, that to attack is a direct derivative of the aggressive drive, while aggression in the service of defense is a learned response mediated via the ego.

2. The second observed item concerns the toddler's attitude to the hurt which he is inflicting. In fact, initially, these children are completely oblivious of the effects of their aggressive actions, and demonstration is needed from

the side of the adults to bring them to their attention. It is popularly believed among many mothers of toddlers that the child has to be "bitten back" before he will appreciate that biting hurts. Nursery workers are used to show to the offender that his victim cries, or bleeds, is angry, cross, afraid, etc., very often to the complete surprise, if not bewilderment, of the attacking child.

This, to my mind, invalidates the assumption that to inflict hurt is the basic purpose of the aggressive act. Rather, we have to conclude that only the aggressive action itself is primary, while its result is accidental initially. However, a conclusion of this kind merely refers us back to one of the unsolved questions posed at the beginning as to the intrinsic aim of innate, primary aggression.

There is more information to be gained if children in their second year are studied systematically, and the findings produced so far are admittedly minute. However, members of the Congress were warned at the outset by their President to keep their expectations at a modest level (Rangell, 1972).

THE THEORY OF AGGRESSION

Psychoanalytic study of aggression has as its starting point Freud's "Beyond the Pleasure Principle" (1920). This publication had the double result, on the one hand, of moving the hitherto neglected topic of aggression into the limelight but, on the other hand, of burdening and hampering its clinical investigation by drawing it into the center of a theoretical dispute. So far as a theory of drives is concerned, the analytic world remained, since 1920, divided into two factions, with convictions ranging from complete or even extreme commitment to Freud's dualistic theory of drives to an equally complete rejection of the assumption of a death instinct with aggression as its representative. Inevitably, these theoretical divergencies had unfortunate results. While on the side of sex, patient explorative work had continued for years before a sexual theory evolved, on the side of aggression whatever clinical finding was made was utilized immediately, before it was even proved or disproved, to validate or attack one of the reigning theoretical hypotheses. It is deliberate that no such attempt was made so far in this paper, which was intended to be clinical.

Nevertheless, each individual analyst, even if not theorizing himself, has to choose his stand somewhere among these far-flung differences, with myself no exception. There are in the relevant analytic literature a number of hints and warnings in this respect to be used for guidance.

To my mind, the most helpful of these are contained in Eissler's already quoted paper on "Death Drive, Ambivalence, and Narcissism" (1971), a paper written with the avowed intention "to lend support to Freud's theory of a death drive" (p. 25). With Schopenhauer and Freud, Eissler asserts that, next to birth, death is the most important event in man's life and that any worthwhile psychology needs to "allocate to death a meaningful place in its overall structure" (p. 26). While relying heavily for his assumption on the German physiologist Rudolf Ehrenberg, Eissler might also have quoted support from poets such as Rainer Maria Rilke, who sees the move toward death as one of the main purposes of life; or support from child analysis, since children who suffer from neurotic fears of death invariably are found to regard every step toward growing up as a frightening step toward death which needs to be avoided.

However, even while basing his own conception on biological speculations, Eissler admits "that no rules have yet been worked out that would tell us when biology may be legitimately called in to serve psychology" (p. 40). He also considers the disentanglement from biological encroachments as important for psychoanalysis as the reliance on some biological and cultural data. In this connection he refers to his exploration of ambivalence, a psychological phenomenon which "presupposes the presence of opposing drives [but] is not sufficiently explained by their presence" (p. 47).

To me it is tempting to apply the last-quoted formulation to some of our formerly mentioned doubts and difficulties in the clinical area. Many of these dissolve or become unnecessary if we observe the warning and agree to acknowledge the gap between clinical fact and biological speculation instead of enforcing direct causal links between the two fields.

The topic of "source" may serve as an example. It was never implied in Freud's dualistic biological theory that the life drive is the actual source of the sexual urges; the latter was always acknowledged as being either hormonal or anatomical. Nor need the death drive be the actual source of aggression. In clinical terms, both have their own material sources, known or unknown, while simultaneously being what might be called the "representatives on earth" of the two supraordinated biological forces with contrary goals, the presence of which they presuppose. We may say equally with regard to "aim," that clinically speaking, i.e., on earth, both libido and aggression pursue their own limited and mundane aims while serving at the same time the vaster biological purposes of life and death.

There is no doubt that our clinical task is rendered more difficult by the fact the neither libido nor aggression is ever observable singly, i.e., in pure culture; except in the most pathological instances, they are always fused and for the purpose of study their respective actions have to be disentangled. But this, I believe, is true for biology as well as for psychology: sexual mastery cannot be achieved without the appropriate admixture of aggression; aggression cannot be integrated in normal life without an admixture of libido; equally, on the higher plane, death cannot be attained except via the vicissitudes of life.

12

Changes in Psychoanalytic Practice and Experience

(1976 [1975])

Members of the London Congress who read or listened to the prepublished papers by Leo Rangell (1975) and André Green (1975) had little chance to bridge the gap between these two widely divergent presentations. Rangell defended the hard-won insights of psychoanalysis and their therapeutic value by quoting their continuing efficiency when we deal with the consequences of the infantile amnesia, with anxiety, pathological defense, guilt, and depression. He pleaded for adding new discoveries to the old instead of

Presented as the opening discussion paper at the Plenary Session on "Changes in Psychoanalytic Practice and Experience: Theoretical, Technical and Social Implications," held at the 29th International Psycho-Analytical Congress, London, July 1975. First published in the *International Journal of Psycho-Analysis,* 57:257–260, 1976. German translation: Wandlungen in psychoanalytischer Theorie und Praxis. *Die Schriften der Anna Freud,* Volume 10. Munich: Kindler Verlag, 1980.

discarding the latter in favor of the former. André Green, on the other hand, deplored the failure of present-day psychoanalysis to effect cures when applied to the psychotic core of human nature or to the more severe, psychotic-type disturbances. He gave proof of experimentation with far-reaching modifications of technique and theory, offering a range of clinical examples.

It was not easy for anyone, under these circumstances, to extract from the authors' formulations what might be valid predictions for the future of the psychoanalytic discipline.

THE PSYCHOANALYST'S MALAISE

My own efforts in this direction fasten on to André Green's description of the "malaise" felt by present-day analytic workers, a frame of mind which I cannot help to contrast with the satisfaction and excitement which governed the attitude of the pioneering, early psychoanalysts, a series of generations to which I myself belong. What caused this elated mood were a whole number of circumstances. We felt that we were the first who had been given a key to the understanding of human behavior and its aberrations as being determined not by overt factors but by the pressure of instinctual forces emanating from the unconscious mind; that we were the first, therefore, to see mental illness as a battle between rationality and irrationality; that we also were the first to possess a method, namely, free association, for breaking down the barrier between consciousness and the unconscious; that this method was applicable to ourselves as well as to our patients, thus reducing the difference between the mentally ill and the mentally healthy and altering the relationship between therapist and patient from one of dominating authority to one of shared endeavor; that our new technique of inquiry and exploration of resistance and transference was identical with our technique of cure; and, finally, that, apart from suggestion and hypnosis, we had no rivals in the field of mental treatment.

It was not surprising that this combination of factors produced an attitude of pride and confidence. We may wonder today why, when, and where such security was lost in the case of some of our colleagues, and also what the chances are for them to reacquire it.

THE WIDENING SCOPE OF PSYCHOANALYSIS

In fact, none of these questions is difficult to answer once a historian of the psychoanalytic movement ventures to approach them. Psychoanalytic therapy had its heyday, obviously, while its application was strictly confined to the mental upsets for which it was devised. It was surest of success where a patient's potentially healthy ego was suffering from symptoms caused by the pressure of internal conflicts and their pathological solutions, but was ready and able to accept help in the struggle against them, so as to restore a state of tolerable inner equilibrium.

Nevertheless, it did not take long until the analyst's understanding went far beyond the states where these conditions were present, i.e., beyond the character deformations, anxiety hysteria, the phobias, the obsessional neuroses. It soon embraced the many, frequently puzzling, sexual perversions; the addictions; the delinquencies; the adolescent abnormalities; the infantile neuroses and arrests of development; the psychoses such as amentia, the schizophrenias, paranoia. It became more or less irresistible for the psychoanalytic therapists to step out of their original, comparatively narrow confines and to embark on the treatment of all these disorders, regardless of the strain this imposed on their technique. Actually, it was this era of the "widening scope of psychoanalysis" which first served to tone down the psychoanalysts' therapeutic optimism by confronting them with significant changes in the atmosphere governing the analyst-patient relationship and, thus, with unfamiliar problems for which they had not bargained.

To mention a few instances only: August Aichhorn (1925), in his psychoanalytic treatment of wayward adolescents, was the first to be faced with patients who presented a severely diminished or wholly absent *treatment alliance,* caused by the fact that, in Freud's words, "the sum of pleasure which the delinquent can obtain as a law-abiding individual can never match the one derived from his delinquent acts." A similar problem awaited all those who treated the perversions and addictions since being cured in their cases was felt to be identical with being *deprived of* what was to them a central *pleasure. Suffering,* named by André Green as essential for the decision to undergo analysis, is nevertheless absent from all cases of character analysis since these patients experience even severe abnormalities not as foreign bodies but as ego-syntonic. *Free association,* designated by Rangell as "the core of technique" and "the center of the psychoanalytic method" (p. 92), is unobtainable in child analysis and needs to be substituted for by other, less efficient means. Further, the psychoanalyst of children can count neither on the patients' *insight* nor on their *sincerity,* just as the analyst of adolescents will meet their typical reluctance to revise and *relive the past,* even though this ability is considered essential for the successful analysis of adult neurotics. So far as the psychoses are concerned, there is in the more severe cases no *intact ego,* normal enough in its functioning to accept, work over, and profit from the analyst's interpretations.

Nevertheless, in spite of such increased technical difficulties in the new fields of work, analysts struggled on and achieved improvements, even if not cures. They accepted the loss of the patients' suffering, of their treatment alliance, of their sincerity, their ability or willingness to produce free associations. They equally accepted the loss of their uniqueness in the field where a whole host of rival therapies, psychological, electric, chemical, made their appearance. After all, to use Rangell's words, it was only psychoanalysis which held the key to the understanding of human problems, and as such its identity could be maintained. There was only one crucial prerogative which they found themselves unwilling to renounce since, more than any other characteristic of psychoanalysis, it seemed to them the hallmark of the method: namely, that understanding a mental aberration automatically implies the possibility to cure it; or, to put it in other words, that, so far as psychoanalysis is concerned, the method of inquiry is identical with the method of therapy.

From then onward, it seems to me, much of the history of psychoanalysis is dominated by two efforts: (1) to deny, even in the face of evidence to the contrary, that analytic understanding reaches further than analytic therapy; (2) to restore by whatever means the former unity between exploration and cure.

Illustration from Child Analysis

Clinical examples to illustrate the aforementioned point can be taken from various areas of work, child analysis among them.

In our categorization of infantile disorders, we have learned to distinguish between two types, intermingled though they are with each other. One belongs to the infantile neurosis and its forerunners, its earliest appearances caused by conflicts between drive activity and environmental forces, its later stages due to purely internal conflicts between contrasting tendencies within the personality structure, both accompanied by fear, anxiety, guilt, inhibition, loss of pleasure or function, and by symptom formation. Experience has proved that psychoanalysis is the method of choice for treating these disorders since interpretation of the repressed, of transference and resistances, enables the child's ego to undo the damage it has done to itself by adopting pathological conflict solutions, and to replace these faulty structures by more adaptive ones.

The second type of disturbance is of a different nature. It arises during the child's early period of growth and maturation and has to be ascribed to direct interference with the course of normal development. Instead of being born with the average expectable physical and mental equipment, reared in an average environment, and developing its internal structure at the usual rate, a child can be subjected to deviations in any or all of these respects and consequently develop deviant, atypical, or borderline features. There is no question here of the child's ego having done harm to itself; on the contrary, harm has been inflicted on it by circumstances entirely beyond its control.

Developmental pathology, no less than the neurotic one, is open to psychoanalytic exploration, explanation, and understanding. In spite of this, it does not respond to psychoanalytic therapy in the same manner. Even the most correct uncovering of past and forgotten circumstances and events (such as physical or mental handicap, neglect, rejection, lack of security and maternal care, precocious or delayed ego or superego functioning) does not blot out their impact on the shaping of the child's personality or eradicate their roots, i.e., does not act as a radical therapy. At best, it helps the child to cope better with the aftereffects of what has happened to him.

But child analysts, no different from their colleagues in the adult field, are reluctant to accept the humiliating fact that the developmental damage which they understand so well and reconstruct so efficiently can be beyond their power to cure by truly analytic means. At present, in spite of setbacks and disappointments, their struggle continues to convert their increasing insight into this type of childhood pathology into an effective analytic therapy.

Illustration from Adult Analysis

The analyst of adults who extends his practice beyond the transference and character neuroses to the borderline cases and psychoses meets, as illustrated by André Green, not only the "basic faults" (Balint, 1968), i.e., the aftereffects of what the child analysts recognize as developmental damage, but also the partial or complete shattering of the mental apparatus, as it is experienced in the psychoses proper. Both conditions fail to fulfill the preconditions for the employment of the classical analytic technique by eliminating insight, ego cooperation, or even secondary process thinking and verbal communication from the patients' response. As such, they represent a challenge to the analytic therapists' ingenuity.

In accord with certain, rather widely held current theories, André Green sees the abnormalities described in his paper as throwbacks to or remnants of the first year of life and ascribes them to failures of the mother-infant interaction at this period. Consequently, he and others pin their therapeutic hopes on the reestablishment of this earliest relationship in the psychoanalytic situation. There are, in fact, far-reaching dissimilarities between the two settings. While the infant demands for his satisfaction body care, need fulfillment, and constancy of exclusive attention, the analytic patient has to tolerate frustration of wishes, limitation to set times, and the existence of rivals. Nevertheless, there is the tendency to regard the two situations as identical and to use the later in an attempt to correct the failures of the earlier one. According to André Green's therapeutic recommendations, the analyst-mother in dealing with the patient-infant needs to respect and, where necessary, to enter with him into his undifferentiated state and meet him on the level of primary process functioning. As happens between mothers and their infants, preverbal manifestations have to be translated into meaningful communications. Affects, such as pain or anxiety, have to be shared, the mother acting as a repository for the infant's feeling state, and vice versa. Further, the analyst-mother lends to the mental apparatus of the patient-infant her own powers of superior functioning, thereby mending structural defects and promoting growth. In this close togetherness, even the external spatial setting acquires importance and plays its therapeutic role. In short, an intimate alliance is created which in its primitive nature outweighs by far the high-level treatment alliance between analysts and their neurotic patients.

CONCLUSION

It is open to doubt whether the foregoing discussion will help members to assess the weight of opinions presented to them at the recent Congress. What it may be able to do, though, is to help them construct their own personal picture of the future of psychoanalysis, following either one or the other of the two protagonists.

With André Green, they may doubt the value of our psychoanalytic tenets if therapeutically they prove to be applicable only to a restricted field. They may stand firm on their conviction that every single piece of analytic insight can and should be harnessed to a technique of therapy, i.e., that any mental affliction which is open to analytic understanding also is open to analytic cure. Their aim will be not to rest until such new techniques are forged, however similar or dissimilar they may be to the technique of therapy used by the majority of psychoanalysts today. In short, they may see a positive future of psychoanalysis as dependent on therapeutic ambition and expansion.

Members in accord with Rangell, on the other hand, will expect the future of psychoanalysis to depend on modesty of aim and intensification of insight. With him, they will wish not only to maintain the identity of psychoanalysis but also its reputation as a valid therapy, with "the core of its technique intact," an end to be reached by "a process of shrinkage and precision, of fitting the method to its applicable field" (p. 95). There is, within this field, according to Rangell, ample opportunity for future research, i.e., for clinical investigation into areas which are currently neglected, the vagaries of superego functioning being one of them. In short, instead of setting out to conquer new territories, they may identify with his aim to recognize an "optimum scope" for psychoanalytic therapy and within this scope "to use psychoanalysis for what psychoanalysis can do" (p. 96).

13

Remarks on Problems of Psychoanalytic Training
[1976]

Since I seem to be here as a representative of the past, I would like to remind you of an event that has much in common with the present discussion. It was in the late 1930s that Max Eitingon, then the head of the International Training Commission, instigated a discussion on the difficulties of training analysis. I was charged at the time with contributing a paper, and I selected as my subject the the question "How far is the training analysis as we are

Discussion remarks presented at an international symposium on The Identity of the Psychoanalyst, coordinated for the International Psycho-Analytical Association by Daniel Widlocher and Edward D. Joseph, and held at Haslemere, Surrey, England, February 1976. These remarks are published here for the first time. German translation: Bemerkungen über Probleme der psychoanalytischen Ausbildung. *Die Schriften der Anna Freud,* Volume 10. Munich: Kindler Verlag, 1980.

forced to carry it out now a 'wild' analysis?"[1] A "wild" analysis was at the time the term for every form of analysis
not strictly following the rules of free association, of absti-
nence, of invisibility of the analyst, of not abusing the
positive transference, of not neglecting the negative transference, etc., i.e., keeping the analysis as free as possible of
contaminations by reality.

I agree with Rangell that in every analysis we have contaminations from reality, so that the analytic process instigated by the work of interpretation and coming from the
unconscious of the patient is substituted for occasionally
by stimulation from the external world, its prejudices, or
hopes, its interference, by chance meetings with the
analyst, etc. But it seems to me that this question of contamination is very much a function of quantity, and that in
a therapeutic analysis, when the external world interferes
too much, we also lose the thread of the analysis.

In the paper that I had to contribute then, I tried very
carefully to point out in what respects the training analysis
offends against the analytic rules. I am sorry to say it, but I
think I covered most of the points that have been raised
here. I have also observed since then how the various
societies in their various countries have made attempts to
diminish the contamination. There was one attempt made,
I remember, that the training analyst should be, if possible, an invisible person — an unknown. On the other hand,
the invisible or obscure people are not always the most ex-
cellent ones! And if you show excellence in any direction,
you become visible, not only to your colleagues but also

[1] See *Writings*, vol. 4, chap. 19

to your candidates. Moreover, training analysts are freely chosen by the candidates, and they are not chosen according to their state of being unknown, rather the opposite; and this, of course, destroys the myth of invisibility. It destroys it from the beginning, and as an ongoing process during the analysis, by what the other candidates report, by what candidates learn in their courses, by what they read in their books, by meetings with their analysts which are unavoidable in an institute that is not very large, and where training analysts at the same time lead seminars or give lectures. So things happen that one would avoid strictly in any therapeutic analysis: you sit at the same conference table, or in the same lecture room, with your candidate, and only a very big institute is able to avoid such confrontations.

Another attempt made by many institutes, and still being made, is to exclude the training analyst from any voice in the candidates' progress in the institute. This, of course, has the advantage that the training analyst cannot give in to pressure from the candidate to promote his progress, or that the candidate cannot reproach him for having hindered his progress. But it also has very adverse consequences— after all, the training analyst is the only one who really knows something about the candidate, and what one can discover in one, or even two, or even three interviews may leave out points which are decisive for this candidate's future contact with his patients. So it neglects the point that the training analyst has to have a double loyalty—to his candidate but also to the institute, and perhaps a third to the future patients of his candidate. Therefore I do not think that this exclusion of the training analyst from all

decisions really works, as it is meant to work. But if he is
not excluded, then one cannot avoid the contamination of
the transference reaction of the candidate by the fact that
the analyst is also the parent, the arbiter of his fate, the
grownup who decides about his life as he did in childhood.
And I have known candidates, or have heard about them,
who through their whole training period were very wary to
reveal facts about themselves which could stand in the way
of their becoming analysts. You have probably all heard
the story of the candidate who finished his training analysis
with qualification by the institute, and who then said,
"And now I'll go into a real analysis — and this time it's for
me, and not for my career!"

And then, of course, there is a major difference at the
end. In the therapeutic analysis, we aim at the dissolution
of the transference, positive and negative, and we know
that a very successful therapeutic analysis is one where we
never see the patient again — he does not need us anymore.
But a training analysis ends with the patient and the analyst becoming colleagues, who may never get rid of each
other again in reality.

The problem does not seem to have changed much in the
last forty-five years. I also got the impression that my colleagues who first advocated the introduction of training
analysis at the Marienbad Congress — if they had heard of
all the dangers, of the positive and negative transferences,
of the splits, and the hates — would probably never have advocated it. They would have said, let them be as they are!

There are two further points to which one can address
oneself here, and for one of them — namely, the question
of the identity of the analyst — I really have no justification

to speak: I have never gone through a crisis of identity as an analyst. I can remember that during my analytic life I have met with several crises, in the external world and in the internal world; but what I have missed out on evidently is that I felt my own identity shaken. After listening to what has happened here, I can only come to the conclusion that this had one particular reason. Valenstein has mentioned the dichotomy between, or the need to bring together, the social identity, the professional identity, and the personal identity, as an analyst. I think that I was probably helped by the fact that with me, those three fell together into one.

I would like to connect this particular point with our former discussion on training analysis, training candidates, and, above all, the selection of training candidates. In the past this was very much a self-selection — we selected ourselves for the profession of becoming analysts, very much on the basis of one particular factor, namely, a burning curiosity about how human beings function, what makes them function normally or what makes them suffer abnormally, and lastly what makes them develop from children into adults. I believe that it is this curiosity, never to be lost, that carries the analyst through his whole professional life, and that creates — if you want to call it that — his identity, or rather his identification with psychoanalysis.

I believe that, when we select candidates, we do not pay enough attention to the fact that before they present themselves to an institute as applicants, they should already have given some proof in their lives of this curiosity. I find that people are very seldom asked in their interviews: What have you read? What have you done in your life so far to show that analysis will be satisfactory for you? The select-ors look for very different qualities and attitudes, and too frequently neglect this all-important one.

Leaving the question of identity aside, I would like to return once more to my earlier discussion and to my con-cern that I may have created a wrong impression when I asked whether had we known all its negative consequences, would we ever have voted for the necessity of a training analysis? This was an exaggerated statement, of course; none of us can now imagine training analysts without a training analysis. But what I wanted to express was my feeling that the whole question has been weighted too much toward the negative. We have heard all about the consequences of the object-relationship attachment to the analyst, the identification with the analyst, the indoctrina-tion of the candidate by the analyst. We have heard very little about the positive side, and my feeling is that in this discussion, we — or you — have undervalued the process of learning. I do not believe that any process of learning pro-ceeds without a personal attachment to the teacher, an identification with the teacher, and something that makes this a lasting identification. And this is not only so in analysis, it is so from early childhood onward, and remains throughout life, so long as we are learning. I would there-fore advocate that, besides identification, and transference, and indoctrination, there also is another attribute of the training analysis which I would call inspiration. I mention, as an example, an older colleague, now in America, who was with a training analyst who was not particularly re-nowned for his technique or for his therapeutic abilities, but who had a deep commitment to psychoanalysis. It is this deep commitment which still lives in his former candidate who is probably now sixty years old, if not older. I have another colleague where I know that what he has picked up from his analyst is a certain correctness in the search for the truth, a certain unrelenting devotion to that. Or another one who picked up from his analyst the love for analysis. Should they really have resolved, outgrown, all that, together with their transference? Or isn't it a residue of the transference, namely, a lasting identification with something good, an inspiration that is allowed to remain? When we talk about the negative side of training analysis, and the dangers, I think we should balance it at the same time by looking at the generations of analysts who have picked up from their analytic forefathers something that is invaluable.

The identity of the analyst, or rather the identification with psychoanalysis, is certainly transmitted from generation to generation in this manner.

14

Fears, Anxieties, and Phobic Phenomena
(1977 [1976])

It is the privilege of age to view present happenings in the light of past experience. This explains why it is natural for me to contrast the present picture of the child analytic movement with its modest beginnings. Whereas discussion groups then were content with no more than ten or twelve members, they now have increased to well above fifty times that number; whereas then child analysis was considered the domain of women—probably because in early times it was regarded simply as play therapy—the seriousness of the venture and of its problems has not failed to attract a con-

Summary remarks presented at the meeting of the Association for Child Psychoanalysis, London, July 1976. First published in *The Psychoanalytic Study of the Child,* 32:85–90. New Haven & London: Yale University Press, 1977. German translation: Furcht, Angst und phobische Phänomene. *Die Schriften der Anna Freud,* Volume 10. Munich: Kindler Verlag, 1980.

siderable number of male analysts. It remains an open question, however, whether these very obvious material changes are matched by an equally impressive increase in knowledge; how far our insight into normal and abnormal development has deepened in the intervening years; whether the technique of child analytic therapy has improved and, with it, its results; whether we have become more accurate in diagnosing disturbances and more skilled in applying knowledge to the areas of upbringing and prevention of mental disorders. I believe that all of us welcome the opportunity to test the answers to these queries against the background of the specific clinical topic chosen for this symposium.

What comes to mind first is a criticism of its title. Its wording "Fears and Phobias," at least so far as terminology goes, seems to be no improvement on our former conceptions of the processes occurring in the child's mind. We have always distinguished between the terms "fear" and "anxiety," using the former exclusively for the attitude toward real dangers threatening from external sources and the latter exclusively for reaction to threats located within the mind, due to clashes between drives and internal opposing forces. While fears, however strong they are, do not develop into phobias, anxiety does so under certain conditions. To ignore this distinction and to treat the effect of external and internal threats under one and the same terminological heading is not a step forward in our theoretical position, but rather implies the reverse. By rights, therefore, the formulation of our title should have been "Fears, Anxieties, and Phobic Phenomena," thus spanning the whole range from reactions to deprivations, frustrations, losses, injuries, accidents, attacks, disasters which threaten safety from the outside to the reactions to conflicts, guilt feelings, and so forth, which upset the mental equilibrium for internal reasons.

Leaving these general considerations, I turn to more specific concerns. With regard to the case presentations, it seems to me that the clinical pictures did not convince us of their phobic character. What one of the patients was suffering from were fears and anxieties from a variety of sources, external as well as internal. Moreover, they were defended against by a variety of means, ranging from primitive need for reassurance to sophisticated obsessional defenses, phobic avoidance merely being one among a multitude of other mechanisms.

The other case history is open to similar objections. Here too we were faced with a whole host of reactions to danger, derived from all levels and ranging from archaic annihilation fears to separation fear and anxiety, castration anxiety and guilt, that is, from the primitive to the sophisticated. As in the first case, the child reacts to them in a variety of ways, including inhibitions, passive compliance, active aggressivity, while the use of phobic avoidance is resorted to in a single instance.

We may agree that neither of these cases presents the picture of a classical phobia, but this leaves us with a number of unsolved problems, the first being their relationship to a full-blown phobia. Would it be correct to say that they represent steps toward phobic development, but that, for some unknown reason, these steps remain abortive? Are there, perhaps, some elements in the psychic makeup which are the necessary prerequisites for phobic development and which are not present in these cases? Or is it much more usual and natural for children to cope with their anxieties by other means, phobic avoidance being the exception rather than the rule, neither attempted nor achieved in the majority of instances?

I believe it is this gap in our understanding which Joseph Sandler and his co-workers in the Hampstead Index Department are trying to fill. On the basis of much clinical material Sandler suggests that it is usual for children to try and deal with their various anxieties by means of profuse internal fantasy activity, using many different defensive means and mechanisms. The construction of these fantasies is aimed at keeping the amount of anxiety at a tolerable level in order to maintain a mental equilibrium. But he believes, as does Peter Neubauer, that the feeling of safety achieved in this manner is a precarious one and is easily upset by a so-called intrusive event — a happening in the external world which brings the warded-off danger back to the surface and creates panic. Only then does the child resort to flight in the face of a threat, a defensive solution made possible only by externalizing the source of danger, that is, by exchanging internal anxiety for an imaginary external threat.

Even this extended formulation for the construction of a phobia, however, seems to need amendment since it ignores an important step in the etiological sequence. At one point of the process, presumably when fantasy activity has failed to protect against massive unpleasure, a different mechanism comes into operation, namely, condensation, which precedes externalization. This means that fears and anxieties do not remain diffuse but are compressed by the child into one encompassing symbol which represents the dangers left over from preoedipal phases as well as the dominant ones due to phallic-oedipal conflicts. It is, then, this symbol (animal, street, school) which, as a supposed part of the outside world, is dealt with by avoidance.[1]

I feel doubtful about another point, namely, the opinion that children who suffer from phobias not only flee from the object of their anxiety but also are fascinated by and compulsively drawn toward it. Even though this may be so in some instances, it is certainly otherwise in the majority of cases. School-phobic or agoraphobic children can be seen to be quite unaffected so long as leaving home is not enforced; the same is true of the animal-phobic ones when the dreaded animal is out of sight. In short, there seems to be overwhelming clinical evidence that the truly phobic defense is effective in blotting out any positive seductive aspect hidden behind the anxiety and in leaving the child peaceful and not agitated in the absence of the phobic object.

I turn next to the much-discussed topic of the role of reality testing in the phobia. The questions raised were whether the phobic child believes in the reality of the phobic symbol, or whether he recognizes it as a figment of his imagination; and, further, whether this belief or disbelief has meaning for assessing, on the one hand, the seriousness of the disturbance and, on the other, for the good or bad chances of therapeutic intervention. Instead of searching for answers to these queries, we should, I believe, remember that not only in phobias but in all neuroses we move in a no-man's land between reality and

---

[1] According to this view, the missing piece in the case of diffuse anxiety would be the mechanism of condensation.

fantasy. As early as 1896, Freud maintained that the forceful character of neurotic formations had nothing to do with the patient's attaching belief to them. Later (1907a) he repeated that the neurotic at one and the same time believes and disbelieves in his creations; that while the rational part of his mind realizes their imaginary character, their existence and their impact on his behavior are upheld by his irrational unconscious in which they are rooted. So far as phobic children are concerned, much evidence for this assertion can be found. For example, Hedy Schwarz quoted a little girl with a phobia of lions. This child countered the well-meant assurances of her father that lions could not climb up to her bedroom by saying plaintively that, of course, her father talked of real lions who could not climb, but her own lions could. Nevertheless, she was afraid of "her own lions," as are the many other children who profess firm belief in the reality of their phobic objects.

Looking back on the symposium as a whole, I feel that no pronouncement on fear and anxiety can be taken as conclusive unless their psychological consequences are viewed from two sides, from their pathogenic as well as from their beneficial aspects. Just as on the physical side the unpleasurable experience of bodily pain is essential for teaching the child to avoid injury from fire, water, cutting instruments, falling from heights, so is the unpleasure aroused by fear essential for promoting certain developmental steps. Archaic fears make the infant cling more closely to the protecting mother, thereby increasing object relatedness; fear of loss of love, of criticism or punishment, is the well-known incentive for compliance with educational demands; anxiety aroused by the strength of the id impulses furthers the construction of effective defenses; fear of the superego, guilt, leads to drive modification and social adaptation. In short, the same unpleasant affects which are the direct cause of neurotic symptom formation are known to be indispensable assets for normal character building.[2]

Finally, it seems that the present discussions will have served a good purpose if they leave us with an increased wish to answer a series of important questions. Where, exactly, is the dividing line between the positive and negative impact of fear and anxiety? Is this determined by qualitative factors, i.e., by the age-adequate or age-inadequate level of the threatening danger? Or is it purely a matter of quantity, i.e., does any fear or any anxiety which exceeds a certain level of intensity automatically become pathogenic, with the extreme unpleasure calling for extreme, namely, phobic, hysterical, obsessional, countermeasures?

It would be wrong, of course, to link these queries with the developmental advance (or its failure) from diffuse panic states to adaptive token anxiety since all defense activity, whether benign or pathogenic, is set in motion by token anxiety. However, it is not impossible to find a link here with the problem of phobias. The child's reaction to the phobic object comes nearer to a panic state than any of the other infantile fears or anxieties. This may be due to the high degree of symbolic condensation mentioned be-

[2]It is interesting to note that uneducated parents have always subscribed to the latter, positive aspects of fear and have used them to frighten their children into obedience, while enlightened parents tend to embrace the opposite extreme and try to eliminate all fear from their children's lives. Of course, neither of these attitudes is either correct or helpful for development.

fore. It may well be that it is the dreaded confrontation with panic proper which accounts for the use of the most primitive of all defense mechanisms, namely, flight. Phobia, seen in this light, could be understood as the child's alternative to traumatization.

15

The Role of Insight
in Psychoanalysis
and Psychotherapy:
Introduction

(1979 [1978])

In introducing this discussion I have a sense of inadequacy, since, during my whole working life as an analyst, I have never made the quality of "insight" my special subject of study. When working with adults, I shared the common opinion that the patient's acknowledgment of his psychic disorder and the desire to cure it are indispensable preconditions for his treatment. I also shared with my col-

Introduction to the Anna Freud-Hampstead Clinic Symposium held by the Michigan Psychoanalytic Society, November 11, 1978. First published in the *Journal of the American Psychoanalytic Association,* Suppl., 27:3–8, 1979. German translation: Über Einsicht in das unbewusste Seelenleben. *Die Schriften der Anna Freud,* Volume 10. Munich: Kindler Verlag, 1980.

leagues the common experience that, at least so far as the neuroses and the character disturbances are concerned, analysis tends to fail where such insight is missing and where entry into analytic therapy is due not to the patient's attitude in this respect but to familial or to social pressure.

When it came to children, I merely classed their lack of insight with the absence of the numerous other characteristics which, for the analyst, distinguish the immature from the mature patient and make child analysis such a hazardous and difficult undertaking. I refer in this respect to the child's inability or unwillingness to embark on free association; to the difference in his transference reactions; to his unreliable treatment alliance; to his diminished sincerity and frustration tolerance; to the preponderance of motor action over verbal expression; etc.

In fact, for me it needed a symposium such as today's to make me isolate the capacity for insight from this larger series and accord it special status for investigation into its role.

I assume Hansi Kennedy's permission when I extract from her paper (1979) the statement that, from the child patient under five, and indeed through much of the latency period, we have no reason to expect either a rational or an objective appraisal of internal conditions since the prerequisites for such insight are not yet developed within the structure. Obviously, thus, child analysis has to proceed without them, a not unfamiliar situation since in its technique we deal generally with substitutes for the tools of adult analysis. The questions which arise in this particular instance are merely whether there are any valid substitutes for the missing insight; how the replacements are made;

how far an individual not cognizant of his own pathology can be induced to wish for its removal, can be made to join in the effort to correct it; how, in short, the whole difficulty caused by the lack of this particular quality can be circumvented.

Such questions are more easily answered in the physical field. Here too, the young child who suffers from an illness is quite oblivious to its cause, is incapable of rational understanding for it, and even replaces the absent reality appraisal with the most fantastic misconceptions. Nevertheless, he is amenable to nursing or medical care under the condition that he feels pain. The child cooperates with doctor, nurse, or mother so long as their actions serve the immediate relief of pain. His cooperation ceases abruptly as soon as the therapeutic measure is a long-term one and is experienced by him as more painful in the present than the pathological condition to which it is applied.

Transferred to the mental sphere, this raises some corresponding expectations. Pain caused by the mental disorder may prove the substitute we are looking for as the basis for the child patient's treatment alliance with his analyst. However, we are right to ask to what extent this is the case.

Much of the symptomatology of the very young causes distress and upset to the responsible adults, while being taken for granted by the child himself. This is true for the psychologically based early sleep disturbances, the disorders of food intake and elimination, the arrests, delays, inhibitions, and defects of motor, intellectual, emotional, and moral development. Understandably enough, under these conditions, insight into the disturbance, wish for its removal, alliance with the therapist, were always demanded from the parents rather than from the child.

However, the nearer to the truly neurotic pattern, as in the anxiety states and the obsessional involvements, the more acute the distress felt by the child himself and, accordingly, the greater the chances of his accepting help. Examples of this are truly numerous. Children may plead to "have the devil taken out who urges them to commit acts" of which they themselves disapprove. They may complain about "the nonsensical actions which something forces them to undertake." They may beg for reassurance that they are "not naughty," "will not die in the night," etc. Such pronouncements when made during diagnosis are usually understood as signs of insight and raise hopes for the child's readiness to embark on psychoanalytic treatment. In fact, they are untrustworthy as heralds of therapeutic cooperation. What is revealed by them is not a realization of internal conflict or of the power of frightening fantasy which blots out reality. The child gives evidence of his panic and upset at finding himself at the mercy of alien powers or of feeling attacked by a nagging, critical authority which he does not recognize as his own emerging superego.

Once the child has entered treatment, it soon becomes obvious how far the analytic method of dealing with psychic pain by following it back to its origins runs counter to the child's own natural inclinations. Quite different from the total helplessness vis-à-vis physical suffering, his whole organism is geared toward dealing with mental pain. The developing defense mechanisms of the ego have as their sole aim the reduction or total abolition of anxiety, unpleasure, and upset. Thus, the child's automatic reaction to danger in the outside world is flight, in the inner world avoidance, i.e., phobic retreat; or denial with consequent counterphobic attitudes. Anxiety arising from drive activity is countered first by externalization; with increasing structuralization, by blotting out the drives' mental representatives, i.e., by repression; the remaining worries to be removed by reaction formations.

These mechanisms need to prove ineffective before the child turns to external help at all. Moreover, when he does, he merely clamors for support to strengthen them, certainly not for their abolition. To replace them by uncompromising confrontation with the root of the trouble itself, as analysis does, increases the very distress the child is eager to avoid. So far as his automatic response is concerned, the remedy is indeed no improvement in the trouble.

Different from adult analysands whose resistances are lodged either in the id, or the ego, or the transference, with children the bulk of their resistance, or at worst their total unwillingness to be analyzed, thus stems from their ego's age-adequate preference for clinging to its own methods for safeguarding or reinstating well-being and for their inclination to reject all others. Analytic insight belongs to the latter category, and it taxes the therapist's technical skill and ingenuity to lead his patients toward accepting it. Finally, as outlined in Kennedy's developmental paper, the child's advancing age and maturity help to unfold a capacity which gradually narrows the gap between the classical psychoanalytic method and the technical modifications forced on the child analyst.

Part III

Introductions to Freud's Writings

16

A Study Guide to Freud's Writings

(1978 [1977])

Introducing lay persons — whether students or readers who have no prior knowledge — to the conceptual world of psychoanalysis is a task that is difficult to solve, no matter how one goes about it. The processes occurring in the psychic life of adults and children, ill and healthy individuals, have many meanings and their infinite variations produce a sense of estrangement. If the instructor wants to spare his student surprises and difficulties, he cannot help but falsify his material. If he wants to do justice to the facts, he runs the risk of demanding too much from his students and

Originally written in German as: Einleitungen und Einführungen zu Sigmund Freud, *Werkausgabe in zwei Bänden*. Frankfurt am Main: S. Fischer Verlag GmbH. The English version is here published for the first time. It combines the various introductions to the selections from Freud's writings into one chapter.

losing their interest and continuing attention.

Freud himself strove throughout his life to take a middle course between these two dangers. His efforts to present the results of psychoanalytic work clearly and as far as possible in generally comprehensible language began in the year 1904 with "Freud's Psycho-Analytic Procedure" and ended only in the last year of his life with the unfinished paper "An Outline of Psycho-Analysis" (1940a) and "Some Elementary Lessons in Psycho-Analysis" (1940b). During the intervening years he wrote numerous other surveys that differ in length and range and are directed to very different audiences; some of these were initiated by his own interest, others were the result of requests. Thus, "Introductory Lectures on Psycho-Analysis" (1916–17) and "New Introductory Lectures on Psycho-Analysis" (1933a) are directed primarily to an academic audience, the first having in fact been presented at the University of Vienna. "The Claims of Psycho-Analysis to Scientific Interest" (1913b) and "A Short Account of Psycho-Analysis" (1924e), and "Psycho-Analysis" (1926c), on the other hand, are highly condensed summaries that were written as contributions to dictionaries and encyclopedias in Germany, Italy, England, and the United States. "On the History of the Psycho-Analytic Movement" (1914a), in addition to describing the basic concepts of psychoanalysis, also serves the purpose of defining the boundaries separating psychoanalysis from the two movements that broke away from it, namely, Adler's individual psychology and Jung's analytic psychology. "An Autobiographical Study" (1925b) deals primarily with the life work of the author and barely touches on his personal biography.

In the middle of this series is the essay "The Question of Lay Analysis" (1926b), a publication that owes its existence to the need to defend the psychoanalytic treatment method against the claim by the medical profession that only physicians can carry it out. This claim, which based itself on the Austrian law against "quackery," threatened all nonmedical psychoanalysts with legal prosecution at that time. It was Freud's task to take up the arms and to justify his view that "the important question is not whether an analyst possesses a medical diploma but whether he has had the special training necessary for the practice of analysis" (p. 251f). In a postscript (1927b) to his extensive tract, Freud then wonders whether he has succeeded in sufficiently clarifying the problem of lay analysis. In fact, the issue of accepting nonmedical persons for training in psychoanalysis still remains unsolved to this day. In Europe and other continents, Freud's exposition led to far-reaching acceptance of his point of view. This is not so in the United States where, however, it is not the official authorities that oppose lay analysis, as had been the case in Austria; rather, it is the psychoanalytic specialty itself that advocates the medical privilege and excludes nonphysicians from the American Psychoanalytic Association.

Apart from possibly pointing the way to a solution of this dispute in the present and the future, Freud's treatise on this topic remains a publication of permanent value which is better suited than any of the above-mentioned introductions to make psychoanalytic teachings accessible to the interested student. In it Freud leads, step by step, an imaginary "Impartial Person" created by him from the conscious surface of mental processes to the depth of the unconscious.

He starts with the meaning of dreams as evidence of the existence of an *unconscious mental life,* of which waking life has no knowledge. From there he leads over to the other elements which comprise that same psychic system and endow it with energy, i.e., the *instinctual drives.* The detailed description of man's *sexual life* from its infantile prestages to its definitive organization in the adult serves Freud as the basis for presenting the conflict between the individual's search for pleasure and the demands of reality opposed to it. He demonstrates how the battle between instinctual urges and the inhibiting external world, a battle that begins in childhood, changes its character with the progressive building up of the *psychic personality.* He divides the latter into an instinctual, unconscious *id,* a rationally oriented *ego,* and an ethical-moral, critical agency, the *superego,* which develops on the basis of identifications. The circumstance that each of these inner agencies pursues its own goals leads to the insight into the *dynamic* aspect of mental life; i.e., to the psychoanalytic concept of *psychic conflict:* the ego mobilizes all methods available to it, in the first line, *repression,* to prevent the instinctual impulses from unrestrainedly gaining their goal. The knowledge of these defensive struggles opens the way to an understanding of those compromise formations between ego and id from which *neurotic symptoms* evolve.

Only after having described these complications of mental life, Freud returns to his original question concerning the practice of psychoanalysis and draws attention to the difficulties inherent in its *technique of therapy:* the patient's ever-present positive attachment to his symptoms, i.e., his need to remain ill; the resistance against the lifting

of repressions and the undoing of the other defensive accomplishments as well as the fear of instinctual break-
throughs, an anxiety that led to the illness in the first place;
the *transference of feelings* originally directed to persons in
the patient's past to the treating analyst and the technical
difficulties in their management. The obvious fact that
there is nothing in the medical curriculum to prepare the
physician for dealing with these psychic complications
becomes the basis for Freud's demand that analysts be required to have special, lengthy, and careful *training* in spe-
cialized institutes which do not follow the traditional medical course of study.

In introducing the student to the elements of psychoanalysis, we cannot find a better arrangement than that
adopted by Freud in "The Question of Lay Analysis." On
the one hand, we can presuppose that individuals wanting
to learn about analysis bring to this task the same critical,
yet open-minded attitude that Freud accords to his partner
in the conversations presented in this essay, and that they,
like the Impartial Person, will welcome the interplay of
questions and answers which encourages the participant in
this discussion to voice his doubts and to seek further clarification of obscure points. For this reason I would suggest
that the study of Freud's writings begin with "The Question
of Lay Analysis."

On the other hand, we would be convinced that a student
of psychoanalysis wishes to learn more than the "higher
functionary," who wanted to use his newly acquired
knowledge solely for deciding a legal question. Thus, we
would use Freud's sequence of themes as a guiding prin-

ciple for introducing students to the major elements of psychoanalysis: starting with the dream, we would proceed to the unconscious, the instinctual and sexual life, the structure of the personality, the defense mechanisms, and symptom formation. Each of these elements is extensively treated in Freud's work. The selections from his writings outlined below constitute a reasonable course of study which will enable the student to penetrate the theoretical structure of psychoanalysis to a certain depth.

PART I
THE BASIC CONCEPTS OF PSYCHOANALYSIS

The Meaning of Dreams

Some students may not be inclined to turn their attention to the meaning of dreams as long as the important problems of waking life have not yet been discussed. For what has since time immemorial directed men's interest to psychology is the hope that they will learn to understand what in the course of every life is determined by external forces and what the individual himself contributes to his fate by his faults and mistakes, his passions, his inclinations and aversions.

I would maintain that no psychologial discipline can answer this question as long as it takes as the object of its study only what transpires at the surface of consciousness. Only when we learn what occurs—to speak with Freud (1950, p. 170)—"behind the official consciousness" do we obtain a realistic picture of the influences that determine human behavior.

Today it is no longer unknown that a large part of our mental life proceeds without our awareness, i.e., that our ego — to speak again with Freud (1917, p. 143) — "is not master in its own house." Gradually it has also become part of everyday knowledge that this unconscious includes the instinctual life whose derivatives in the form of wishes strive for satisfaction.

Another characteristic of the unconscious is less well known, however; namely, its predominant mode of thought which in many respects differs from our waking thought processes. While our conscious thinking and planning are subject to the rules of reason and logic and also take into account the conditions in the external world, the mode inherent in the unconscious follows its own paths that are directed solely to the gain of pleasure. It uses a picture language that has no words at its disposal; it does not distinguish between past, present, and future; it treats opposites as though they were one and the same; it does not hesitate to displace affects such as anger and rage from one target to another; it creates mixed figures from a number of single individuals; and so forth.

This mode of expression is strange to us and, in order to understand it, we must laboriously translate it into our own, much as we would with the language of some primitive tribe. Mothers who observe the language development of their young children are familiar with at least some of these phenomena. They know that in the young child laughter and tears are close together; that anger and rage at one person can easily flow over to another; that at this age cause and effect are not yet being connected with each other; that the gain of pleasure and the avoidance of unpleasure are the paramount motives of all actions.

We understand that this form of thinking its age-appropriate and primary and that only with increasing maturation will it be overlaid by a secondary, logical and rational thought process. This does not imply that the primary mode then becomes extinguished. It continues to exist, but hidden, and can again gain dominance over the psychic life whenever the reasonable ego is for some reason weakened. The fantasies of feverish patients and the deliria of the mentally ill provide evidence of such reversion. Only the healthy adult steadfastly adheres to the secondary mode of thinking as long as he is awake and in full control of his mental forces. For him, it is only sleep that nightly turns him back to the primary process. It is the function of sleep to inactivate conscious thinking; to abolish, for its duration, the moral censor whose task it is to guard the access of the unconscious to consciousness; to let wishful impulses deriving from the earliest infantile period rise to the surface again — in short, that the sleeper returns to a primary state and attempts to experience in the dream that which during the day he kept under strict control for the sake of reality considerations.

Viewed from this perspective, the preoccupation with the dream is far from an idle intellectual pursuit. At the beginning of his psychoanalytic work, the dream represented for Freud the most important road to the subterranean forces which determine the parapraxes in everyday life, the choice of the partner in love life, and symptom formation in neurosis and psychosis in mental illness. His *Interpretation of Dreams,* published in 1900, proved to be a trailblazing study of the role of dreaming in the mental life of the healthy; the infantile and actual sources of the dream; the language of the dream; the thought processes prevalent in the unconscious; the distortion of wishes in the dream, which is necessary to disguise the inadmissible and forbidden aspects characteristic of these wishes and to hide them from the sleeper's critical judgment, which never entirely ceases to operate.

The Interpretation of Dreams itself, which in view of its length may not be feasible in an introductory course of study, can in part be replaced by Freud's own summary of it, "On Dreams" (1901a). But even in this necessarily abbreviated form, the section on "The Meaning of Dreams" offers the student the main ideas that should serve to introduce him to this important area of his mental life; without a thorough knowledge of it everything that can be observed on the surface must remain unintelligible.

Not all of Freud's followers share his high estimation of the dream as an aid in psychoanalytic treatment. Today the patient's behavior in the psychoanalytic hour and, above all, the revival, in the psychoanalytic relationship, of repressed childhood conflicts in connection with long-vanished persons compete for the outstanding position of the dream. As important as this emotional transference by the patient to the analyst is and as much as it can contribute to the reconstruction of the patient's past, however, the dream retains *one* prerogative that no other measure of psychoanalytic technique can even remotely attain to: only the penetration into the nature of the dream is capable of clearly bringing into our view the language of the unconscious; that is to say, to convince us of the existence of a primitive mode of thought which all men have in common, which continues to live on in the unconscious long after our conscious mind has learned to acknowledge the supremacy of reason and logic.

Freud only touches on the relationship between sleep and dreaming, which since then has attracted the attention of many investigators. Without contributing to the problems or the content of the dream, the language of the dream, of dream distortion, these mostly physiological studies carried out under laboratory conditions have nevertheless yielded numerous results of interest to psychoanalysis. We now know that there exist two types of sleep, which are scarcely less different from each other than they are from the waking state. The first type, which occurs in periods of roughly 90 minutes, is characterized by rapid eye movements; experiments have established that in this the eyes follow the movements of the objects hallucinated in the dream. Paradoxically, this relatively light sleep is otherwise accompanied only by weak body movements, which is to say that in this respect the sleep state is "deep." Dreaming is confined to this type of sleep which is called "paradoxical" and which, on the basis of its wish-fulfilling hallucinatory activity, is in fact the "guardian" of sleep.

The second type of sleep, called "orthodox," has physiologically entirely different characteristics, and the thought activity associated with it is much closer to waking thought. In this phase, problems of the previous day can be dealt with logically, though the path leading to their solution cannot be remembered after awakening. In this respect every thought activity that occurs in orthodox sleep is more evanescent than the content of dreams during the paradoxical period.

Physiological research into the nature of sleep continues, but we can already say that it has led to far-reaching agreements with Freud's work on the interpretation of dreams. One example is the role played by day residues in the content of the dream, a role which in the meantime has been demonstrated experimentally. Most significant, however, is the experimental confirmation of Freud's hypothesis that the dream serves the important function of relieving tension in the psychic apparatus and thereby ensures the continuation of undisturbed sleep.

The Concept of the Unconscious

Students who were ready to be introduced to the previously enigmatic realm of the dream now confront the task of penetrating deeper into the complexities of human thought activities.

Psychoanalysis has frequently been reproached, though without justification, for incorrectly claiming priority for its assumption of *unconscious* mental activities. In its defense, I refer to words which Freud wrote in the last year of his life: "The concept of the unconscious has long been knocking at the gates of psychology and asking to be let in. Philosophy and literature have often toyed with it, but science could find no use for it. Psycho-analysis has seized upon the concept, has taken it seriously and has given it a fresh content" (1940b, p. 286).

Those who make the effort to pursue psychoanalytic teachings can themselves gain an impression of the characteristics of this new content. It does not in any way consist of a low estimation of conscious psychic activities and their role in mastering the tasks of life. On the contrary, it is the task and the goal of psychoanalytic work to enlarge the domain of conscious thinking, to fill gaps in it, to uncover and dissolve resistances against permitting psychic contents to gain consciousness. It is a triumph for every analyst when he succeeds in making unconscious processes conscious.

The historian who immerses himself in the prehistory and early history of psychoanalysis is impressed by the contrast in attitudes to the mentally ill before and after the assumption of unconscious thinking. Cold water packs and faradization, in the past the only aids in the fight against psychic suffering, simultaneously were evidence of the physician's lack of understanding hysterics, obsessional neurotics, and hypochondriacs. Nothing that occurs in conscious thinking opens up a path to the irrational and abnormal thought processes which underlie psychic symptoms.

It was this, for Freud unbearable, darkness which was illuminated for him by the work of three men. The first was, in 1885–86, Jean-Martin Charcot in Paris, who succeeded in uncovering the meaning of hysterical attacks. Next Freud was influenced, in 1889, by Hippolyte Bernheim in Nancy, who in his demonstrations with hypnosis proved that human behavior and action can be motivated by thought processes of which the person is unaware. The decisive step, finally, is linked to the name of Josef Breuer, a respected Viennese physician, who, in painstaking work with his patient Anna O., was able to trace back her numerous hysterical symptoms to their origins in psychic experiences that had become unconscious.

Breuer and Freud (1893–95) both realized that an individual's hysterical illness was triggered by a return to the past, a finding that was succinctly put in the formulation: "Hysterics suffer mainly from reminiscences" (p. 7). In his earliest works, Freud attributed this "reminiscence" to sexual seduction in childhood, a view which he already abandoned in 1897. He replaced it with the realization that the recollection to which the hysteric is tied is not of real events but goes back to fantasies. We can say that the hysteric regresses to infantile wish-fantasies.

In their pioneering efforts Freud and Breuer also shared the discovery that what occurs in consciousness constitutes only a part of human mental life and that the logical mode of thinking with which we are familiar extends no further than the surface of consciousness. What transpires behind it and rises to the surface in the form of pathological symptoms is as irrational, distorted, and compressed as the phenomena of dream-life. It is not "nonsensical" in the usual sense of this word; rather, it follows its own sense, which is alien to us, in its own form of expression, which is alien to consciousness. The psychoanalytic interpreter of dreams who can unravel the dream distortion and translate the latent content of the dream into manifest thoughts is the model for the psychoanalytic therapist who understands the language of symptoms and traces the pathological manifestations back to their actual origins.

The first person who, following Breuer's example, took this path was Freud. The *Studies on Hysteria,* authored by both Breuer and Freud, document the painstaking work involved in proceeding from consciousness to the thoughts lying behind it. At that time it was still hypnosis which was called upon to remove the obstacles in this path. Soon, however, hypnosis proved to be an unreliable aid; its therapeutic effect was tied too closely to the person of the hypnotist and his suggestions; therefore, it always carried with it the danger that the therapeutic effect would be extinguished with the resolution of the patient's emotional tie to the therapist. A new method to reach the unconscious had to be found — a method, moreover, which was in keeping with Freud's rationality and nonauthoritarian attitude. The commands of the hypnotist who autocratically intrudes into the patient's inner world were to be replaced by the patient himself who by his own act of will and free decision resolved to put his conscious, logical, and goal-directed thinking out of action and to give his thoughts free reign, which soon leads them away from the rational exigencies of everyday life and subjects them to the pressing urges of instinctual wishes and fantasies with which we have become familiar in the theory of dreams. Today we regard the replacement of hypnosis by so-called "free association" as the real birth of psychoanalysis. Free association is, next to the interpretation of dreams, the second *via regia* to insight into the unconscious.

For the serious student of psychoanalysis the assumption of unconscious thought processes represents only a first step. Four further steps serve to lead him into a world of hard-won clinical insights and theories derived from them.

The first fundamental insight of this kind concerns the contrast between psychoanalysis and all earlier psychological theories. For the latter, it was axiomatic that consciousness equaled psychic activity, an assumption that was in full accord with the popular opinion that people knew what went on in their ideational world, were aware of the origins of their emotional attitudes and fantasies, and were informed about the motives of their actions. It is this familiar notion, lulling man in deceptive security, which decisively contrasts with psychoanalysis. Its findings, as described above, not only aim at the psychic processes occurring *outside* of the conscious realm; they also change the proportion between awareness and unawareness of one's own self. They teach that our psychic activity proceeds for the most part unconsciously; that only fragments of this activity emerge temporarily into consciousness; that we, far from controlling our inner life, are in many respects subject to domination by it — in short, to use Freud's formulation again, that psychologically we are "not master in [our] own house" (1917, p. 143). On several occasions Freud compared the injury which he inflicted upon man with his findings with the effect of the unwelcome realization (by Darwin) that man descended from the apes and the no less welcome discovery (by Copernicus) that the earth is not the center of the universe (e.g., 1925a, p. 221). No other finding of psychoanalysis, with the exception of the revelation of infantile sexuality, earned it more enemies and elicited more resistances.

A second insight further complicates matters for the student: there is not one but two kinds of unconscious. It is possible to demonstrate thought processes which temporarily disappear from the surface of consciousness and which descriptively are therefore unconscious, though they do not change their character by disappearing. They merely make room for other, at the moment more relevant thought processes, but for this purpose they leave the realm of consciousness only temporarily; they can at any

time without difficulties again return to it. In psychoanalysis they are called *preconscious*, a term that is meant
to characterize their position of waiting in the forecourt of
consciousness. We distinguish the preconscious thought
processes from the unconscious ones — *unconscious* in the
real sense of the word — which lead their existence in a
different realm of mental life and which are cut off from
consciousness by strong counterforces, i.e., resistances
that can be overcome only with the aid of dream interpretation or free association. This classification of psychic
processes into conscious, preconscious, and unconscious
proved to be an important advance in a new orientation to
the mental life of man.

A third insight concerns the characteristics of the mode
of thought dominant in the realm of the unconscious — an
insight for which our students have already been prepared
by the discussion of dream processes. I repeat: we are dealing here with modes of expression that are closer to hallu-
cination than they are to thinking in words; opposites become one and the same thing; temporal relationships and
sequences are disregarded; logical thinking and consequen-
tial cause-effect connections are missing; emotions are easily displaced from their real object to another; mixed
figures are formed as the result of condensation of several
single figures. Altogether this mode of thinking characteristic of the unconscious strikes one as extraordinarily primitive; it is not different from what we assume to prevail in
the infant before the acquisition of language. In psychoanalytic terminology, we call it the *primary process,* in contrast to the later evolving conscious thought process, the
secondary process. The differences between these two

thought processes are decisive for man's inner life and cannot be overestimated.

The fourth, necessary advance is the interest in the mutual relations between conscious, preconscious, and unconscious processes, especially the interchange between these two different systems. While the preconscious and the conscious can without difficulty pass over into each other and exchange their elements, there are at the border between the system conscious (system *Cs.*) and the system unconscious (system *Ucs.*) guardians which examine and censor the elements emerging from the depth with regard to their admissibility and turn back everything that is objectionable to consciousness. In the personifying language of psychoanalysis, these guarding forces are in fact compared with a political censor; the method employed to keep objectionable elements away from consciousness is called *repression.* Whenever elements from the system unconscious circumvent the censors and undefended penetrate into the system conscious, anxiety arises, not different from what happens in the anxiety dream in which a forbidden instinct derivative without being distorted succeeded in entering the manifest content of the dream. Much psychic suffering of man derives from nothing other than the continuous struggle between the instinct derivatives that are held in check but strive to rise to the surface and the system conscious that wards off these invaders or, when the defense miscarries, attempts by one or another means of disguise at least to minimize their harm. A person who—like the analyst— once has learned to follow such a defensive struggle in all its details will forever remain fascinated by the never-ending variations and complications of man's psychic life.

The student who has followed us thus far should now be in a position to undertake the study of Freud's "A Note on the Unconscious in Psycho-Analysis" (1912c), "The Unconscious" (1915c), and "Some Elementary Lessons in Psycho-Analysis" (1940b).

The Instinctual Drives

We assume that our students have by now become convinced of the existence of an unconscious mental life and have gradually approached four further pieces of knowledge: insight into the overwhelming range of the unconscious processes which is in no way comparable to that of conscious experience; the difference between what is genuinely unconscious and what is only descriptively and temporarily separated from consciousness; an understanding of the extraordinarily primitive mode of thinking dominant in the unconscious. one which is suggestive of the psychic processes in very early childhood; a first impression of the disharmony between the different psychic agencies which as "inner conflicts" aggravate and burden human life. What we now expect of the student thus prepared is a fifth step: a look at the *content* of the unconscious, i.e., at the elements comprising this system, because it is only an understanding of their characteristics which explains why they must be barred from consciousness and why man must be continually on the alert against their emergence.

In seminars of our training institutes the candidates are frequently told that psychoanalysis is essentially a drive psychology. But this does not mean that psychoanalysis also claims to have formulated a theory of instinctual drives which in comprehensiveness, specificity, and usefulness surpasses all previous attempts aiming in that direction. On the contrary, Freud repeatedly stressed that he regarded the state of the psychoanalytic instinct theory as unsatisfactory. He referred to the drives themselves as "mythical entities, magnificent in their indefiniteness," their description being not much more than "so to say our mythology." At the same time, however, he asserted that the analyst in his work "cannot for a moment disregard them" (1933a, p. 95). It is precisely this constant preoccupation with the existence and workings of the instinctual drives that gives psychoanalytic work and theory their special character. The investigation of the unconscious by means of the dream, free association, and interpretation of the transference behavior in the analytic situation is at the same time research work aimed at the understanding of the drives. It goes beyond the realm of psychology to the extent that the sources of the instinctual drives lie in the biological and somatic sphere from which the instinctual drives merely send out their derivatives into the psychic realm. In their search for satisfaction these derivatives reach the unconscious, the system closest to them, and from there attempt to force an entry into conscious thinking and action. The above-mentioned "inner conflict," which causes trouble for the individual and his analyst, is accordingly the incompatibility between the demands made by the instinctual drives and the moral, ethical, and social side of the human personality that opposes them.

Freud's lifelong, persistent, and tentative attempts to create his own drive theory led him far away from his predecessors. He regarded the single instincts described by other authors, such as the instinct for power, imitation, play, or the sociable instinct, as too unimportant to explain the outstandingly significant occurrences dominating human mental life. His search was directed to a dualism, to two supreme opposing forces with the demands of which the psychic processes had to contend: self-preservation versus preservation of the species, ego instincts versus sexual instincts, life instinct versus death instinct. Freud's view was directed to biology, the area lying behind the psychic sphere, i.e., to the vital processes themselves which are only reflected in the psychic processes.

Each of these attempts to solve the riddle of the instinctual drives dominated whole phases of Freud's life work and productivity. At times these were close to clinical observations, supported and required by them; at others, they were far removed and more akin to biological speculations than descriptions of clinical facts. It was the fate of these different advances to evoke as much agreement as disagreement, not only in wider circles but especially among Freud's immediate followers. In particular, the dualism between life and death instincts postulated by him became a matter of dispute; many psychoanalytic clinicians regard the hypothesis of a death instinct as a foreign body; others welcome it and consider it to be the basis of all psychic conflicts. Be that as it may, Freud felt that with his last formulation of instinct theory he had come closer to a factor which, extending far beyond individual psychic life, was responsible for the life processes in their widest sense.

For the general student it would be too difficult to follow

in detail the sequence of instinctual drive concepts in analysis. I would therefore assign first "Instincts and Their Vicissitudes" (1915a), drawing attention to the fact that this paper is a relatively early attempt of Freud's to treat the topic comprehensively. It has remained a fundamental work, not in the least for an understanding of the subsequent changes in the classification of instinctual drives. Freud's last formulation, expressed in the contrasting pair of Eros and Thanatos, can then be studied in "Beyond the Pleasure Principle" (1920).

Human Sexuality

The scientific readers in Freud's times may have been put off by his assumption of an unconscious psychic life and his supposition of a dualistic instinct theory. But these reactions were far from evoking the hostilities that, beginning with the investigation of human sexuality, decided the fate of psychoanalysis.

Even the first hunches that sexual impulses might be at the bottom of hysterical symptoms cost Freud the collaboration and friendship of Josef Breuer, who in the pioneering treatment of his patient Anna O. uncovered the previously unrecognized relationship between suppressed memories and pathogenic manifestations. That Freud questioned his neurotic patients about the details of their sexual life offended the conventions of the bourgeois world in which he lived and worked, without sharing its hypocritical denials. What he himself regarded as resolute exploration others construed to be perverse pruriency. The situation grew worse with the publication of *Three Essays on the Theory of Sexuality* (1905b). This work contributed considerably to Freud's social and scientific isolation from his environment.

Today readers can scarcely imagine the outbursts of indignation aroused by this book. What in our days is counted as everyday knowledge of the instinctual side of human nature was then a shocking and prohibited attack on human dignity. It made no difference that the data presented in this book did not stem from the author's fantasies but were derived from laboriously won and painstakingly assembled clinical facts. The topic of sexuality itself was taboo, and the sufferings caused by the sexual difficulties and abstinences were to remain barred to all physicians.

Conceivably, the situation might gradually have been changed in view of the relief which Freud brought about in his patients by requesting that they speak openly about their sexuality. But it was the details he described in the *Three Essays* which had the opposite effect on his adversaries. Apparently, the most offending factor was the extension of the concept of sexuality, which was most important to Freud and which he himself described as follows: "That extension is of a twofold kind. In the first place sexuality is divorced from its too close connection with the genitals and is regarded as a more comprehensive bodily function, having pleasure as its goal and only secondarily coming to serve the ends of reproduction. In the second place the sexual impulses are regarded as including all of those merely affectionate and friendly impulses to which usage applies the exceedingly ambiguous word 'love'" (1925b, p. 38). Since then Freud was repeatedly implored, by well-meaning adherents as well as strangers, to drop this "extension" or at least to substitute a harmless term for the word "sexual." But he remained firm. For him, the restriction of sexuality to the genital function constituted "inexpedient limitations of the concept" (p. 38), which glossed over the fact that the feelings and relations named above have their roots in the very same sexual impulses that manifest themselves in various forms and degrees. He was convinced that large areas of human life become intelligible only when this common instinctual foundation is recognized, an insight that was to be illuminated and not obscured by the terminology.

Another thesis, however, carried even more weight. The detaching of sexuality from the genitals enabled Freud to trace the development of sexual functioning from its manifestations in the adult to its first beginnings in early childhood. What had until then been deemed infantile demeanors or misdemeanors—thumb sucking, interest in the excrements, masturbation—appeared in this new light as the search for sexual pleasure, though not connected with the genitals but dependent upon specific bodily zones which in the course of childhood development successively gain significance in view of their excitability; these are, at first, the mouth, then the anus, and later the penis. Oral, anal, and phallic strivings, together comprising infantile sexuality, were characterized as physical accompaniments of the child's affectionate tie to his parents; this allowed for including the concept of sexual excitation in the early relationship to the mother and later in the triangular relationship to mother and father.

The world as it was then could not accept the statement that the child's love for his differently sexed parent resembles in many respects the adult's love for his sexual partner. This assertion contradicted the widely held popular view of the "innocence of the child"—i.e., of a prestage which is devoid of any sexual knowledge and feeling and which comes to an end only with the stirrings in puberty; all sexual activities that could be observed in the preceding phase, especially masturbation, were taken as signs of moral depravity. The notion of infantile sexuality found its most stubborn opponents among the official German psychiatrists, who outdid each other in heaping accusations on Freud. Especially the concept of the so-called oedipus complex (love for the mother and jealous and hostile impulses to the father, in the case of the male child) represented for them "a poisoning of one of the few human relationships which mankind still regards as sacred." They rejected psychoanalytic theories as a degenerate form of "European nihilism, as dissolution of all accepted values," and called for its boycott and denunciation, i.e., a call to arms for a bitter and fierce fight against psychoanalysis (Editorial, 1931).

Even the publication of "Analysis of a Phobia in a Five-Year-Old Boy" (1909a), which appeared about four years after the *Three Essays,* contributed little to convince Freud's opponents and to take the edge off their enmity. This description of the illness and treatment of Little Hans for the first time opens up a path to the otherwise inaccessible world of feelings and thoughts of a young child, to his fantasies, anxieties, passions, and death wishes, with all their bizarre entanglements, displacements, and compromise formations. Anyone who has the slightest readiness to look at something so entirely novel will find here the picture of an infantile neurosis — not as a theoretical construction deduced retroactively from a neurosis in the adult, but as an individual, immediate, actually occurring event. The ideational world of Little Hans, though drastically accentuated at the height of his illness, is essentially not different from that of other — perhaps of all — children of his age. Since the publication of this case history, psychoanalytically informed parents have learned to observe their own children carefully, to understand the pregenital sexual manifestations as indications of a prescribed developmental course, and to connect the frequent anxieties, inhibitions, and developmental disturbances with the conflicts to which they give rise. Within the psychoanalytic movement, the analysis of Little Hans thus became the starting point for two important branches of the discipline: on the one hand, for child analysis, which steadily gained in importance; on the other, for psychoanalytically oriented direct observation of infants. But for the psychiatric world, hostile before and after, even this clinical advance in the understanding and treatment of childhood disturbances was just another grave reason for defamation.

The opposition to including childhood in the study of sexuality was so violent that it could be equaled only by the rejection of another thesis contained in the *Three Essays*. The detachment of the concept of sexuality from the genital zone and the study of its infantile prestages enabled Freud to gain a better understanding of perverse sexual activities as well. From the viewpont of conventional genitality in the adult, all pregenital sexual pleasure was after all perverse; i.e., the entire infantile sexuality was polymorphously perverse. Seen in this light, the adult pervert was nothing other than a sexually disturbed person who failed to attain the sexual aim and who in its place was condemned to seek his orgastic satisfaction in the pregenital sphere. As convincing as this insight was for the psychoanalytic clinician, and as often as it was confirmed in analytic treatments, however, the psychiatric world persisted in its moral repudiation of the perversions as well as of psychoanalysis. Freud, who in general paid little or no attention to polemics and accepted even determined rejection with equanimity, once characterized this attitude by saying: "German science will not have cause to be proud of those who represented it." While the fact that they rejected psychoanalysis was understandable to him, there could be no excuse "for the degree of arrogance which they displayed, for their conscienceless contempt of logic, and for the coarseness and bad taste of their attack" (1925b, p. 49).

It is characteristic of the resistances to and attacks on psychoanalysis that in the course of time their rationalizations and place of origin change, while the intensity and passionateness of the antagonism remain more or less the same. In today's academic world, the combative attitude to psychoanalysis has given way to peaceful coexistence, occasional collaboration, or some degree of indifference. The fact of infantile sexuality and the consequences it has for the normality and abnormality of adult sexuality has been widely recognized by the medical, psychiatric, and lay world. Homosexuals struggle with more or less success for public toleration and freedom from legal persecution. Such perversions as fetishism, transvestitism, and compulsive exhibitionism and voyeurism are regarded as symptoms of an illness and no longer as signs of moral depravity.

One can no longer imagine the absence of descriptions of even crass or daring forms of sexuality in the literature, the theater, and the mass media. Disbelief and indignation now come from a new side and are directed to different aims: the side of the modern women's liberation movement which disputes Freud's theory of female sexuality and its development. Representatives of this movement experience this theory as an affront and depreciation, very similar to how formerly the representatives of the ideal of "innocent childhood" reacted to the theory of infantile sexuality.

In fact, psychoanalysis and the women's movement differ in their essential presuppositions. On the one hand, Freud stressed the bisexual disposition of all human beings; on the other, he was convinced that anatomy determined whether predominantly male or female qualities would be developed and prepare the individual for his or her differing future life tasks. As little as the sexual manifestations of boys and girls differ from each other in the oral and anal phases, as significant is the marked dissimilarity in the phallic phase during which the anatomical equipment of the female child puts her at a disadvantage in relation to the possessor of the phallus, as far as masturbatory and exhibitionistic pleasures are concerned. While the boy who highly values his sexual organ is exposed to castration anxiety, the girl in turn develops penis envy and the wish for a substitute for what has been withheld from her, a wish that ultimately culminates in the wish to have a child.

The prestages of female sexuality which Freud reconstructed, piece by piece, on the basis of data gained in the analysis of female patients, are simply brushed aside by

liberated women as the result of male chauvinistic preju-
dice. They deny the existence of any inherited difference
between man and woman and explain the appearance of
early unlikeness as the exclusive result of social influences
on upbringing which push the girl to play with dolls and
propel the boy toward interest in motors, soldiers, and war
games. The anatomical difference between penis and vagi-
na, between impregnation and giving birth, and its decisive
impact on psychic development are pushed aside in the
passionate efforts to free women from the subjugation in
which they have in fact been held for centuries and to put
women in a position that in every respect equals that of
their male partners.

Some of Freud's remarks relating to the attitude of
women to cultural tasks are a consequence of the exclusion
of women from the professional life of men in his times
and as a description are no longer valid in our times when
all possible professional activities, in business, medicine,
the law, or as a head of state, are open to women.

The feminist battle, much like the early attacks on psychoanalysis, is being fought out by means of rigorous and
wholesale condemnation. Thus, in the arguments of the
women's movement, there is, for example, not a single
appreciative reference to the facts that the equality of the
sexes for which they strive existed in the analytic movement from the beginning, that analytic training institutes
do not discriminate between male and female applicants,
that at all times women played an important role as
authors contributing to the psychoanalytic literature and
as respected collaborators of Freud. The data that psychoanalysis laboriously won in order to throw some light on

the difficulties and frequent disturbances of female sexual functioning are taken out of their narrow sexual context by its enemies and blindly applied to the general significance of woman as a social being and professional worker.

Today modern research into sex has resulted in further opposition. It was Freud's effort and merit that in the creation of his libido concept he welded together somatic and psychic processes into an inseparable unit. In contrast, Masters and Johnson (1970), for example, attempt to demonstrate that physical processes in isolation are amenable to therapeutic interventions. Thus, they once again divorce the sexual and the love life from each other and put the stamp of a purely physical process on the former.

In this way they undo what Freud accomplished with his *Three Essays,* which is still the central work in this area. After studying it, the student might proceed to some of the briefer writings (1908b, 1923b, 1924a, 1925c, 1931a) as variations on the theme and as evidence for the fact that Freud continued until the end of his life to work out and elaborate on specific elements of his theory of sexuality.

The Structure of the Psychic Personality

Freud's readiness to change his theories as soon as they no longer met his requirements occasionally posed some problems for his followers and pupils. Those who had just begun to familiarize themselves with the theory of the unconscious and to evaluate all psychic processes in terms of their relationship to conscious perception must have found it difficult to give up this point of view again and to exchange it for a new one. And those of Freud's collaborators who were wholly committed to depth psychology were scarcely inclined to turn at least part of their interest once more to the surface of consciousness and to the influences of the external world.

Freud himself, however, had no such misgivings. In the 1920s he was concerned with integrating into his theory two new insights gained in his analytic treatments. The ego which until then had in its entirety coincided with the system conscious now appeared to have distinct unconscious parts; the system unconscious, on the other hand, seemed to contain more than the repressed that Freud had assigned to it. Both observations contradicted the previously adopted simple division of psychic life into spatially separated systems (unconscious, preconscious, conscious) that were clearly demarcated from each other. This classification, then, did not do justice to the newly observed facts and therefore had to be replaced by another one.

In his new formulation which he presented at length for the first time in *The Ego and the Id* (1923a), Freud restricted the concept of unconscious to a quality of psychic processes, i.e., to a characteristic of mental activity that can be found in every part of the psychic apparatus. The psychic apparatus itself was now conceived as a structure consisting of several agencies or institutions. In short, the earlier topographic model of psychic life was superseded by the structural model.

Freud's opponents repeatedly reproached him with proceeding unscientifically because he gave these newly postulated agencies names of their own (namely, ego, id, and superego); they disparagingly compared this terminological characterization with a description of mythological

figures. Nevertheless, it was precisely this obvious per-
sonification of theoretical constructs which for the analyst
as well as the lay reader brought into focus the contradictions contained in his own person and perhaps made
them clearly visible for the first time. That no human individual is a unity, that inner disharmonies are unavoidable, becomes intelligible only when we can clearly discern
the different origins, the different contents, the different
mechanisms and aims of each single agency. Freud set himself this task of clarification in *The Ego and the Id,* and
subsequently once again summarized his solution in his lecture on "The Dissection of the Psychical Personality"
(1933a) (which should both be assigned).

According to the new concept, the inner collisions and
conflicts are no longer simply between conscious and
unconscious elements; rather, other, no less serious contrasts are decisive. The blind search for satisfaction by the
drives, which are given at birth and determine the nature of
the id, is not compatible with the nature of the ego whose
task it is to register conditions, requirements, and dangers
in the outer world and to take them into consideration.
The ego agencies in their turn are naturally, as it were, divided according to their double origin. For the ego itself is
nothing other than a remodeled part which, having split off
from the id, is adapted to the external world; the superego,
again, is a precipitate of the child's prolonged dependency
on his parents and their demands with regard to drive restriction and socialization.[1] Thus, in every individual,

[1] The significance and the genesis of the superego, and especially the
role played by identifications in its development, also are discussed by
Freud in *Group Psychology and the Analysis of the Ego* (1921) and

the search for pleasure, for adaptation, and for morality clash with each other and over and over confront each of us with the task of reconciling the irreconcilable and, all contradictions notwithstanding, to strive for inner harmony. When these efforts succeed, psychic health is assured; when they fail, we see inhibitions, symptoms, and morbidly increased anxiety—pathological manifestations.

These introductory words stress the important advances in the formation of Freud's theories. At the same time, however, students should also be warned that the new structural model of the psychic apparatus does not neglect the old classification conscious/unconscious. Modern analytic authors easily forget that Freud's own estimation of the significance of the unconscious mental life did not decisively change with the introduction of the structural model. He was and always remained convinced, as he himself said, that the "division of the psychical into what is conscious and what is unconscious is the fundamental premise of psycho-analysis" (1923a, p. 13), "our own beacon-light in the darkness of depth-psychology" (p. 18). The practicing analyst is in fact frequently tempted, now as ever, to understand his efforts in terms of the old topographic theory. Again and again he is made to realize that the psychic contents that shun the light of the conscious surface must laboriously be coaxed out of the dark room of the unconscious and furnished with word-presentations, as is the case with the preconscious, before they can take their place in consciousness. In descriptions of this sort, all theoretical advances notwithstanding, the concepts of un-

---

Civilization and Its Discontents (1930), both of which are assigned reading in the section on the applications of psychoanalysis.

conscious and id, and of conscious and ego, obviously coincide once again.

Pleasure Principle and Reality Principle

It is one of the premises of psychoanalysis that psychic processes are subject to laws and that the regulatory laws governing them undergo development. Freud described one such progressive regulatory step in "Formulations on the Two Principles of Mental Functioning," a brief but fundamental paper which was written in 1911, long before he introduced the structural model discussed above. Stated simply, this paper deals with mankind's advance from the blind search for pleasure and instinctual satisfaction to the capacities to recognize the conditions in the external world and to take reality factors into account — an advance that in the childhood of each individual must be repeated and newly accomplished. Freud assigns the primary search for pleasure of the earliest times to the hallucinatory thinking of the system unconscious, and the subsequent phase of reality observation and evaluation to an adaptation of the psychic apparatus, i.e., to the equipment of the system conscious with such functions as attention, notation, passing of judgment, and action. The progression from the pleasure principle to the reality principle is described as a transformation of the ego: from pleasure ego to reality ego.

It is important for the student to recognize that this highly condensed work forms a bridge between Freud's early conceptions and his later formulations. The initial postulate that the mastering of stimuli is the task of the psychic apparatus, "which has the function of getting rid of the stimuli that reach it, or of reducing them to the lowest possible level" (1915a, p. 120), belongs to the early phase of Freud's thinking, as does the notion that phylogenetic acquisitions must be attained anew, in abbreviated form, in ontogenesis. On the other hand, "Formulations on the Two Principles of Mental Functioning" already contains the first hints of his subsequent division of the psychic personality into distinct agencies.

The pleasure principle which, according to the topographic point of view, originates in the system unconscious but extends its influence to the conscious ego, obviously is, in the later structural theory, the regulatory principle which dominates the id and to which the instinctual id contents are subject. Thus, the pleasure principle is coordinated not only with hallucinatory thinking but with the entire primitive mode of thought characteristic of the id—the so-called primary process which operates with thing- rather than word-presentations; without knowledge of the conditions in the external world, indeed, without access to them; without understanding of causal relationships; and, insofar as the access to the motoric sphere is open to it, purely impulsively in action; and, finally, without the capability to evaluate the consequences of actions and to anticipate dangers. The reality principle, in contrast, reigns, according to the structural viewpoint, in the ego, and the functions that enable it to operate are those of the so-called secondary process—perception, thinking in word-presentations, memory, reality testing, control of motility, etc.

In "Formulations on the Two Principles of Mental Functioning" as well as on other occasions, Freud emphasized that "the substitution of the reality principle for the pleasure principle implies no deposing of the pleasure principle, but only a safeguarding of it. A momentary pleasure, uncertain in its results, is given up, but only in order to gain along the new path an assured pleasure at a later time" (1911b, p. 223). Seen from this vantage point, the aim-inhibiting activity of the reality ego is friendly to the instinctual drives. As every practicing analyst knows, this objective assessment does not always coincide with the judgment of the individual in whose inner life these processes are enacted. In the case of the derivatives of the sexual instinct, in particular, the restrictions required by the reality principle are experienced as inimical to the drives. Here lie the causes of the individual's conflicts between the id's adherence to the instinctual aims appropriate to it and the postponement, inhibition, and transformation of the instinctual impulses which the ego considers to be necessary.

Repression

For Freud, repression was the fundamental problem from which "the study of the neurotic processes took its whole start" (1937, p. 236); the "theory of repression became the cornerstone of our understanding of the neuroses" (1925b, p. 30). Throughout his working life Freud persisted in his attempts to explain the phenomenon that there are psychic processes capable of excluding other psychic processes from consciousness. What he described in the later-abandoned "Project for a Scientific Psychology" of 1895 (1950) as a failure in the translation of an earlier mode into a subsequently superimposed mode of psychic expression appeared, in the topographic theory, as hindering the passage from the system unconscious to the systems preconscious and conscious — specifically, as the withdrawal of the quantity of cathexis which alone would make the emergence into conscious perception possible; and finally, in the structural model of the psychic apparatus, as the result of the dynamic interplay between the psychic agencies. The element which in these successive attempts remains constant is the motive of repression, namely, the prevention of the arousal of anxiety or unpleasure in the system conscious, respectively, in the conscious ego.

Where these purely theoretical expositions may perplex the student or lay reader, Freud's allegorical descriptions come to his aid. In the topographical model, Freud uses the picture of the censor who guards the border between unconscious and conscious, severs the connections between the forbidden drive derivatives and the feelings accompanying them or the thoughts and images representing them, and thereby prevents their rising into the higher systems. In the structural model, it is the picture of the ego which is hard pressed by the instinctual claims of the id, the conditions in the external world, and the moral demands of the superego, and which takes refuge by resorting to the defense mechanism of repression. These lively descriptions reflect something of the individual's actual and immediate experience: a dim intimation of pressing impulses at work; a sense of being at odds with oneself; in short, the distress connected with an internal conflictual state.

As is usually the case in psychoanalytic investigations, the study of repression started not with the successful but with the miscarried defense. Where repression achieves the desired aim, namely, to keep the unwelcome psychic elements more or less permanently away from consciousness, there are on the surface of consciousness no visible indications of what has occurred; at best, there are breaks in the psychic connections and such gaps are frequently enough disregarded. On the other hand, where repression does not succeed or succeeds only partially, symptoms are formed and the conflict between impulse and defense, between the upsurge of the repressed material and the repressing forces, continues before the eyes of the observer; this makes it possible for us to gain an understanding of all the stages, forms, and mechanisms of the defensive struggle, beginning with the extensive withdrawal of cathexis from the conscious representatives to the return of the repressed in its original or distorted form.

Repression is not the only possible form of defense; there exist other mechanisms of defense which support and augment and also succeed it. Freud only hinted at this in the paper we shall study next, namely, "Repression" (1915b), a relatively early work (written before the introduction of the structural model), but he elaborated on it in later publications. In 1926, Freud speaks of defense as "a general designation for all the techniques which the ego makes use of in conflicts which may lead to a neurosis, while we retain the word 'repression' for the special method of defence which the line of approach taken by our investigation made us better acquainted with in the first instance" (1926a, p. 163).

It will be obvious to every reader of Freud's case histories what Freud means by "the line of approach taken by our investigation." In the early *Studies on Hysteria*

(1893–95), it is the defensive device of repression followed by conversion of the repressed into somatic innervation which is convincingly demonstrated. In the later "Notes upon a Case of Obsessional Neurosis" (1909b), the same occurs with regard to the mechanisms of defense characteristic of this illness: obsessional thinking, compulsive actions, doubts, indecision, undoing, isolation of affect and ideas, turning into the opposite, reaction formations. "Analysis of a Phobia in a Five-Year-Old Boy" (1909a) throws light on psychic displacement and flight, and "Psycho-Analytic Notes on an Autobiographical Account of a Case of Paranoia" (1911a) primarily on the defense mechanism of projection.

The avoidance of anxiety and unpleasure is the overriding principle that dominates the individual's life from the very beginning; accordingly, the development of a reliable chronology of defensive processes is a task of psychoanalytic theory which has high priority but which, for the time being, has not yet been solved. It is obvious that there can be no repressions in the period of complete immaturity, i.e., prior to the division of the psychic apparatus into the systems conscious and unconscious, ego and id. The defensive devices commonly used in this early period are primitive — flight, denial, reversal into the opposite, turning against the self. As soon as psychic differentiation between the self and the surrounding world, between inner and outer, has taken place, unpleasant elements of the inner life can be displaced into the outer world. When later on genuine repressions are accomplished but remain unreliable, they are reinforced by the cathexis, in the realm of the conscious ego, of representatives of the opposite of the repudiated elements (e.g., compassion instead of cruelty, disgust instead of pleasure in soiling, etc.). Finally, under the influence of the superego, primitive impulses are transformed, inhibited in their aims, and the drive energies belonging to them deflected to moral, ethical, or socially higher aims.

The fact that such defense mechanisms as denial, reversal into the opposite, turning against the self, projection, reaction formation, and sublimation develop and are used does not diminish the outstanding position of repression in psychic life. Repression is and remains "something quite peculiar and is more sharply differentiated from the other mechanisms than they are from one another" (1937, p. 236). Although these other mechanisms may bring about deflections, changes in direction, and transformations of drive derivatives, only repression succeeds in completely obliterating their appearance in the conscious material. For this reason, repression is the most stable and highly developed defense.

Symptom Formation

Those who have studied the preceding material (especially 1915c, 1905b) will not find it difficult to understand the complicated ways of symptom formation and their end products. Drastic changes in the course of psychic processes, such as those enforced by repression and the other mechanisms of defense, cannot remain without serious consequences. What starts out as seemingly harmless, namely, in the service of avoiding unpleasure, ends more or less intractably in ego alterations, character distortions, and pathological manifestations.

The student who has followed us thus far must by now have gained a clear notion of the conflict between drive satisfaction and defense against the drives. At this point he needs to be introduced to two new concepts — regression and fixation.

An individual who finds the path to an instinctual aim of adulthood blocked by internal or external obstacles can respond to such a frustration by reverting to childhood forms of satisfaction; i.e., he regresses in his search for pleasure. Which one of the old forms of satisfaction will in this way be revived depends upon the real or fantasied occurrences of his own repressed early childhood, i.e., on the quantity of libidinal energy attached to or fixated at specific developmental phases. The larger the quantity is, the stronger is the pull exerted by the phase involved and by the forms of satisfaction in question. But that which in childhood was a legitimate part of the infantile drive constitution is for the adult, nonregressed ego a piece of perversion and as such inadmissible and unpleasure-provoking. A defensive struggle ensues and comes to an end only when a compromise between instinctual drive and defense has been found. The compromise solution is the neurotic symptom, which is two-faced. On the one hand, it represents a partial success of the defensive forces which contrived to prevent the instinctual drives from attaining their aim; on the other hand, it serves as a substitute for the instinctual satisfaction, though in a "very much reduced, displaced and inhibited" form (1926a, p. 95).

The path to the neurotic symptom thus proceeds via several steps: from the demands of the instinctual impulses to their frustration; from the frustration of satisfaction to regression to the fixation point in infancy; from the infantile fantasied satisfaction to anxiety and unpleasure; from anxiety and unpleasure to defense; finally, from defensive struggle to compromise formation. It is impossible to overestimate the role played by anxiety in this context. Where the individual's ego acquiesces to the infantile satisfactions and does not object to them, that is, where no anxiety arises, neither defense nor symptom formation comes about. Instead the individual's entire behavior reverts to an earlier level.

As the main work illustrating these formulations I would select Freud's lecture on "The Path to the Formation of Symptoms" (1916–17). The processes involved are further illustrated in Freud's case histories (1905a, 1909a, 1909b, 1911a, 1918), which, according to his own account, "read like short stories" (1893–95, p. 160). As mentioned in the section on Repression, different combinations of defensive processes are at work in each of the different neuroses described by Freud. It is the choice and mixture of mechanisms which in hysteria (repression, conversion), phobia (flight, displacement, avoidance), obsessional neurosis (repression, reaction formation, isolation, undoing), paranoia (projection) determine the form of symptom formation.

Neurosis and Psychosis

Freud's field of work was the neuroses, his observational material being limited by the conditions of his medical practice. For this reason, his ventures into the area of psychosis were few, instigated by the occasional psychotic episodes of his patients or the intensive study of publications such as Daniel Paul Schreber's *Denkwürdigkeiten eines Geisteskranken* (1903). Freud explores, on the one hand, the common factors and, on the other, the considerable differences between these two forms of illness (1924c, 1924d). In his opinion, both have their onset in the frustration of a vital instinctual wish. Their difference lies in the nature of what is substituted for the frustrated wish.

As was demonstrated in the previous section, the neurotic's relationship to reality is an important chapter in Freud's theory of the neuroses, though he had stressed that "in the world of the neuroses it is psychical reality which is ... decisive" (1916–17, p. 368). Or, put differently, he does not discriminate whether "the infantile experiences to which the libido is fixated and out of which the symptoms are made" (p. 367) actually happened or whether they belonged to the patient's fantasies; the pathogenic effect is the same in both cases. In "The Loss of Reality in Neurosis and Psychosis" (1924d), on the other hand, Freud explicitly emphasizes that it would be wrong to conclude from this finding that he believed neurotics to be incapable of clearly distinguishing between fantasy and reality, between inner and outer reality. On the contrary, it is in fact a defining characteristic of the neuroses that the ego function of reality testing has for all practical purposes remained intact and that the equivalence and equality of inner and outer reality are confined to the processes of symptom formation. The neurotic, e.g., in obsessional neurosis, behaves as though he truly believed in the omnipotence of his death wishes; or he may believe that some harmless everyday utensils contain dangerous substances which might pass over to him and from which he must protect himself by avoiding contact with them. At the same time he knows that these apprehensions are only a product of his fantasies; and it is precisely this reality-adequate knowledge which forces him to fashion his symptomatic substitute formations in such a way that they simultaneously take into account the pressure of the instinctual wishes and the demands by the external world represented by the superego which has adopted them.

As "Neurosis and Psychosis" (1924c) shows, Freud sees the significant difference of the psychoses in the circumstance that the frustration of the instinctual wish is from the very beginning experienced as intolerable and therefore leads to a rupture in the relations to the external world which is held to be responsible for the nonfulfillment. Depending upon the form of the psychotic illness, the cathexes are withdrawn from the real perception, the real persons, and even the real memories, as a result of which the external world no longer has any influence on psychic processes. Unlike the neurotic, the psychotic then is free to evolve symptoms and substitute formations that need to be adequate only to the demands of the id and no longer to those of reality.

In his paper on the Schreber case (1911a), Freud demonstrated that psychoanalysis can reach beyond the area of neurosis and illuminate diverse psychic mechanisms and their ways of operating and unravel such pathological forms as amentia, schizophrenia, and paranoia. On the other hand, he did not base any therapeutic claims on this understanding. He was convinced that psychotics lack the fundamental prerequisite that makes a patient suitable for psychoanalytic therapy: a more or less normal ego that has retained the capacities of reality testing, self-observation, and insight into the illness; the libidinal cathexis of real persons, which makes the emotional transference to the analyst possible; the readiness of the inner world to perceive, acknowledge, and at least partially to subject itself to external influences. Since these functions are not at the disposal of the psychotic, he was, in Freud's opinion, not amenable to psychoanalysis and at best accessible only in periods of remission between psychotic episodes.

Freud's pupils and followers who in general uphold his views do not share this one, which they regard as therapeutic nihilism. Today the therapeutic ambitions of many analysts extend far beyond the frame of the symptom neuroses and character disturbances to the so-called borderline cases that lead over to the psychoses and to the psychoses themselves. It is difficult to decide how much of this is to be ascribed to general human interest in the bizarre phenomena of psychosis, how much to the thorough psychiatric training of medical analysts, and how much simply to the desire to advance beyond the frontiers of what has already been explored to new territories. In any event, preoccupation with the psychoses now constitutes a special field of interest in the psychoanalytic literature dealing with problems of theory and technique of therapy. In view of certain technical considerations, many believe that it is possible to arouse in the psychotic enough of the still-present remnants of object libido so that a transference relationship from the patient to the therapist can be established; to compensate temporarily for the patient's ego defects by means of the analyst's putting his own intact psychic apparatus at the disposal of the patient; and in general to enter together with the patient into the primary thought processes and phantasms of his id before the patient is gradually urged toward and made capable of replacing id processes by ego processes, in the tradition of psychoanalytic therapy.

Whether the treatment of psychotics by psychoanalytic means can be successful is still a matter of debate in psychoanalysis. It remains a task for the future to find a middle course between therapeutic pessimism and therapeutic optimism in this area.

Freud's work on the psychoses had serious consequences for a central aspect of psychoanalytic theory, namely, libido theory, i.e., the theory of the vicissitudes of the psychic energy emanating from the sexual drives. What Freud previously conceived of as an antithesis between sexual instincts and ego instincts (1915a) became, in the new conceptualization (1914c), the different deployment of one and the same sexual energy, on the one hand for the cathexis of real or fantasied persons in the external world (object libido) and, on the other, for the cathexis of one's own somatic and psychic person (narcissistic libido).

The introduction of the theory of narcissism in 1914 led to the explanation of many previously ununderstood phenomena. In this new conception, the paranoiac's megalomania, for example, is understood as caused by the withdrawal of cathexis from objects and the hypercathexis of his own person and its functions; the same process also is held responsible for the "end of the world" anxieties of these patients because, for them, the external world is devoid of libidinal cathexis. Hypochondriasis, on the other hand, is thought to develop when all libido is concentrated on the body or a specific part of the body or a specific body organ. A complete counterpart to this is the impoverishment of a person in the state of being in love in which all libido is withdrawn from narcissistic purposes and transferred to the love object that as a consequence is overvalued. The love life of adults also is thought, in many respects, especially in the choice of a partner, to be determined by the difference between object-libidinal and narcissistic impulses.

In his explanation of this phenomenon, Freud goes back to childhood, i.e., to "the idea of there being an original libidinal cathexis of the ego, from which some of it is later given off to objects, but which fundamentally persists and is related to the object-cathexes much as the body of an amoeba is related to the pseudopodia which it puts out" (1914c, p. 75). The intense ego cathexis which the child and the psychotic (as well as primitive peoples) have in common also explains their own "over-estimation of the power of their wishes and mental acts," the so-called grandiose "omnipotence of thought" (1914c, p. 75). The hypothesis that the same libido is capable of object-libidinal as well as narcissistic deployment — i.e., is mobile — is one that can no longer be dispensed with in Freud's theory. As valuable as the more recent studies of narcissism may be for the theory and practice of psychoanalysis, the assumption of an autonomous narcissistic libido independent of object libido cannot be reconciled with the conceptualization described above.

Psychoanalytic Therapy

The psychoanalytic method of therapy described in a series

of papers (1912a, 1912b, 1913e, 1914b, 1915d) is the end result of Freud's prolonged attempts to break through the barrier between the unconscious and conscious and to enter into the realm of the unconscious, and thereby to aid the release of the quantities of excitation dammed up in it. Under the influence of Charcot in Paris, Bernheim and Liébault in Nancy, and Breuer in Vienna, Freud at first made use of hypnosis, i.e., a method that pushes aside the patient's own conscious, defensive and censoring psychic activities, replaces them with the hypnotist's commands, and thereby opens a path to the deeper layers of the psyche. As Breuer and Freud demonstrated in the jointly published *Studies on Hysteria* (1893-95), this method has the advantage of making possible a broadening of consciousness, to an extent previously unimagined, which permits the filling in of gaps in memory and the abreaction of affects adhering to the symptoms; i.e., they can be led to more normal forms of expression.

Although much could be learned from hypnosis about the prestages of symptom formation, its disadvantages were the decisive factor in Freud's abandonment of it. Not only is the number of hypnotizable patients restricted; even in those who could easily be put in hypnosis the therapeutic success of this "cathartic method" lasted no longer than the personal, positive relationship of the patient to the hypnotist. Each separation from him, each emergence of hostile impulses to him, inevitably led to a return of the former symptoms. Apparently, in the psychic household of the patient, the therapy remained a foreign body; it was carried out without his conscious participation; hypnosis could only temporarily inactivate the resistances to it;

clearly, the patient's conscious personality had not accepted the entire procedure.

Based on these experiences, Freud in his next step was primarily concerned with creating a method that did not depend on the authority of the therapist but relied on the cooperation of the patient. The broadening of consciousness, until then a result of hypnosis, was to be accomplished by an act of will on the part of the patient, i.e., by the deliberate elimination of all restrictive considerations which direct ordinary conversation, guard against indiscretions, and protect the speaker from "wandering all over the map." It is precisely this freedom from all restraints which is the essence of "free association." Freud followed his conviction that with the cessation of all censorship, the thought processes could not escape from coming under the domination of unconscious mental activities and from exposing the repressed thoughts, impulses, and emotions. He made use of the psychological fact that the association of thoughts proceeds unhindered only so long as it does not encounter any inner critique and that it will falter or break off when it gets close to the repressed. In this way the resistance which in hypnosis subsequently had destroyed every success achieved by it already becomes apparent during the treatment and thus is accessible to analytic interpretation and resolution.

Freud's new method of free association was in its early phases still tied to certain instructions and starting points. In a fashion similar to C. G. Jung's later association experiments, Freud at first invited the patient to fix his thoughts on the symptom itself and to follow the ideas connected with it; for a while he also used the so-called pressure technique in which the chain of thoughts was started by the physician putting his hand on the patient's head. Only an additional step liberated the working method from these last remnants of hypnosis. In the fully developed psychoanalytic technique of therapy (see 1912a, 1912b, 1913c, 1914b, 1915d), it is left entirely to the patient to start and end where he wants; to let himself go; to tell everything that occurs to him, in whatever form; without regard to whether he supposes it to be important or unimportant; and without concern for the feelings of the analyst or the patient's own feelings of shame and embarrassment. What becomes visible in this way is an unretouched picture of the past and current internal life. The only, but therefore particularly important, restriction imposed upon the patient concerns his motility. He is asked to lie down and associate freely without moving around. Nothing that is brought up, including the revived past, has the freedom to leave the world of thought and reach over to the real world of action.

Freud's technical papers written between 1912 and 1915 contain recommendations and directions concerning the most prominent hazards encountered in every analysis. They are far from offering the student a "general technique of psychoanalysis," which Freud occasionally thought of writing. That his intention was never carried out is not an accident but is due to Freud's growing conviction that the psychoanalytic process is too complex, too different in each individual case, and too variable to be pressed into a definitive systematic presentation.

In accordance with this view, Freud's definition of the psychoanalytic method is deliberately broad: every therapy that is based upon the interpretation of resistances (to the

repressed) and transference (of past emotional relationships to the analyst) deserves, in his opinion, to be called
psychoanalysis. Apart from these two principal factors,
which also remained decisive for his followers, the technique had in the course of time to put up with many
changes in emphasis and innovations which are supported
by new theoretical assumptions, or the widening scope of
the applicability of psychoanalysis, but also by the personal idiosyncrasies of their advocates. Some of these advances are logical extensions of Freud's revolutionary beginnings, e.g., the longer duration of analysis and the
deepening of its content that extends beyond the oedipus
complex to its repressed prehistory, especially the early
mother-infant relationship. Others are due to altered eval-
uations of the psychoanalytic instruments; this is especially
true of the dream, which has ceded to the transference phenomena much of its role as the preferred road to the unconscious. The most significant changes, however, are undoubtedly in the handling of the transference itself. What
in Freud's method appeared as an autonomous revival of
the past and was the spontaneous production of the patient
is today all too often a phenomenon which the analyst has
foisted upon the patient from the very beginning, behind
which the patient's other spontaneous contributions to the
analysis, such as his free associations, his memories, disappear and remain excluded from the interpretive work.
The reconstruction of the past, for Freud a principal part
of the analysis, is thus replaced by the current interplay between analysand and analyst, between transference and
countertransference. Even the real relationship between
analyst and patient, which Freud never denied, was with

the almost exclusive preoccupation with the transference pushed so far into the background that it required special efforts on the part of other analysts to rescue it, almost as a novelty, from oblivion.

In view of this confusing and often confused variety of opinions, it is important not to lose sight of several fundamental thoughts: the rules that Freud established and that many others defended are valid, above all, for the analysis of adult neurotics or neurotic characters. The further the analyst moves away from this legitimate field of psychoanalytic work — whether from the adult to the adolescent or child; or from the neuroses to the borderline states, psychosomatic illnesses, and the psychoses — the greater are the technical changes, and occasionally they go so far that the modification diametrically contradicts Freud's model of therapy.

The Training of the Analyst

For Freud, it was axiomatic that neither the medical degree nor the prior training in psychiatry entitled a person to practice psychoanalysis. Analytic technique, like every other therapeutic measure, must be specially learned as such. The study and teaching of psychoanalysis are, however, in many respects different from the educational process in other medical specialties. The direct demonstration on the patient, so informative for all students, is precluded because the intimate relationship between analyst and analysand does not permit the presence of a third party. Since it can be comprehended neither through verbal descriptions nor through the reading of books, the analytic candidate must take himself as the example and experience in his own case how difficult and also how painful it is to relinquish resistances to the impulses which until then had been kept in the darkness of the unconscious and to look, without illusions in the light of consciousness, at his own person, with all its weaknesses and faults, its sexual desires and aggressive hostilities.

Freud's initial opinion that students, following his own personal example, might succeed in exploring their inner life by interpreting their own dreams was not confirmed in the ensuing years. What persons with extraordinary integrity and relentless love of truth — like Freud himself — might accomplish is too difficult an undertaking for the ordinary person. It requires the help of another who assumes the role of the interpreting analyst while the person to be analyzed himself becomes the patient. The so-called training analysis then proceeds as in the case of every therapeutic analysis: with efforts to facilitate free association and interpretation of the resistances that bring it to a halt, the gradual uncovering of the repressed, and the revival of forgotten childhood experiences through the transference of emotional attitudes to the analyst.

The significance of the training analysis in the traditions of psychoanalysis cannot be valued too highly. In 1922, at the International Psychoanalytic Congress in Berlin, it was declared by unanimous decision to be a prerequisite of all analytic training. In contrast to the time when the first official training institutes were being established, today the training analysis no longer coincides with the entire training. While in the beginning it was left to the individual student to find his way in the then easily surveyed psychoanalytic literature, it is now the task of the institute to develop a curriculum representative of the different theoretical subjects and to illustrate them by selections from the overabundant publications. Only after the study of theory, and only when the training analysis has sufficiently progressed, does work with patients begin; and this work is supervised in the so-called control analyses in which the candidate once a week discusses his first cases with an experienced training analyst.

In the course of time admission to this tripartite training program (training analysis, study of theory, supervised analyses) also has undergone significant changes. As long as the local psychoanalytic groups were small and each individual member had to struggle for his existence, each new arrival was welcomed and everyone who seriously applied for membership was sure of acceptance regardless of his preparatory training. It is relevant to the future development of psychoanalysis that with its growing recognition by the outside world and the increasing membership number of the International Psycho-Analytical Association, this attitude has vanished. In the endeavor to guard against psychoanalysis being practiced by unqualified or emotionally unstable persons, the admission requirements of individual institutes have steadily become more stringent. In the United States this occurs, above all, under the auspices of restricting admission almost exclusively to physicians, in stark contrast to Freud's opinion stated explicitly in "The Question of Lay Analysis" with which we began. Other institutes include preparatory training in academic psychology, as little as the latter has in common with psychoanalysis. This exclusion of educators, clergy-

men, social workers, lawyers, historians, and those interested in literature and art has led to an increasing narrowing of psychoanalytic interest to pathology and a growing alienation from the humanities and social sciences to
which psychoanalysis after all belongs.[2]

In one of the few places where Freud dealt with the topic
of psychoanalytic training (1927b, 1937), he refers to the
high expectations that at times were tied up with the
analyst's own analysis and rejects them as unjustified. The
main object of the training analysis is not to make the analyst into a "perfect" human being but to give him "a firm
conviction of the existence of the unconscious ... a first
sample of [the correct] technique" (1937, p. 248), and to set
in motion a process that guards against his refraining from
making the same demands on himself as he makes on his
patients. Where a training analysis cannot in this way lead
over to self-analysis, it was Freud's advice that every analyst should periodically again accept the analytic help of a
colleague in order to keep in check the complexes stimulated by the constant exposure to the unconscious.

PART II
APPLICATIONS OF PSYCHOANALYSIS

Medically trained analysts who spend their working lives in
treating patients are inclined to overestimate the therapeutic applications of psychoanalysis or even to regard
them as the only important ones. Psychologically trained
persons with little clinical experience, on the other hand,

[2]See the section on Applications of Psychoanalysis to gain an impression of the original variety and breadth of these endeavors.

see in psychoanalysis, above all, a theoretical system the theses of which need merely to be deepened and developed further. What disappears only too easily behind this attitude is the relevance of psychoanalytic findings to areas of applicability to which the traditional psychology of consciousness is not entitled to lay claim.

Those who have studied Freud's works referred to in Part I have familiarized themselves with the knowledge that the division of the psychic apparatus into different agencies and the ego's endeavors to do justice to the demands of the external world are responsible for the existence of inner psychic conflicts and their solution in the form of neurotic symptoms. But these ideas have not yet enabled them to obtain an understanding of the extent to which psychoanalytic insights — and, above all, which of them — have led not only to a new depth psychology but also to revolutionary changes in such nonpsychological sciences as philology and philosophy, biology, the history of religion and civilization, sociology, and education.[3]

Psychoanalysis would not "have 'disturbed the sleep of the world'" — to use one of Hebbel's phrases cited by Freud (1914a, p. 21) — if it had not gone beyond working with neurotic suffering to the general problems of mankind and the development of humanity, which it clearly illuminated and discussed anew. In "The Claims of Psycho-Analysis

[3]In applying psychoanalytic knowledge to legal problems, Freud himself wrote several important comments (e.g., 1906, 1916, 1931b). His suggestions were subsequently taken up by some of his pupils and followers, e.g., Alexander and Staub (1929). A more recent application of psychoanalytic insights to family law (e.g., Goldstein and Katz, 1965; Goldstein et al., 1973, 1979) would undoubtedly have interested Freud and received his recognition.

to Scientific Interest" (1913b), Freud not only presents a brief outline of the fundamental principles of psycho-analysis but also impressively describes the positive relations that can be established between psychoanalysis and different branches of science, while in "The Resistances to Psycho-Analysis" (1925a), he examines the negative reactions that psychoanalytic findings evoked among scientists and the lay public.

It is significant for Freud's attitude to literature that, according to his own words, his case histories "read like short stories" (1893–95, p. 160), that he referred to a contemporary writer as his "double" (1960, p. 339), and that in 1930 he was awarded the Goethe prize. Freud himself explains this affinity by the circumstance that he and the dramatists, poets, and writers work with the same human material, the latter in creative intuition, he himself in the laborious piecing together of clinical details. In his essay on Jensen's *Gradiva* (1907b), Freud shows that the poet, without himself having explored the rules of psychic functioning — indeed, without even knowing them — subjects the actions of the persons created by him to these laws. The same commonality is generally valid for the themes dealt with by psychoanalysis and world literature. What Freud recognized as the central complex of the neuroses, i.e., the jealous triangular relationship of the child to mother and father, appears in Sophocles as the drama of Oedipus, and in Shakespeare as the tragedy of Hamlet (see Freud, 1900, pp. 260–266).

As much as Freud throughout his life was attracted by the mystery of poetic creativity, he was equally convinced that the solution of its riddle lay beyond the limits of what psychoanalytic investigation alone could accomplish. He himself was content with contributing something to the explanation of the motives which are the wellspring of all artistic productivity (1908a). He traced the path which leads from man's dissatisfaction with a disappointing reality to play in the child and to fantasying in the increasingly mature person. The wishes that reality interdicts find their fulfillment in daydreams and in fantasy. Freud calls the realm of fantasy a "reservation," which has been interposed in the painful transition from pleasure to reality principle (1925b, p. 64) and in which the drive derivatives, impulses, and wishes can without interference and punishment attain their ends, though only as long as they do not resort to motility and also maintain affectively determined economic barriers. The energies expended in daydreams and fantasies must not compete with the libidinal and aggressive cathexes which anchor the individual in his relations to reality and to his fellowmen and enable him to fulfill his real tasks in everyday life.

The meaning that fantasy and daydream have for their inventor is not difficult to demonstrate in the analytic investigation of the individual. What they accomplish is purely personal; they are rooted in the individual's own experiences and aim toward making good disappointments in love, gratifying ambitious and grandiose strivings, and so forth. They are not, or only in the rarest cases, designed to be shared with other persons (shared daydreams).

The situation is different in creative writings in which, according to Freud, an as yet not understood transformation takes place; in this, psychic processes occurring in the realm of the individual are lifted to the sphere of the general and made accessible to a large audience. Freud leaves open the question whether the aesthetic depiction or the choice of fundamental themes common to all men is responsible for this.

As in the case of the poets and writers, Freud turns in his interpretive work as though naturally to the greatest among the artists and sculptors. Here again his interest is focused not on the problem of the creative act itself but on the theme that underlies the creation and finds its elaboration in the completed work of art. In Leonardo da Vinci's picture "St. Anne with Two Others," Freud (1910) recognizes the painter's fantasies which revolve around the unconscious and repressed image of his mother who vanished early in his life and which permit insight into an otherwise puzzling and contradictory personality.

Freud's retranslation of the language of the dream in which negation is absent, compromise formations occur frequently, opposites are treated as one, and symbols as remnants of old concept formations play an outstanding role—this accomplishment of Freud's uncovered the existence of a primary psychic function which belongs to the unconscious mental life of man. This unconscious, which in Freud's view constitutes a large part of mental life, is the common factor responsible for the unexpected connections between the immature infant and the mature adult, primitive and civilized men, the mentally healthy and the mentally ill. The study and the recognition of the existence of the unconscious also constitute that aspect of psychoanalytic theory from which the decisive transformations of certain preconceived views in other scientific areas started. In philology it was possible to demonstrate correspondences between these archaic modes of expression of the unconscious, the thought processes and language of seriously disturbed mental patients, and the oldest roots of the historical languages disclosed by philologists. What psychoanalysis has to offer philosophy is a revaluation of the term "unconscious" as it had customarily been used until then by the representatives of different schools of philosophy: "Either their unconscious has been something mythical, something intangible and undemonstrable" or it was something wholly to be excluded from psychic activity for "what is unconscious cannot be mental or a subject of psychology" (1913b, p. 178). Freud was convinced that this attitude was "highly unpractical" (p. 179) and could be corrected only by a thorough knowledge of unconscious phenomena such as was made possible by psychoanalysis.

Even more important than the applications mentioned above are the contributions made by psychoanalysis to the understanding of religion and cultural manifestations. Freud views man's religious desires as anchored in the individual's childhood. During the period of their immaturity children enjoy parental protection, and not every growing individual finds it easy to forego it in adulthood. This attitude is, according to Freud (1923a, p. 37), "the germ from which all religions have evolved." The all-powerful spiritual being to whom the yearning believer submits is, like the superego, ego ideal, and conscience, an heir to the father complex and preserves the character of the father relationship. In this respect as well a correspondence between the religious believer and the neurotic can be shown to exist, as Freud did in his paper on "Obsessive Actions and Religious Practices" (1907a), in which he analytically examines the ceremonies and rituals which both have in common.

For the cultural historian and anthropologist the comparison between the developmental processes in children and the formative processes in the prehistory of peoples is of special interest. In *Totem and Taboo* (1913a), Freud traces the path from psychic ontogenesis to phylogenesis and demonstrates surprising correspondences between infantile elements, on the one hand, and primitive customs, practices, and ways of functioning, on the other hand, and finally between these and the injunctions, prohibitions, inhibitions, and restrictions that occur in the neuroses. The attentive reader will here find a narrowing of the gulf which earlier generations put between the mental life of primitive man and that of civilized man today, between child and adult, between mentally healthy and mentally ill. In Freud's view, every immature child of our culture is a primitive individual; every mentally healthy person can more or less at any time join the ranks of the mentally afflicted if the pressure of internal or external circumstances or conflicts becomes unbearable to him. In *The Future of an Illusion* (1927a) and *Civilization and Its Discontents* (1930), Freud explains the measure of renunciation and drive curtailment and the demands for rationality, insight, and adjustment which every society imposes on the individual as the unavoidable by-products of culture and civilization. He sees hope in what he expects to be mankind's progress from illusion and religiosity to sober recognition of the real conditions and a relationship to reality that is determined exclusively by reason.

In its clinical applications Freud's psychoanalysis never

was anything but an "individual psychology" in the best sense of this term, i.e., insight into the complicated psychic processes of the individual and his relations to the inner and outer world, hence far removed from the present concerns with analyses of groups, family, and society. Only in his role of applying psychoanalytic insights did Freud take the step from the individual to the group and the mass. *Group Psychology and the Analysis of the Ego* (1921) deals with the individual's identification with his fellowmen on the basis of common superego figures and shared ego ideals. This substitution of a personal internal agency by one that belongs to the external world and is shared with others transforms the single individual into a member of a group and subordinates his actions to the requirements of the group without regard to his own predilections, values, and idiosyncrasies. Freud considers group formation to be "an inherited deposit from the phylogenesis of the human libido" (p. 143), its indispensable prerequisite being the differentiation between ego and superego which makes possible the externalization of the superego onto persons or ideals in the environment. Finally, in "Why War?" (1933b), Freud examines, on the basis of his concept of a destructive drive introduced into instinct theory in 1920, the conflicts between already formed societies and their solutions by aggressive actions, which cultural progress has not yet precluded.

In comparison to the phenomena essential to or threatening life such as group formation and war, the brief essays on mythology appear at first glance to be of less interest. But here, too, Freud points from the manifest end product to the important underlying motives. In "The Occurrence in Dreams of Material from Fairy Tales" (1913c), Freud is concerned with uncovering the relationship between personal childhood recollections, neurotic conflicts, and fairy tales that are meaningful to generations of children. Behind the theme of "choosing among three" (1913d), which occurs with equal frequency in literature and mythology, Freud sees a presentation of man's attitudes to the forces of destiny, to death. In "The Acquisition and Control of Fire" (1932), he describes the struggle between instinctual wishes and renunciations which occur in every individual.

In the same manner as Freud's "The Question of Lay Analysis" was chosen as a guiding principle for Part I, Part II is oriented around "An Autobiographical Study" (1925b) and the "Postscript" (1935) to it. After some preliminary discussion of the attitudes to psychoanalysis, Freud gives in these papers an overview of the different nonmedical applications of his theory — from the history of literature and art, psychology of religion and theory of civilization, social psychology and mythology to education — and comments on his own contributions. Thus we start this course of study with Freud's own outline of his contributions to applied psychoanalysis (1925b, 1935). This will be followed by sections on The Attitude to Psychoanalysis (1913b, 1925a), Literature and Art (1900, pp. 260–266; 1907b,[4] 1908a, 1910), Psychology of Religion and

[4]Those who have studied the works referred to in Part I will be especially interested in reading Freud's study, "Delusions and Dreams in Jensen's *Gradiva*" (1907b) because this essay demonstrates with particular clarity how the theoretical elements of Freud's conception of the dream are applied in the concrete analysis of dreams. Moreover, this essay has the advantage of reading like a case presentation. Freud be-

Theory of Civilization (1907a, 1913a, 1927a, 1930), Social Psychology (1921, 1933b), Mythology (1913c, 1913d, 1932).

As was true in Part I, this selection from Freud's writings leaves out some important works in the area of applied psychoanalysis, namely, *The Psychopathology of Everyday Life* (1901b), *Jokes and Their Relation to the Unconscious* (1905c), and *Moses and Monotheism* (1939), all of which can be assigned as supplementary reading.

Education

This leaves one area to which psychoanalysis has been applied, namely, education. Since the world of the child has a privileged position in psychoanalysis, this topic warrants a special introduction. "Children have become the main subject of psycho-analytic research and have thus replaced in importance the neurotics on whom its studies began" (1925d, p. 273). What Freud legitimizes with these remarks has in the past half century grown into a movement which counts a considerable number of analysts as its members and whose practical and scientific findings balance the scale of the technical and theoretical advances in the study of neuroses and psychoses.

The theory and practices of child rearing already were discussed in the early period of psychoanalysis. What the treatment of neurotic symptoms, anxieties, and inhibitions

---

lieved that Jensen's imagination "enabled the author to construct his 'phantasy' in such a way that we have been able to dissect it like a real case history" (p. 91). For those who were unable to study Freud's major case histories, this essay will at least somewhat make up for this omission.

made visible for the first time were forgotten, submerged, repressed childhood experiences such as strict prohibitions of sexual activities (thumb sucking, masturbation, voyeurism and exhibitionism), anxiety-arousing castration threats, unwillingness on the part of the parents to give sexual enlightenment, traumatic repudiations of oedipal wishes. These findings which pointed to educational measures as being responsible for psychopathology and neuroses led, seemingly in a logical fashion, to the demand for a new form of upbringing that deserved to be called "psychoanalytic," i.e., educational practices based on freedom for instinctual drives, avoidance of anxiety, and prevention of neurosis.

It indeed took a thorough investigation of the relationships between education and psychoanalytic efforts — one foreseen by Freud (1925d) — to correct the errors of this initial period and to turn back the exaggerated hopes of analysts, educators, and parents to a reasonable degree.

Therapeutic work with juvenile delinquents made it perfectly clear that the absence of drive curtailment and moral orientation in childhood did not result in psychic health as expected, but rather had delinquency as its consequence (Aichhorn, 1925). Group work with homeless children and adolescents led to the recognition that all educational work, regardless of its direction, has far-reaching limitations (Bernfeld, 1925).

The realization that anxiety could not be banished from the life of children was a result of child analysis, which began to be practiced in the 1920s: *archaic anxiety* such as fear of being alone, fear of the dark and loud noises is a result of the initial immaturity and weakness of the childish ego,

whose protective shield is still undeveloped, and this anxiety can never be entirely eliminated even by the most reliable maternal protection. The absolute necessity of this
maternal or parental protection itself gives rise to a new
anxiety, *fear of object loss,* i.e., of the absence or total disappearance of the parental persons; where *fear of punishment* has been avoided as a result of permissive upbringing, another anxiety, *fear of loss of love,* takes its place;
where the child is assured of the unshakable love of his
parents, he will either become uneducable or produce anxiety wholly as a result of inner reasons, i.e., *conscience
anxiety (guilt),* which is evoked by the tension between instinctual wishes and ego and superego demands. Where
none of the anxieties mentioned so far arises, the ego develops, purely automatically, *fear of the overwhelming
strength of the instincts* which the ego experiences as
threatening its total organization.

The realization that even the best-intentioned *sexual enlightenment* could not inactivate the effect of the infantile
sexual theories came as a further disappointment. The
child might be intellectually capable of bringing some understanding to the sexual activities in the life of adults, but
emotionally he understands them only so far as his own
physical and psychic organization permit it. Before genital
maturity is reached in puberty, it is the pregenital ero-
genous zones (mouth, anus), as child analysis has shown,
and the sadistic-aggressive fantasies of the infantile psychic
life which determine the child's conception of the nature of
adult sexuality and which make the observation of parental
intercourse, the so-called primal scene, a pathogenic event.

Such insights as the one that the development of neurosis was not due solely to mistakes in upbringing but was caused by the difficulties inherent in the process of maturation, the complexities of the psychic apparatus, and the conflicts between instinctual wishes and cultural demands led, in the next period, to a more modest program: there were no longer attempts to "liberate" the child, which were recognized to be impossible under the conditions of civilization and adaptation to a social community; rather, psychoanalytic knowledge was to support the "work of education, whose aim it is to guide and assist children on their forward path and to shield them from going astray" (1925d, p. 273). A reasonable middle course between gratification and frustration, between strictness and indulgence, between abandonment of threats, force, and physical punishment and maintenance of moral guidance and the need to transform instinctual drives appeared to be the best means of realizing this intention.

The desire to know more about the details of early development induced child analysts to perfect their technique and to put it on a par with that used with adult patients — no easy task in view of the immaturity of child patients, their limited insight into the illness and lesser readiness to cooperate, their refusal to associate freely, their instinctive flight from anxiety and pain, their tendency to act out, i.e., automatically to put into action impulses reawakened in the transference. These difficulties notwithstanding, the findings of child analysis were able gradually, step by step, to augment, correct, and confirm the picture of childhood obtained by reconstruction in the analyses of adults. What the child analysts, supported by psychoanalytically oriented

direct observations of infants and young children, brought
to light were such facts as:

- the significance of the first year of life and of the early
  tie to the mother;
- the connection between ego maturation and the emotional object relationships;
- the devastating effect of object loss at the time of the
  biologically determined unity between mother and
  child;
- the vacillations between the symbiotic unity with the
  mother and its relinquishment;
- a chronology of the defense mechanisms in childhood
  development from flight and denial via identification
  and projection to repression, reaction formation, and
  sublimation;
- the prephallic prehistory of the oedipus complex;
- the prestages of the infantile neurosis; and so forth.

On the basis of these findings educational theory developed different prescriptions for the behavior of adults,
geared almost to every developmental phase of the child:

- the right of the infant to reliable maternal help in mastering anxiety and distress;
- the avoidance of separations, e.g., during hospitaliza-
  tions;
- cleanliness training that does not start too early and is
  carried out leniently;
- understanding of and tolerance for the libidinal and
  aggressive drive derivatives during the phallic-oedipal
  stage;

—stimulation and furthering of the ego functions in close connection with the libidinal interests during all developmental phases; and so forth.

What we now expect of the application of psychoanalytic knowledge to education and upbringing is indeed more than prophylaxis of pathological manifestations. Today we see it at work building up a psychoanalytic psychology of normal development, i.e., following the developmental lines which—apart from neurosis, psychosis, and delinquency—lead from emotional immaturity to maturity of feelings, from dependence to independence, from the pleasure principle to the reality principle, from somatic to psychic discharge of excitation, from asociality to adaptation, from play to the capacity to work. In this it is again the task of the child analyst to demonstrate that all these acquisitions are won step by step and that they, like neurotic symptom formation, proceed under a combination of influences, i.e., as compromises between instinctual wishes, ego and superego prescriptions, and real demands of the external world.

In his preface to August Aichhorn's *Wayward Youth,* it is true that Freud emphasizes, "My personal share in this application of psycho-analysis has been very slight" (1925d, p. 273). Yet, these remarks should not deceive the reader or student about the fact that in some short papers (1907c, 1913f), but especially with "Analysis of a Phobia in a Five-Year-Old Boy" (1909a), Freud opened up a first path to the understanding of the child, for analysts as well as educators.

17

Foreword to
"Analysis of a Phobia in a Five-Year-Old Boy"
(1980 [1979])

For the first generation of analysts, Freud's own works were trailblazing and decisive. Future historians of psychoanalysis will not find it difficult to trace the lines connecting his advances in technical, clinical, theoretical, and applied respects with the publications of his collaborators and pupils. The road leading from *Three Essays on the Theory of Sexuality* to the intensive work on homosexuality and the perversions is as clear as the fact that the "Psycho-Analytic Notes on an Autobiographical Account of a Case

First published in German as: Vorwort to Sigmund Freud, *Analyse der Phobie eines fünfjährigen Knaben ("Der kleine Hans")*. Frankfurt am Main: S. Fischer Verlag GmbH, 1980. The English version is published here for the first time.

of Paranoia" opened the way to the exploration of the psychoses, or that "Delusions and Dreams in Jensen's *Gradiva*" and "Leonardo da Vinci and a Memory of His Childhood" led to the appearance of other psychobiographical studies.

Among these direction-giving publications of Freud's, the "Analysis of a Phobia in a Five-Year-Old Boy" (1909a) has a special position. This paper represents more than a specific case history and the illumination of a clinical syndrome which, like "Fragment of an Analysis of a Case of Hysteria" or "Notes upon a Case of Obsessional Neurosis," furthers understanding and suggests the treatment of specific forms of neurosis. What the analysis of Little Hans opened up is a new branch of psychoanalysis, more than the extension of its therapy from the adult to the child — namely, the possibility of a new perspective on the development of the individual and on the successive conflicts and compromises between the demands of the drives, the ego, and the external world which accompany the child's laborious steps from immaturity to maturity.

What Hans documented for his father and for Freud were the by now familiar elements of the phallic-oedipal phase of infantile sexual development: the high valuation of the male genital as a source of pleasure; the love for the differently sexed and the rivalry with the same-sexed parent (who in other respects is also loved); scoptophilic and exhibitionistic pleasures; ruminations about the differences between the sexes, about sexual intercourse between the parents, about pregnancy and birth; jealousy; death wishes; castration anxiety.

We would be greatly underestimating the significance of

this presentation, however, if we saw no more in it than what the analyst at that time hoped to obtain from it—the confirmation of "hypotheses as to . . . infantile sexuality . . . in the components [of which] he believes he has discovered the motive forces of all the neurotic symptoms of later life" (p. 6). At the same time as Freud introduces the reader to the stirrings of infantile sexuality, he demonstrates the painful and anxiety-arousing contradictions in the inner life of the young boy. In spite of his pressing death wishes, Hans is not a "bad," uninhibited, rebellious child who has passed beyond the control of his parents. On the contrary, he is amiable, affectionate, easily moved, compassionate, attached to and dependent upon his parents, and seeks, to the extent that he can, to obey their demands and prohibitions. It is only the clash between these so different sides of Hans's personality that makes Freud's description uniquely important. Here the observer—and the reader—witnesses for the first time, not by way of reconstruction but directly in the child, the struggle to transform the drives and learns about the means at the disposal of the human ego and superego for the socialization of the individual. In the case of Little Hans, it was the task of *repression* to remove the aggressive wishes (stemming from the anal-sadistic phase); it is the task of *reaction formations* to transform jealousy of siblings into love for them, exhibitionism into modesty, pleasure in soiling into disgust. *Displacement* from humans (father, mother) to animals (lions, giraffe, horse) is the order of the day, at the same time as attempts are made to divert threatening instinctual dangers from the parental home to more distant parts of the external world. *Identification with the aggressor* determines the role play in which the child takes on the part of the dangerous, biting, kicking horse. *Projection* externalizes his own bad impulses and makes him experience them as coming from his father. *Denial in fantasy* or *in action* serves to assuage the narcissistic injury sustained by the realization of the better physical equipment of the father and the child's own inferiority in relation to the bigger, stronger, and perhaps omnipotent and omniscient man.

We may ask why such an arsenal of functioning defense mechanisms did not suffice to keep Hans's castration anxiety in check and prevent the retreat from the normal activities of the child. It is Freud's answer that raises the description of this infantile syndrome beyond its relevance to pathology and gives it momentous value. The issue in this paper is not the illness of a child who may be hereditarily tainted, or sexually overstimulated, or abnormally precocious, or otherwise individually predisposed; rather, it is a more or less typical occurrence which demonstrates "the unavoidable difficulties by which the child is confronted when in the course of his cultural training he is called upon to overcome the innate instinctual components of his mind" (p. 143). The generally valid factor is the relative weakness of the childish ego in comparison with the urgency of his instinctual wishes and the unavoidable demands, no matter how attenuated, of the external world that is subject to its own rules. Little Hans sacrifices those instinctual satisfactions which every child is called upon to forego as the price for entering the community of adults. That he, like many other children, cannot accomplish this step without neurotic entanglements and that he requires external help to make him symptom-free again may have to be ascribed, as in the case of many other children, to a quantitative factor — namely, the discrepancy between the strength of his own drives and the strength of his own ego.

However that may be, with the case history of Little Hans psychoanalytic theory took a decisive step in bridging the gap between pathology and normality, between mental illness and mental health; its further evolution then took the direction from a psychopathology to a developmental psychology.

Having followed Freud's road thus far, we must also be prepared to acknowledge that his statements about the insuperability of the technical difficulties in the way of conducting an analysis in early childhood have not proved to be true. Since 1909, a considerable number of analysts have learned to adapt the method of psychoanalysis to the intrinsic nature of the child and to replace the factor of "authority of a father and of a physician [being] united in a single person, and ... both affectionate care and scientific interest [being] combined" in him (p. 5) by their own interest in the developmental processes and their own empathy with the different modes of expression used by the child. Freud remains right in asserting that the technique so laboriously gained in the analyses of adults is not directly applicable to children; that children are unwilling or unable to associate freely; that they neither make nor keep a contract with the analyst to be candid and honest; that they are unreliable collaborators; that they shun insights offered them through interpretations; that they rebel against renunciations; and that they prefer to act out transferences rather than use them to gain understanding of past emotional relationships. That despite these obstacles it was possible to forge an analytic-therapeutic access to the child could not be predicted more than half a century ago.

It was the task of child analysts to replace the unsuitable parts of adult therapy, piece by piece, by appropriate ones and thus to create a new, independent, and independently to be learned treatment method — that is, child analysis. In this context it is worthwhile to emphasize that the father in the case of Little Hans is today replaced by the analyst. It is also important to realize that even today the efforts to perfect child analysis cannot yet be regarded as complete and still are the central interest of many practicing analysts. Each technical advance in child analysis, as in the analysis of adults, brings us closer to the analysand and his conflicts which without assistance are inaccessible to him.

The pioneering work performed by Hans's father and Freud in this area provides evidence, on the one hand, for the difficulties, and, on the other, for the need and fruitfulness of such an undertaking.

Part IV

Applications of Psychoanalysis and Brief Writings

18

On the Interaction Between Pediatrics and Child Psychology

(1975)

Among the innumerable advances made by the medical profession in recent years, the forging of links between pediatrics on the one hand and child psychiatry, child analysis, and child psychology on the other seems to me worth mentioning. There are by now some regular meetings between leading pediatricians and child analysts where problematic cases are discussed and illuminated by relevant

This paper was first published in German as: Die Beziehung zwischen Kinderheilkunde und Kinderpsychologie. *Hexagon* (Roche), 3(7):1–5, 1975; also in *Die Schriften der Anna Freud,* Volume 10. Munich: Kindler Verlag, 1980. Translations of this paper also appeared in the English, French, Finnish, Norwegian, Polish, Portuguese, and Spanish editions of *Hexagon* (Roche), in 1975 and 1976.

The author addressed the same topic on receiving the C. Anderson Aldrich Award (see Anna Freud, 1975a).

contributions from both sides. There are some children's wards where child psychiatrists or analysts are welcome as advisers to the medical and nursing staff. There is at least one prominent university in the United States where the departments of pediatrics and child psychiatry are under the chairmanship of a single head.

These beneficial innovations — however few and far between — seem to be derived from a variety of causes: from new light shed on the effects of specialization in the approach to children; from new knowledge unearthed about the processes at work in the first year of life; from increased understanding of psychosomatic phenomena; and from increases of knowledge in the field of psychoanalytic developmental child psychology.

THE NEED FOR A UNIFIED APPROACH TO CHILDHOOD FUNCTIONING

So far as medicine is concerned, specialization is as inevitable as it is beneficial since the amount of knowledge amassed in each branch precludes expertise in more than one specialty. This is in contrast to the experiences in child psychology or child psychiatry where at all times a unified approach to the child's total functioning is essential and where the existent trend toward specialization already has had some unfortunate effects. Thus, it took the educational world some time to realize that school teachers are bound to fail in their objectives if they concentrate exclusively on their pupils' intellect and fail to understand that a child's capacity to learn also depends on the fulfillment of his physical needs and on the deflection of his curiosity and inquisitiveness from the instinctual to the intellectual sphere. Similarly, child guidance workers, probation officers, and judges in juvenile courts had to learn that a child's or adolescent's moral behavior, i.e., his social adaptation, does not exist in isolation but needs to be seen and assessed in the light of his emotional relationships within the family. Nurses in children's hospitals had to become convinced that their patients' recovery is influenced not only by their physical state but also by their separation distress, by their irrational anxieties, and by their fantasies. In short, as our experience increased, there was accumulated evidence for the close ties between a child's mind and body, his intellect and his emotions, and for the realization that neglect of these interactions had harmful consequences for the child's well-being and developmental progress.

PSYCHOSOMATICS:
THE POWER OF MIND OVER MATTER

What had been learned in this respect from viewing older children's behavior in school, in the hospital, and before the courts was corroborated and extended by the observation of infants in the first year of life. This is a period in human development before any strict division between physical and mental processes has taken place. Every mental excitation of the infant, such as frustration, impatience, rage, or anxiety, is discharged via the body, i.e., finds expression in disturbances of sleep, feeding, or elimination; every physical upset on the other hand leads to changes of mood, diffuse excitation, and anxiety reactions. This mode of functioning persists until, with the beginning of the second year, the development of speech and of other higher functions opens up new pathways for the discharge of mental stimuli which are purely mental. But even then the psychosomatic regime does not vanish without leaving some of its traces. A number of these interactions between mind and body persist in all people. Also, there are individuals who retain throughout childhood and carry into adult life a predilection for the somatic discharge of mental excitation, i.e., who convert especially their aggressive impulses, their irritations, and their disappointments into physical symptomatology.

The medical practitioners of our days have learned to take psychosomatic interaction seriously and to include the mental contributions to physical illness in their diagnostic assessments. Likewise, the pediatricians have ceased to expect that somatic manifestations are due exclusively to somatic causes. It had become evident all too frequently that children's headaches, stomachaches, nausea, digestive and respiratory upsets, eczemas, etc., were their reactions to fears, conflicts, and difficulties in home relationships. The power of mind over matter became too obvious here to be ignored any longer.

THE INFLUENCE OF PHYSICAL PROCESSES ON THE DEVELOPMENT OF THE CHILD'S MIND

Nevertheless, whatever the pediatrician may extract from psychosomatic medicine remains insufficient for his purposes unless he considers simultaneously the reverse side of the process, namely, the impact on mental development of whatever happens in the bodily sphere. There is ample evidence to support the latter, and here child psychologists and child analysts can come to the pediatricians' help by sharing with them the examples which they have collected.

As it happens in the realm of the psychosomatic processes, the significance of the body for the mind makes itself felt from the outset, i.e., from the time when the mental processes unfold first. At this period, the infant's life is restricted to the awareness of pleasurable sensations on the one hand and of unpleasurable, painful ones on the other. Pleasure arises when the infant's needs for food, care, and comfort are ministered to and satisfied. Unpleasure and pain are experienced on the occasions when, more or less inevitably, mothering falls short of fulfilling the infant's demands, and equally inevitably when physical upsets such as colic send out their sensations. So long as the pleasurable moments outweigh the painful ones, or at least hold their own with them, all is well. The infant then begins to relate to the caretaking mother in a positive manner, gradually detaches his feelings from his own self-regarding concerns, and includes in them a figure in the external world. We consider this early move as essential for the development of a human individual's capacity to love his fellow beings.

All is not well if events take the opposite course and when pain and unpleasure outweigh the pleasure moments. This may happen to infants who are badly mothered. It happens only too frequently to those who incur some painful illness during their early life or to infants whose physical equipment necessitates surgical intervention for repair. In the latter instances, it is the infant's own body on which his feelings remain concentrated, and there is little or no reason for him to reach out toward the environment which, according to his limited perception, has failed him in the provision of comfort and the alleviation of pain. There is the danger that the sum of unpleasure arising from the body will seriously delay or block altogether the moves toward mental progress. Perhaps we should not be surprised by this experience. Popular opinion has always maintained that only a healthy baby is a happy, attentive, and responsive one.

There are many areas in a child's life where the interactions between body and mind tend to be ignored, the sphere of feeding being one of them. Mothers, nannies, and doctors regard the child's intake of food only too frequently as a purely physical matter, i.e., from the aspect of weight gain or weight loss. What is ignored by the adoption of this attitude is the infant's own conception of the feeding process, i.e., the initial mouth pleasure connected with sucking; the equation of food with mother (in the second year) which leads to food refusal whenever the child feels hostile; the psychological repercussions of hunger or of the enforced intake of unwanted food. It is only the child analyst who can trace the way in which such early experiences with food become transformed into elements of the psychic personality and may appear in later childhood and adulthood as personal characteristics that usually conceal their origin. Thus, individuals who suffered hunger pains in infancy, for whatever reason, may prove insatiable later, not only for nourishment but for gratification of every kind, ranging from the sexual to the intellectual sphere. Individuals who were force-fed in infancy may become averse to any kind of intake in later years, frequently with very unfortunate consequences for the capacity to learn, i.e., for the intake of intellectual stimuli.

What is now known regarding feeding has been known to psychoanalysts for a much longer time with regard to the psychological consequences of the various ways of handling toilet training. While the adult world concentrates on the child's control of his sphincter muscles, the child himself is concerned with urethral and anal pleasures and their threatened loss. He does not give up easily and, when forced to do so either prematurely or with undue severity, reacts with a characteristic form of obstinacy which may extend far beyond the sphere where it has arisen and dominate his general relations with the world around him. For the pediatrician, moreover, it is important to realize that any interference with a child's anal zone denotes interference with the normal course of sexual development. Enemas administered to relieve constipation increase anal sensitivity and act as a temptation for the child to linger unduly in this phase of sexual experience instead of moving forward to the next stage, namely, phallic sexuality. Surgical repairs in the rectal area, especially with boys, may have dire consequences: they are frequently the cause of later sexual deviation, i.e., of passivity, impotence, and homosexual inclinations.

Beyond these very extreme examples of the impact of physical occurrences on the mind, there are other, less vital ones which, for this very reason, may be more readily accepted by the pediatrician. It is easy to observe, for instance, how badly young children react to being confined to bed. In fact, any restriction of free movement at an early age has repercussions on the child's mental advances. Especially in the second year of life, children never keep still voluntarily, and they become distressed when made to do so. At this time of life, motility is their main pathway for the discharge of libidinal and aggressive energy. When they are deprived of it, mental functioning in specific areas may become affected, especially the acquisition of speech. Young children who are immobilized for whatever reason may talk later than is normally expected.

Another area where physical illness and mental progress are at odds with each other is the child's distribution of feeling between his own body on the one hand and the people around him on the other hand. As described above for the infant, we expect the growing child to turn his emotions increasingly toward the external world, i.e., to advance from self-love to loving others. However, ill children take the opposite course and may even undo their initial advances. Their ailing body clamors for their attention and this reduces the strength of their positive attachments to their objects. We are not surprised to find that ill children are often egocentric, inconsiderate, and withdrawn from contact, even though this is not true for all cases. There are also children who are unable to assist their bodies on their own and who look to the environment for help, comfort, and support. Such children become clinging and dependent to a degree which is far from age-adequate.

Another sphere where illness interferes with developmental progress is that of exhibitionism. We know that young children show off their naked bodies happily and unconcernedly and do not hesitate to urinate or defecate in front of others. We then regard it as an important step forward when feelings of shame and modesty are acquired and when the child begins to hide his private parts and bodily functions from the eyes of adults. However, these expectations are changed when the child is ill. Pediatricians are not pleased when their young patients stubbornly refuse to take off their clothes for a medical examination, just as hospital nurses take it for granted that even older children will accept help when put on the bedpan.

In fact, being ill means that the child has to undo one of his significant developmental advances: after learning to take responsibility for the safety and management of his own body, he has to return once more to the position of the helpless infant whose body is wholly under the control of other people. Young children feel that their bodies do not belong to them but to their mothers. It is the mother's task to look after the child's physical safety, while it is the child's privilege to be carefree and to court all kinds of danger. The child's progress from the latter to the former attitude is by no means fast, and full independence in body management usually is not achieved until late adolescence. At least, this happens while the child is healthy. Prolonged illness interferes with this course of events in one way or another. With diabetic children, for example, many pediatricians welcome their patients' ability to administer their own insulin injections, disregarding the fact that such care for their own bodies is not age-adequate and that children are entitled to be cared for, even if their reason and abilities already point in the other direction. Or, the opposite may happen. The more severe the illness, the less the adults will be inclined to respect whatever advances toward physical independence have already been achieved by the child. His ill body is totally withdrawn from his own control and belongs once more to the adults: to the mother, the nurse, or the pediatrician.

To the rational mind of the pediatrician, it may come as a surprise that the children's reactions do not depend on the severity of the illness or the extent of a surgical procedure. Nor do the children distinguish between the effect of the illness itself and the effect of the medical or nursing measures devised for its cure. Some children dread the mere exposure to a sunlamp as much as they dread an operation, a pain-relieving injection no less than the pain itself. Many children regard a necessary diet or bed rest as punishment, all the more so if in their families deprivation of a favorite dish or confinement to bed is still in use as a disciplinary measure. Operations and amputations confirm the child's worst fears that important parts of the body such as the sex organ can be cut off and be lost. When children are isolated because of an infectious disease, they feel rejected and deserted as if they were moral lepers. They cope better even with severe illness if they can be nursed at home and spared the separation distress aroused by hospitalization. Even the pain caused postoperatively or after burns may prove less devastating to the child's mind than the immobilization of his hands. While this is intended as a beneficial, protective measure, it is understood by the child as an intolerable restriction of freedom and of his personal right to touch his own body for his own purposes whenever and wherever he feels like doing so.

Whatever advances are made in the medical field, illness and pain will remain part of every child's life experience. Even though children's diseases such as measles and German measles, scarlet fever, diphtheria, and whooping cough are significantly reduced in incidence and importance owing to preventive measures, there remain heart and lung defects, asthma, diabetes, cancer, and the results of burns and other accidents. Some people feel that illness is a necessary adjunct to human life since it teaches the individual to bear pain and unpleasure and to use the mental means at the disposal of his mental apparatus to cope with them. It also is true that some children mature surprisingly in a period of illness. Nevertheless, their number is small compared with those who react negatively to the physical experience and suffer setbacks and arrests of their developmental progress.

If pediatricians are ready to believe in the interactions of body and mind described above, they may be ready to take the next step: to learn to distinguish between the consequences for the child of the illness as such and the consequences of the medical and nursing procedures carried out for the sake of therapy. While the former are necessary, the latter are open to scrutiny and to changes aimed at diminishing discomfort and at avoiding its increase. There may be many ways of doing this. Hospitalization will be less dreaded as soon as free visiting for mothers is introduced in all children's wards. Operations will prove less traumatic if they are preceded by careful mental preparations. Confinement to bed and restriction of motility can be dispensed with wherever they are not absolutely essential. Irrational and anxiety-arousing fantasies regarding the physical events can be kept in check by patient unraveling of misconceptions and explanations adapted to the child's level of understanding.

CONCLUSION

There is no doubt in my own mind that we are only beginning to make inroads; that pediatrics and child psychology need to come much nearer to each other before children can profit fully from the insights increasingly being gained in both disciplines.

19

Concerning the
Relationship with Children
(1977)

The further specialization in the work with children proceeds, the more difficult it is for professional workers to establish a personal relationship with the children in their care. Pediatricians and pediatric nurses, teachers, social workers, psychologists, and child therapists are taught from the outset of their training to concentrate their interest on the specific side of the child's person which is in need of their attention. On the other hand, parents frequently complain that their child who, for them, represents something precious and unique, has a very different meaning for the professional people. For them, it may be no more than

First published in *Acta Paedopsychiatrica,* 43:5–6, 1977. German translation: Über die Beziehung zum Kind. In *Kindergesichter,* ed. W. Dreifuss. Basel: Schabe, 1977, p. 125; also in *Die Schriften der Anna Freud,* Volume 10. Munich: Kindler Verlag, 1980.

an intellect which needs stimulating and teaching; a body in need of medical care; a mass of neurotic symptoms and inhibitions, or developmental disorders in need of psychotherapy.

However, the limitations of interest, though regretted by the parents, have their own justification. What is necessary here is to stress the differences between the parents' bond to their own child and the attitude of pediatricians or teachers to patient or pupil. Parents' feelings for their children arise from the depth of their inner lives and are based on procreation and pregnancy, on the emotional dependence of the child, and on the unquestioned proprietary rights of the parents. None of these feelings have any significance for the professional. The children with whom he or she deals are transient, one followed by another too frequently and quickly to give rise to deeper dependency on their side, or deeper bonds from the side of the adult.

Difficult as it is for parents to cope with the loss of a child, for the pediatrician or therapist to part from a patient is not a loss, but rather a sign that the child is no longer in need of help from him, i.e., a sign of professional success. Seen from these aspects, we may well doubt whether perfection in any of the branches of work named above is possible at all without the professional worker losing touch with the essential personality of the child, his good and bad sides, his inclinations, his talents, or his fantasies.

Nevertheless, my own experiences with workers from the various professions named above render me less pessimistic. I believe that it is possible to combine the two aims which, at first glance, seem contradictory. All we have to do is to drop the expectation that professional workers could, and should, love the child in the way his parents do. This cannot be done; it would be as fruitless as it is inappropriate for them to tie their feelings to a particular child. What should happen instead is that every child to be dealt with is regarded by the professionals as an important representative of his own species. There are in our world many phenomena which tax or defy our understanding, the phenomenon of childhood having high priority among them. Each child has a long way to go until the immaturity of the newborn changes into the mature adult state, a path which is full of hindrances and obstacles, advances and regressions, external and internal conflicts, deviations from the norm, etc. Once alerted to these complexities, people cannot help being fascinated by the problems connected with them; by the questions where on this developmental road a particular child has arrived at the time in question; what mental mechanism he has developed for coping with his difficulties; whether body and mind, impulses and emotions, intellect and conscience are in harmony with each other, or whether they clash and endanger the child's present and future mental health.

I cannot help seeing it as our task to arouse this type of interest in all the people who work with children. Not love, for which there is no real basis, but an insatiable curiosity to learn more about the problems of child development seems to me the appropriate bond which ties the professional workers to the child in their care, irrespective of the fact whether work is located in school, in the hospital, in a social agency, or in the child therapist's office.

20

Children Possessed

Anna Freud Looks at a Central Concern of the Children's Bill: The Psychological Needs of Adopted Children

(1975)

It seems to me that the forthcoming Children's Bill can be viewed and reviewed from three different viewpoints: from that of the parents within our community who are anxious to see their parental rights safeguarded against invasion;

First published in *The Times Educational Supplement* (London), March 7, 1975, p. 21. German translation: Kinder als Besitz. *Die Schriften der Anna Freud,* Volume 10. Munich: Kindler Verlag, 1980.

from that of the authorities whose concern it is to diminish the percentage of casualties, misfits, neurotics, and delinquents in the next generation; and from that of the children who, at least in their earlier years, are the most helpless and least vocal members of the population. As co-author of a recent book, *Beyond the Best Interests of the Child* (Goldstein et al., 1973), I address myself predominantly to the third of these aspects.

For the purpose of inquiring into the position of children before the law, I combined forces with two professors from Yale University, one law, one pediatrics and psychiatry. Together, we started out from the idea that there is nothing more vulnerable than the developmental processes of human beings between the date of birth and the attainment of maturity. That, during a prolonged period, the immature body needs constant care, shelter, food, and, in illness, medical attention, is by now an acknowledged fact. That the same is true for the immature mind is still waiting for the same recognition. It takes public opinion longer to agree that, comparable to the physical field, developmental progress will be arrested or distorted unless certain basic developmental needs are respected and fulfilled.

As the prototype of such basic needs we take the child's requirement for emotional and intellectual stimulation, for reciprocity of affectionate relationships, and for the unbroken continuity of his ties with parental figures.

We agree with all other workers in the field that children born into healthy, intact families have the best chances for unfolding their potentialities. Parental concern for the existence of their offspring guarantees the exacting *day-to-day care* needed for survival. *Parental affection* arouses in the child the answering unfolding of positive emotions so that the child *wants* and cherishes the parents to the extent to which he is *wanted* and cherished by them. Parental ambition and pride in the child's progress lead to the indispensable *stimulation* of his faculties. It is true, of course, that no family is perfect and that every lack or weakness in the parents' personalities cannot fail to affect the child's prospects in one or the other direction, i.e., emotional, intellectual, or moral. Nevertheless, so long as the family setting itself is intact, it will at least provide the unbroken continuity of relationships which allows emotional ties to develop into the identifications which give structure and stability to the child's emerging personality. There is no doubt that normal family life is in the best interest of the child's developmental processes.

Children who come before the court after the breakup of their family are thus, by definition, already deprived and at risk, no matter whether neglect, ill-treatment, abandonment, custody, or adoption proceedings have brought them to the attention of the law. With their interests already jeopardized, what is left for the authorities is to search for the least harmful alternative setting to salvage as much as possible from the wreckage of the best developmental prospects. Unfortunately, experience shows that there is no satisfactory substitute. Institutional upbringing in which the authorities used to place their trust half a century ago has been found wanting: while providing for the child's body and, under favorable circumstances even for his intellect, it cannot provide for the one-to-one emotional exchange with an adult guardian which is an essential requirement for character formation. Foster care, which replaced the institutions with high hopes, is found wanting in another direction. The fostering couple who are expected to offer their ward full parental care receive in return only a limited parental ownership of the child, i.e., one to be shared with the responsible agency and the biological parents. This inbuilt contradiction leads, on the one hand, to the repeated breakdowns in fostering which deprive the child of any continuity of surroundings and relationships or, on the other hand, to the unhappy dilemma of concerned foster parents who develop a true parental involvement with the child in a situation where their feelings are not backed by any legitimate claim to his possession.

There is, thus, only one valid substitute for the benefits children receive in their biological families and that is assignment to an adoptive family at the earliest feasible moment. Unfortunately, this is also the point where the interests of children and their parents go farthest apart — in fact, are in direct opposition to each other. In the mind of the biological parent who has either born or begotten the child, his ownership is not in doubt. The offspring remains an unquestioned possession, a being of his or her making, from whom one can separate, whom one can rejoin, whom one can claim for one's own purposes of revenge or bargaining or, in the case of separation enforced by illness, fate, or war conditions, for the fulfillment of benign parental fantasies. In contrast, the young child has no comparable loyalties to the biological parents. While length of separation may matter little to father or mother, the child has a different sense of time, not based on clock or calendar but on the urgency of his wishes, needs, and desires. The earlier the age, the shorter is the period during which a child can live in a no-man's-land of emotional indifference, i.e., the greater will be the haste with which he attaches himself to an adult caretaker who can act as a parental substitute. With the blood tie wholly ignored at this age, he recognizes as his parents the adults who fulfill the parental task in the psychological sense, i.e., who serve his growth by day-to-day interchange of continuous care, affection, and stimulating involvement.

As the law stands today, the rights of such an acquired "psychological" parent fade into nothingness when clashing with the rights of a biological parent who asserts his or her claim to the child, regardless of what anguish is suffered or what harm is done to the particular child's development. Thus, children can be forced away from psychological parents, to whom they are deeply attached and under whose guardianship they prosper, and with continuity broken, be made to adapt to biological parents with whom no ties are in existence. This happened to Maria Colwell, who struggled unsuccessfully against this inhuman process with all the means at a young child's disposal. It is a sobering thought that it was only her body which was finally killed by her newly acquired stepfather. Her spirit was broken earlier when, in a long-drawn-out process of so-called readaptation, she was forced to exchange her psychological parents for totally unwanted strangers.[1]

It is alleged by some people that return to the biological family is truly in the "best interest" of the child, who thereby will be spared an identity crisis in adolescence when all adopted children begin to question who they are and insti-

---

[1] The case of Maria Colwell is discussed in detail in *Before the Best Interests of the Child* (Goldstein et al., 1979).

tute a search for their biological origin. It should not be too difficult to expose this belief as a fallacy. The truth is that in adolescence most children undergo what may be called a crisis of identity when they have the difficult task to grow beyond the parents of their childhood and enter the world as prospective adults. Adopted children merely clothe this conflict in terms fitting their specific fate: when outgrowing their adoptive (psychological) parents, they take the intermediary step of turning to the fantasy image of lost biological parent figures until these have served their purpose of facilitating the step toward adulthood.

In a less dramatic way, young children's interests also clash with those of their parents after a family breaks in two parts after divorce. Where parents agree privately how to divide possession of their children, this remains outside the law, with the children's reaction to divided loyalties, divided lives and influences, harmful partisanship for either father or mother largely unexplored. Where there is legal dispute about custody, with visiting rights for the noncustodial parent enforced by the court, the developmental harm done especially to the very young becomes more obvious. So long as a family is intact, the young child feels that parental authority is lodged in a unified body and, as such, a safe and reliable guide for later identification. The child of divorced parents, even where visiting is amicable, has to deal with two such sources of ideas and ideals, commands and prohibitions, i.e., sources often in contrast with each other. After custody proceedings the children have to deal with three, the court adding its authority to that of father and mother; where visiting is imposed by a judge, against the wishes of the custodial parent, there is no doubt that this undermines the latter's authority. Seen from the vantage point of development, it would not be surprising to see such children grow up without any firm belief in and identification with any kind of adult guidance and authority.

21

Dynamic Psychology and Education

[1976]

I assume that there are few people in this audience who, like me, were privileged to watch and accompany the changes and upheavals in educational work over the last sixty years. It was during this time that the attitude to childhood changed dramatically and, from very orthodox beginnings, arrived gradually at the tenets which dominate this symposium today: at acknowledging the pressures under which every human being labors during the period of his immaturity; at accepting the psychoanalytic view of

This paper was prepared for the symposium on Dynamic Psychology and Education: Contributions from a Modern Psychoanalytic Perspective; American Educational Research Association, San Francisco, April 20, 1976; Harry L. Summerfield, organizer and chairman. It is published here for the first time. German translation: Dynamische Psychologie und Erziehung. *Die Schriften der Anna Freud,* Volume 10. Munich: Kindler Verlag, 1980.

different agencies within the child's personality; at exploring the implications of these insights for the upbringing of children in general, and for the imparting of knowledge to them in particular.

For my own part, I entered the educational world during the First World War, approximately at the time when August Aichhorn first developed, and then published, his new approaches to the work with *Wayward Youth,* and when Siegfried Bernfeld, taught by his experiences in a home for derelict children, first explored the limits of education (1925). I was lucky to share with both pioneers their first attempts to apply psychoanalytic knowledge to these problems. After some early work in a day care center, I qualified for elementary education and taught school for several years until, in due course, and after further qualification as a psychoanalyst, I became a consultant for nursery school teachers in the city of my birth, and also took part in the psychoanalytic training course founded and directed by Willie Hoffer. Graduates from this course are still carrying the message of modern education through many centers of the United States.

The educational doctrines from which we departed at that time were one-sided and narrow ones. If there was a dawning recognition of the complexity of infantile nature, there was still the belief that each area of the child, his body, mind, drives, emotions, conscience, intellect, could be approached by itself, as a separate unit, with neither help nor hindrance forthcoming from the rest of the person. Actually, it needed the experience with undernourished and badly housed war children on the European continent to convince people that a child's mind does not function independently of his body and that insufficient food, insufficient rest, and general lack of physical care play havoc with the wish and ability to learn. For the authorities, this served as an incentive to provide school meals for the poor. For the teachers, the new insight ended their belief that attention to the child's physical state, his infirmities, his hunger, his tiredness, etc., was beneath their dignity. Concern for the body, its health and its exercise, from then onward began to play a part in every school's program.

It took even longer before teachers realized that taking an active interest in their pupils' home surroundings was a legitimate part of their duties; that children were not to be thought of merely as beings by themselves, but to a large extent as products of their family backgrounds; that they should not be dealt with or assessed without knowledge of that background; that social adaptation and law-abidingness are not subjects taught in a curriculum but the outcome of the child's emotional interaction with his parents and identification with their attitudes, beliefs, ideas, and ideals. Hard as the teachers tried to enter their pupils' lives as completely new persons, they had to recognize that the children's reactions to them were due as much to feelings transferred from home as they were responses to their own attitudes and actions. In fact, working with the nursery school teachers of postwar Vienna in the early 1920s, I and my co-workers could demonstrate to them how often their playrooms became stages where sexual and aggressive scenes in the parental bedroom were acted out by the children, and that understanding of this nonverbal communication offered a key to the children's confusions, distresses, anxieties, unruliness, and uncooperativeness, i.e., to behavior problems which remained inexplicable otherwise.

To deal with the child's whole person, not only with his intellect, gradually became an exacting and in many ways surprising task. There was hardly a school subject which we did not learn to harness to one or the other of the children's instinctual or emotional concerns so that it could profit from drive energies transferred to it. Sexual curiosity could be deflected from its aim and sublimated into a general wish for knowledge. Involvement with anatomical explorations led, unexpectedly, to an interest in geography. Fantasies of parental omnipotence translated themselves into active pursuit of facts of natural history, with lions, tigers, elephants, and other impressive big animals serving as symbols for the parents' might. Boyish games of fighting, shooting, and killing promoted interest in the wars of history. When not forced to draw straight lines or copy prescribed patterns, even the less gifted children became capable painters; when allowed to spin out their own imaginings, some turned into reputable authors.

Seen in these terms by us teachers, the whole curriculum became a challenge, an attempt to tap and divert the drive energies underlying the child's private fantasy world, thereby to ban dullness, boredom, and learning by rote from our programs. What we strove to do was to turn what had formerly been chores into exciting adventures for the child.

It is not easy after more than half a century to recapture the mood in which such pioneering work was undertaken. What dominated our actions then was the spirit of discovery, the wish to open up more and more of the potentialities which lie dormant in each child, to free intellectual capacities which had been stifled rather than enhanced by outdated teaching methods. I remember how much we enjoyed our successes in this respect and that we were not overly dismayed by setbacks and disappointments. Most of them were inevitable, after all, since, from the wide range of psychoanalytic principles at our disposal, we had applied to our problems no more than a few: the concept of transference (from parents to teacher); of displacement of energy (from sex and aggression to learning); of sublimation (from prohibited to socially accepted aims). In our eagerness to make school attractive for the children, we had also tried too hard to turn all work into play, neglecting the fact that play, developmentally essential as it is as the precursor of work, is nevertheless governed by the pleasure principle and stops whenever hindrances arise and enjoyment ceases; work, on the other hand, is governed by the reality principle, which means that it also is pursued in the face of difficulties until an intended aim is reached. School cannot do without the latter. Thus, too much effort in this direction was one of the mistakes which had to await correction.

As concerns myself, I have learned in the intervening years to view a child's normal growth toward adulthood not in terms of action by single mechanisms, nor one-sidedly in terms of either successive phases of drive development (oral, anal, phallic), or of growing sophistication in ego functions and defenses, or of increasing independence of superego authority. Instead I see it as a series of steps on a number of developmental lines which, on their part, come about through interaction between three influences represented by endowment, environment, and the internal structure of the child's personality. Examples of them are the line of growth from the infant's complete emotional dependence on the mother to adult object love; the line from the infant's complete egocentricity to the older child's peer relationships; from being physically in other people's care to growing independence in body control and hygiene; from being fed and equating food with love to rational eating; from play to work, etc. Each line reaches from the immature state of the individual infant to the highest level of achievement which the same individual can attain as an older child or adult. Some steps on the lines are made easily, merely being the result of growth, provided that endowment, environment, and inner structure cooperate peacefully with each other. Other advances are hard won and represent compromises between conflicting forces.

Not all the developmental lines mentioned above affect the child's adaptation to or success in school. Some are more relevant than others in this respect.

For example, no young child should be considered ready for entry into nursery school before, on the developmental line toward adult love, the stage is reached where trust can be detached partially from the familiar figures in the home and attached to the unfamiliar, i.e., when the teacher is acceptable to the child as an extension of the parent. Likewise, young children will react with distress to the eating, sleeping, or toilet arrangements in the nursery school until certain stages are reached on the line toward developing independence in body care and control. They will remain isolated in nursery school while their advance on the line toward peer relationships is poor, i.e., while they remain essentially egocentric and treat other children as inanimate objects, or as hindrances, or as rivals for the adult's love. To be popular in the nursery school group, they have to reach at least the stage where other children are welcome as temporary playmates. To be popular in the higher grades, the child needs to advance still further, i.e., attain the level where classmates are regarded as persons in their own right, are loved or hated as such, are admired or competed with. On the all-important line from play to work, what is needed for nursery school is no more than the steps from soft toys and cuddly animals to constructional toys and from motor activity to role and fantasy play, carried out with or without material props. School, as mentioned before, demands more in this respect. No child can be a successful scholar unless he has advanced further on this line, has outgrown the mere search for immediate pleasure, and has attained functioning governed by the reality principle. It is only this step which guarantees uninterrupted application to tasks and the wish for their mastery.

Teachers are only too aware of the fact that not all children respond to their efforts according to expectation. If they can regard a child's failure to do so in terms of insufficient advance on one or the other developmental line, this may lessen the teacher's tendency to criticize and blame and instead increase his or her understanding of the hazards and complexities of growth. Positive developmental progress in any individual case presupposes that the three interacting influences which determine it remain somewhere within the limits of an expectable norm. They do not always do so, by any means; any one or all of them may fail in this respect. Endowment may include handicaps on the physical, sensory, or intellectual side. Environmental influences may be distorted by parental absence, abandonment, death, physical or mental illness, indifference, rejection, cruelty, overprotectiveness, failure to stimulate, etc. The child's own inner structuralization into id, ego, and superego with the appropriate borders between them may be precocious or delayed. Whenever any of this happens, the developmental lines will be thrown into confusion, advance on them will be uneven, and progress toward maturity will be reduced. It will not be the teacher's fault if even the most enlightened teaching methods fail with cases of this kind.

In our analytic work with the infantile neuroses and other psychopathological manifestations of childhood, we had occasion to learn something about the borders between child education and child therapy.[1] Provided that developmental progress is intact to an acceptable degree, educational and teaching efforts are appropriate and effective. If, on the other hand, developmental advance is disrupted severely, therapy needs to come to the rescue and restore a situation where school and teachers have some chances of success.

[1] In this context, see Anna Freud (1975b) and Rose Edgcumbe (1975).

22

The Nursery School
from the Psychoanalytic
Point of View
[1979]

When I speak of a plan for a nursery school based on psychoanalytic insights today, this is not a new task for me but merely continues efforts begun some fifty years ago. At that time Vienna already was far ahead of other European countries in making provisions for the next generation. What I have in mind is not only the School Reform, which goes back to even earlier years and which fundamentally

Presented at a symposium, Der Kindergarten aus der Sicht der Tiefenpsychologie, at the City Hall, Vienna, May 1979. An author's abstract appeared in the *Sigmund Freud House Bulletin,* 3:29–31, 1979. This paper was originally written in German (Der Kindergarten aus der Sicht der Tiefenpsychologie) and is included in *Die Schriften der Anna Freud,* Volume 10. Munich: Kindler Verlag, 1980. The English version is here published for the first time.

changed life in the elementary school. I am thinking, above all, of the provisions for preschool children and the after-school hours of older children. At that time the representatives of these two directions of work were the inspectors Tesarek and Jalkotzsky, two progressive men who were influential in the Department of Youth. They upheld the idea that organizations created for children should not serve external aims, such as aiding working mothers or keeping older children off the streets, but engage in the far more important task of furthering education and development. One of them made a statement that is characteristic of this attitude and which I have always remembered: that schools have no concerns about their existence, which is guaranteed by compulsory education, no matter what the schools are like; but that nursery schools and day care centers, being voluntary institutions, must by their quality convince parents that it is worthwhile to attend them; that, on the other hand, quality of this kind can be achieved only on the basis of extensive and intensive knowledge of childhood development and children's needs.

At that time psychoanalysis was not very popular in Vienna. I was therefore greatly surprised and pleased by the willingness of these two inspectors to obtain the necessary information from me and my colleagues. On my part I did not hesitate to cooperate with the Department of Youth; the results were the four lectures for teachers and a continuous seminar for nursery school teachers which provided the occasion to discuss difficult cases and to work on developmental difficulties. Participants in this seminar could then get further education by enrolling in a course on psychoanalytic education which Willie Hoffer conducted.

This kind of work, as I said, goes back half a century. When I speak about the same topic today, in the same place and in the same city, I can add knowledge gained in the meantime.

I had the opportunity to continue my previous work with children and the application of psychoanalytic findings to such work in England. During the five war years I directed a home for eighty children, ten days to five years old, who had lost their homes due to bombings. In the course of this work my collaborators and I were able to learn much. While earlier in Vienna I had directed the teachers' attention, above all, to the instinctual development of young children and its consequences for their personality as a whole, I can now add material pertaining to the individual development of different ego functions and thus to the more general topic of the young child becoming a mature human being.

Before discussing this topic as it relates specifically to the nursery school, I first make a detour via the elementary school.

I have always found it very interesting that teachers of the first grades of elementary school, in whatever country, want their pupils to enter school with as little preparation as possible. When mothers are concerned that their children will not be able to hold their own in school unless the children have carefully been taught in advance, the teachers reassure the mothers that they have no expectations whatsoever of the new entrants and that the teachers regard it as their prerogative to introduce the children to school life. I believe that in saying this, the teachers forget that this attitude applies only to the learning of reading, writing, and arithmetic; and that beyond that, with regard to the child's personality itself, they have very high expectations.

For example, they take it for granted that a six-year-old child will without difficulties leave the parental home for a period of time; will be willing, at least temporarily, to put the authority of the teacher in the place of parental authority; and also understand that the school day is not endless and that he will return home. Teachers are not surprised when a child indicates that he has some concept of punctuality and, for example, urges an unpunctual mother not to make him "too late" for school. They expect that the child will without further ado accept his status of being one among many, without special privileges in relation to his classmates; that he has fully acquired clean habits, will not wet or dirty himself, and will take care of his physical needs without assistance and without being reminded. They expect that the child will be able to express his wishes, concerns, and fears in words, and not by crying and screaming, as he did in former times; that he is able to sit still for the period of instruction and take pleasure in freely moving about when this is permitted; that he will respect the possessions of other children; that he will protect his own body and his own exercise and school books from his own destructive inclinations; that he will turn his curiosity away from all bodily processes and direct it to the prescribed goal of learning; and that from beginning to end he will carry out the tasks assigned to him, regardless of whether other activities appear more desirable to him at the moment.

We need only translate these expectations of the teacher

into the language of the psychoanalyst to recognize that these apparently natural achievements are in reality the end products of significant developmental lines. These achievements take on a different meaning when viewed from this vantage point.

The child who, for example, can separate from his mother and spend part of the day in school has achieved a certain degree of *emotional self-reliance*. He has taken a step away from the original biological unity with his mother, i.e., from the state in which he experiences panic when he does not see the mother's familiar face and therefore does not know how his next need will be fulfilled.

In order to be one among many, the child must have begun to take a step on the difficult road from *egocentricity to objectivity*. For the young child, rain, for example, which spoils a planned trip, may mean a punishment for having been "bad"; and sunshine, a reward for "good" behavior. It takes several years before he realizes that he is not the center of the world and that natural events such as the weather apply equally to all people.

As far as the child's *attitude to the body* is concerned, there is a lot more to be learned here than the control of the elimination of body products. His motility, previously solely in the service of physical needs and instinctual wishes, must become goal-directed and serve learning, play, and other functions. The protection of the body should no longer be wholly in the hands of the adults. The child should have learned not to endanger himself unnecessarily, not to eat inedible matter, not to touch electric outlets, not to bend too far out of windows, not to jump down more steps than he can manage.

Similar considerations apply to the *control of drives,* the transformation of which should by that time have begun. When a child is tired, fretful, or bored in school, we do not expect him to start to suck his thumb or play with his genitals or take out his sandwich and begin to eat it. Nor do we expect children to exhibit themselves and to inspect each other on the toilet.

Before a child has achieved full *verbal capacity,* he must be able to think; i.e., the discharge of all stimuli impinging upon him must no longer occur exclusively within the body but proceed via the mind.

That a long stretch on the road from *play to work* must have been traversed before one can be a good school child is of course obvious.

You see that we are justified in warning the teachers not to underestimate what is expected of a child. Far from being slight, these expectations are in fact tremendous. And the teachers would be justified in objecting that basically they have no possibility of properly aiding the child in these developmental steps. All this must be accomplished before entry into school. Yet, it is apparently a task that also exceeds the capabilities of many families. Here the nursery school can intervene and help in leading the child part of the way on this difficult road.

Having completed my long detour and having once again arrived at the task of the nursery school, I want to emphasize, above all, the following: what the child has to acquire between his first and sixth year of life is more than he ever will in his subsequent life; never again will similarly great demands be made. We have reason to be astonished that this very important fact has for so long remained unrecognized, to the detriment of children. It was the prevalent misunderstanding that the acquisitions described above were the result of maturation; that the child need only become bigger, stronger, and more intelligent to be capable of all these accomplishments I have demonstrated to you. I believe, however, that there is no greater misunderstanding than this. Developmental achievements of this kind are won only in hard battles which are fought among a series of influences. We know today that the human personality is composed of several agencies — of the instinctual drives, on the one hand; the reasonable ego, on the other; and the awakening morality and conscience in the third place; all three constantly interacting with the power of the parents in the external world.

It would not be so difficult for the child if each of these agencies did not have its own goal and if these goals were not so different from each other. The drives strive only for fulfillment and satisfaction. The ego strives for moderation, adaptation, and avoidance of unpleasure. The parents demand compliance with their wishes and the conditions of the external world. Normal development presupposes that these divergent aims are somehow reconciled and unified — a difficult task to which not every child is equal. The child needs active help to make the forward steps and gradually advance toward the final desired goals. This is the point at which the nursery school can supplement the parents' efforts. But such support and assistance can be effective only when there is full understanding of the conflict situation in which the child finds himself. Those who are still inclined to believe in the myth of untroubled happy childhood will not be in a position to promote the solution of conflicts.

I return from these general considerations to more specific descriptions to bring out more clearly the stations on individual lines of development.

THE SENSE OF TIME

How does the child acquire, for example, the sense of time, which we expect as a matter of course to be fully formed in the normal adult? We find a first station on the way toward it in the infant or young child, i.e., before entry into nursery school. What strikes the observer most at this time of life is the impatience that dominates the entire existence of the child. Every need that arises, every wish that is felt, every drive urge must instantly be fulfilled. For the feelings of the child, it cannot be done fast enough. Waiting is intolerable and with each delay in obtaining satisfaction, the child becomes angry, tearful, begins to cry and kick. If an infant is left waiting too long for food, his hunger will not increase; on the contrary, his appetite will disappear and be replaced by dislike of food and unwillingness to eat. It is advisable, certainly in infant nurseries but even in the first months of nursery school, to put the food on the table before the children are asked to sit down and not the other way round — to let the children who are already sitting at the table wait for the food. In theoretical terms, this means that the young child measures time on the basis of the urgency of his needs. He experiences as short what satisfies forthwith; as long, what increases the instinctual needs until they become unbearable. Remnants of such attitudes, surprisingly, are still retained in adult life; even then time seems to stretch when we are waiting or are in pain, and it passes unduly rapidly when we experience joyful events.

The child reaches a second station on the way toward developing a sense of time with the help of the daily routine in a well-run household or nursery school. Long before children understand the clock, they know that morning is the time when they go to nursery school; noon, when they are called to have their meal; afternoon, when they are fetched from school; Sunday, when the nursery school is closed. The more regular the routine, the more strongly it supports the understanding of time.

A third step then leads from the routines to the intellectual understanding of the passing of time and, in this respect, to being grown up. Translating into theoretical terms, we say: the developmental line of the sense of time proceeds from being dominated by instinctual needs to the domination by the reasonable ego; i.e., time is measured by clock and calendar.

FROM EGOISM TO COMPANIONSHIP

Another, even more important developmental line, which can easily be followed in the nursery school, is that from egoism to comradeship. At the beginning the other children in the group are for the newcomer at best rivals and at worst not much more than things that are pushed aside when they are in the way.

It takes some time before they become playmates, though in the beginning there may be no more than silent parallel play. One child, for example, may eagerly empty a cupboard, while a second one puts the objects back in without disturbing the first child.

Only on a third level will the side-by-side play be turned into playing together, i.e., working together toward a common desired goal. But this cooperation again falls apart at the end of the play.

Only after a fourth step does the playmate become a comrade, another human being who is accorded to have the same feelings and wishes; who has possessions of his own; someone whom one knows, with whom one agrees or disagrees, whom one loves or hates, admires or envies, imitates and respects. Only then has the child attained the final aim — the capacity for friendship with equals. In the life of the child this is an important step which restricts his egocentricity and expands his understanding of the world around him. When a family is too small to afford the only child the opportunity for this developmental step, the role of the nursery school is in many cases a decisive one in promoting this progress.

FROM UNRESTRICTED INSTINCTUALITY
TO SUBLIMATION OF INSTINCTS

Among the first and most thoroughly studied findings of psychoanalysis is the description of the road from the unrestricted freedom of instincts in the infant to the transformation of instinctual drives and feelings of which the older child is capable. Much of this occurs in the parental home and proceeds under the influence of the parents' guidance, but some of these developments are especially apt to be promoted by the nursery school. The child's curiosity which initially is directed exclusively to the body should be transformed into a quest for knowledge and pleasure in discovery. When the nursery school teacher succeeds in enlisting this sexual curiosity, the latter turns into desire for knowledge and pleasure in learning; when she fails to mobilize it, the child very easily remains bored and uninterested.

With regard to aggression, we know that it reigns freely in the infant. Yet, with the internal imitation of sensible external admonishments, aggression is transformed into effective and useful energies by the ego's mechanisms of defense. The child's natural inclination to cruelty to other children (and animals as well) easily changes in the community of the nursery school and under the influence of the nursery school teacher into readiness to help other children.

FROM PLAY TO WORK

Apart from mothers who witness the first phase of the infant's play (on his own body, on the body of the mother, with cuddly toys which symbolize partly the child's own body and partly that of the mother), nobody is in a better position to observe the development of the child's play than the nursery school teachers. The child's play activities proceed from motor play with sand and water, to building, construction, and mechanics, to role and fantasy play. Nursery school teachers may have a very good idea what each newly emerging play interest means for the child; what constitutes the expression of instinctual concerns, such as the filling and emptying of vessels; what serves reasoning; what manly ambition, imitation of motherliness, or the wish to be grown up in general. On the other hand, nursery school teachers may not sufficiently appreciate the tremendous significance of the development from play to work. In the final analysis, it is this progressive step which makes the nursery school child capable of functioning in school.

Play lasts only as long as it affords pleasure; work must continue until the predetermined goal is reached. Translated into psychoanalytic language, this means that the pleasure principle must be superseded by the reality principle before individuals are able to work, i.e., can temporarily manage without gaining pleasure: the lack of pleasure must be compensated for by the gain or success of the work performed.

We can best understand the significance of pleasurable play when we consider that the normal adult also cannot entirely do without it: in later life, sports, hobbies, and, above all, fantasy activity create a kind of protected area that is reserved for pleasure gain as a counterweight to the reality-oriented discipline of work.

THE TOTAL PERSONALITY OF THE CHILD

The examples presented, only a few among many, are meant to emphasize how important it is for the nursery school teacher not to view her pupils one-sidedly. The child is more than the sum of his capabilities, i.e., his sensory development; more than his reason, i.e., his intellectual development; more than his behavior such as his ability to wait, or not to demand precedence but accept equal status; more than his beginning understanding of the difference between good and bad, i.e., more than his emerging conscience. Only the totality of the inner agencies comprises the child's personality; and it is only this totality that makes it comprehensible why the individual child complies with or defies the educational efforts of the adults and the extent to which he does so.

DIFFERENCES BETWEEN NURSERY SCHOOL AND SCHOOL

Schools have a prescribed curriculum, though such plans have lost much of their rigorous strictness since the school reform. School children, at least as far as their purely intellectual development is concerned, are predictable and capable of mastering a specific pensum at specific age levels. The majority of children in a class reach the planned goal, even though a few who are less well endowed intellectually may be left behind.

Conditions are different in the nursery school where long ago we discarded the practice of giving all the children in the group the same occupation, teaching them the same song, letting them repeat the same rhyme, or handing out the same folding papers. With regard to the developmental lines sketched above, each child has reached a different step on the ladder and seeks different activities. Developmental lines have no date that can with any degree of certainty be predicted. They follow the interplay between the above-mentioned three influences: the hereditary constitution, the internal agencies (drives, ego, and superego), and parental demands. Accordingly, the child may have reached a very high level on one developmental line (such as intelligence) and only a very low one on another line or on several of them (such as friendship, cleanliness, drive curtailment). Many very well-developed children, for example, learn only late in life to protect their bodies from dangers and harm or to obey the rules of hygiene.

NORMAL AND ABNORMAL DEVELOPMENT

What we call the normality of the child is dependent upon the discrepancies between the various developmental lines not being too great. On the other hand, these remain within the desirable limits when two conditions are fulfilled:

Constitution, personality structures, and family background should qualitatively not stray too far from our average expectations. Each one of these influences can, if it deviates too far from the norm, delay or distort development and, in the worst case, bring it to a complete halt.

The rate and timing of the growth of the drives, the ego, and the moral part of the personality must be in harmony with each other, on the one hand, and in harmony with the timing of demands made by the external world, on the other. When the reasonable ego develops too quickly, it prematurely comes into conflict with the drives. When drive development outstrips ego development, a tendency to delinquency arises. When parents demand of the two-year-old what only the five-year-old can accomplish, the child will be in unavoidable difficulties. In contrast, when a five-year-old is given leave to do what should only be permitted to the two-year-old, social adaptation will fail.

The correspondence in the timing of the maturation of

the inner agencies, on the one hand, and of the achievements and demands of the inner and outer world, on the other, can hardly be overestimated in its decisive influence.

REGRESSION IN DEVELOPMENT

Another important difference between the school-aged child and the nursery school-aged child is the degree to which their acquisitions are stable.

We do not expect children who already have learned to read or count to 100 suddenly to revert to the early stages of their developing faculties. But we must be prepared for a nursery school child who is tired, ill, anxious, or otherwise troubled to be thrown back to the early stages of his development. In such circumstances states that had long been left behind may again make their appearance. The child who has already learned to express his thoughts verbally will suddenly cry and scream again; the child who already has mastered cleanliness habits will soil; the child who could wait and share with others will suddenly and stubbornly insist on his rights. We have no reason to be alarmed by regressive movements of this kind. The nursery school child is entitled to such interruptions of forward movement — it is in fact their very occurrence which insures progressive development. The child is endangered only when such regression ceases to be temporary and becomes permanent. This also marks the border between the children who can be helped by educational means and those who require psychological therapy.

CONCLUSION

You may have gained the impression that the application

of psychoanalytic knowledge to nursery school work makes education not easier but rather more difficult. The more one knows, the more there is to observe, to consider, and to do. On the other hand, the chances of the work being successful and gratifying are also enhanced.

I have the feeling that for many decades the nursery school as an institution has led a rather uncertain life. It has been influenced, on the one hand, by the crèche, whose task it is to satisfy the baby's physical needs, and, on the other hand, by the school, which must further the child's intellectual development. If the nursery school and the work of the nursery school teacher move between these two extremes, at times more toward one and on different occasions more toward the other, I believe the time has come for the nursery school to define its own tasks and to adhere to them. Work in the nursery school is work for the child who is at the age when he makes the greatest demands on adult help. The demands on the teacher are therefore great. But of all educational work, this is the most interesting one.

23

Address on the Occasion of the Unveiling of the Freud Statue

(1978 [1977])

I greet all those assembled here and express my special thanks to the official representatives who by their presence honor the unveiling of the statue.

My own address is not a simple matter because I am here in a triple role: as the representative of my father and my family; as the representative of the European Federation of Psychoanalysis; and as myself. In each of these respects something different is to be said.

First, for my father: I think that every young author

Presented in Vienna on May 6, 1977. First published in German: Ansprache zur Denkmalsenthüllung am 6. Mai 1977. *Jahrbuch der Psychoanalyse,* 11:8-9. Bern: Verlag Hans Huber, 1978; also in *Die Schriften der Anna Freud,* Volume 10. Munich: Kindler Verlag, 1980. The English translation is published here for the first time.

who commits his thoughts to paper, whether these serve literature or science, has the wishful expectation that the product of his endeavors will be recognized as important and that not only his contemporaries but also the following generations will be counted among his readers. We also know that many of these men never see the realization of their ambition and that the place where they worked receives no notice. That today my father's jocular youthful dream is being transformed into reality is therefore an exception, and we may ask how he himself would have reacted to the realization of his fantasy.

His attitude throughout his life provides an answer to this question. Whatever he encountered in the course of his working life as rejection, as critique, or as honors conferred by the outside world, he related these not to his own person but to his work. Thus he would say even today: the unveiling of this statue in the presence of so many interesting and interested people is not really meant for him; it is meant for the discipline of psychoanalysis that he created and it can be regarded as a sign of the increasing trust in its validity.

The European Federation of Psychoanalysis in its turn welcomes this festive occasion as a step of recognition for its work in Europe and, above all, in Vienna. Perhaps one may venture to express the hope that Vienna is once again on the road to becoming a scientific center of psychoanalytic work, as it had been in former times.

And finally, my own person and my old connection with the locale where the statue has been placed. In past times I have been here twice: the first time in the year 1895, four months before my birth; the second time, at the age of four years, on the date of the letter to which the memorial inscription refers.[1] Regretfully I cannot say that my memory has retained anything of the significant events of that time. Nevertheless, I am gratified by the thought that they are not alien to me; and that, even though as an unknowing eyewitness, I already was a participant then. This may be the reason why today I also could not stay away on this festive day.

[1]On May 12, 1900, Freud wrote to Wilhelm Fliess: "Do you suppose that one day one will read on a marble tablet on this house:

Here, on July 25, 1895,
the secret of the dream
revealed itself to Dr. Sigm. Freud."

24

Inaugural Lecture for the Sigmund Freud Chair at the Hebrew University, Jerusalem

(1978 [1977])

When I received President Harman's invitation to provide an Inaugural Lecture for the Sigmund Freud Chair at the Hebrew University, I felt surprised and deeply honored. I also felt overawed when finding myself faced with the responsibility of putting the final seal on the realization of a venture which, up to now, has existed merely as a wish-fantasy in the minds of some psychoanalysts.

Presented at the 30th International Psycho-Analytical Congress, Jerusalem, August 1977. The paper was read for Anna Freud by Arthur F. Valenstein. First published in the *International Journal of Psycho-Analysis,* 59:145–148, 1978. German translation: Antrittsvorlesung für den Sigmund Freud-Lehrstuhl der Hebräischen Universität, Jerusalem. *Die Schriften der Anna Freud,* Volume 10. Munich: Kindler Verlag, 1980.

Obviously, this particular inaugural lecture bears little resemblance to the usual one. Traditionally, the newly elected chairman of an old-established branch of science uses this occasion to present himself and his plans to his colleagues. But here, the author of the lecture and the elected man are not identical; the latter's name (at least at the time when this was written), is still unknown; so are his plans. And what requires introduction is therefore not the new incumbent but, surprisingly enough, the discipline itself.

PSYCHOANALYSIS INTRODUCED

In our time, of course, psychoanalysis is no longer the unknown quantity which it was eighty years ago, when its theory of the unconscious mind met with disbelief and its emphasis on the role of the sexual drive aroused moral indignation. By now, a degree of familiarity with its tenets has seeped through, even to the general public. Not that this simplifies a formal presentation. There are too many aspects to consider, all of them important. It leaves the presenter with a threefold task: to enumerate what is basic in psychoanalysis, by-passing for the present purpose the many developments, innovations, departures, and distortions built on the essential; to select what may appeal to the academic community which psychoanalysis now proceeds to enter; and, incidentally, to substantiate the claim that psychoanalytic work fares best in the freedom which it has arrogated to itself from the beginning, and some of which it wishes to retain even within a university curriculum.

THREE ASPECTS OF PSYCHOANALYSIS

1. The aspect of psychoanalysis most familiar to the world at large, and probably of least concern to the university, is the clinical one. To the public it is known as a method of treatment, originally devised for the neurotic disorders of adults and, since then, widened in its scope to include other ages and, one hopes, also the more severe aberrations such as the perversions, the delinquencies, the borderline cases, some of the psychoses. In its dealing with patients it is recognized as being different from earlier methods, such as hypnosis and suggestion, by being non-authoritarian, i.e., based not on persuasion or coercion but on cooperation with the patients. It is this latter circumstance which limits its application to those individuals who possess at least a kernel of healthy rationality and who, from this vantage point, can ally themselves with the analyst's therapeutic efforts.

The treatment method itself is known to be a complex one. The patient's compulsive need to reactivate and relive the remote and forgotten past as well as his strenuous resistances to the therapeutic process are regarded not as threats and hindrances which have to be overruled, but as valuable psychic material which, when worked with, can supply keys to understanding, i.e., as indispensable weapons in the battle for recovery. The repressed items of psychic experience, when presented to the patient, are integrated by him with the remainder of his self-knowledge and serve to widen the area in his mind where reason dominates over fantasy and unreason, to reduce anxiety, to resolve formerly insoluble internal conflicts, and thereby to lessen the need for symptom formation.

There exist, as is well known, two divergent appraisals of the method's efficiency. By some, it is acknowledged that no other mental treatment achieves, or even attempts to achieve, a similarly radical therapy, namely, one aimed not at removal of the symptoms but at removal of the need for their formation. Others blame psychoanalysis for being laborious and cumbersome as a method, restricted to the few, expensive where it is not provided by a public service, with its results by no means guaranteed. As for the psychoanalysts themselves, they are only too ready to concede that there is, certainly, nothing magical or miraculous about an analytic cure. ("For a miracle," my father used to say, "it is much too slow.")

However that may be, my main contention concerning the relations between psychoanalysis and the university are the following: if psychoanalysis were no more than a treatment for mental disorders, whether simple or complex, effective or ineffective, slow or fast, it would not qualify for a Chair of its own. The appropriate allocation of it would be to the medical faculty where, in the department of psychiatry, it would have to take its place among the dynamic psychotherapies developed alongside or derived from it, such as group therapy, family therapy, community therapy, down to the abreaction of tension via the primal scream. Its demand for status among the recognized sciences would be totally invalid.

2. This situation alters somewhat when we turn from the clinical to the theoretical aspect of psychoanalysis. What concerns the scientist here are the efforts, pursued from the beginning, to arrive at increasingly satisfying de-

scriptions of mental functioning. These are commonly described as a series composed of three steps. First, the move away from a psychology based on brain anatomy to one based exclusively on mental data, with the biological drives and the energies emanating from them remaining as the only physiological substratum. Next, a topographical division of the mind into systems, characterized qualitatively by their distance from, or nearness to, conscious awareness, i.e., the systems of the unconscious, the preconscious, and consciousness. And, finally, the conception of a mental apparatus constructed of agencies (personified as id, ego, and superego) which are differentiated from each other by their origin, their contents, their modes of functioning, and their aims. It was this last-mentioned, structural model of the mind which earned for psychoanalytic psychology the title of metapsychology, since it made it possible to regard every psychic process from a variety of angles: genetically, according to its antecedents; dynamically, according to the forces struggling with each other; economically, according to the quantities of energy involved; adaptively, according to the degree of harmony achieved with the external and within the internal world.

Nevertheless, however impressive this elaborate structure may be thought to be, and however different from the traditional, even these characteristics by themselves would not yet warrant the separate recognition which psychoanalysis is accorded here today. From the point of view of departmental disposition, psychoanalytic metapsychology could also be made out to belong in the same faculty as other psychological theories.

3. In fact, it is a third aspect of psychoanalysis which

has prompted my colleagues to wish for, and to subscribe to, a Chair for its representation. This aspect is the existing, exceptionally close connection and interrelationship between the two areas described before, i.e., between its practice and its theory. Unusually enough, both are served by the same working method. To bring unconscious processes to conscious awareness is the established therapeutic tool. It also is, simultaneously, the essential tool for scientific exploration. Thus, whatever psychic content is unearthed from the mind of an individual patient becomes a legitimate item for incorporation into the theory. And, vice versa, every item of the theory becomes in this manner a tool for understanding the problems of life.

To remind ourselves of some of the practical conclusions drawn from one or the other piece of psychoanalytic insight:

— that the major part of mental activity proceeds without conscious awareness has explained much about the day-to-day irrational behavior of human beings; about their insufficient self-knowledge; their limited control of their actions; their frequently being oblivious of their own motivations;

— that, in the earliest years, there is unity between mind and body, with mental excitation discharged via physical pathways, has thrown light on the later psychosomatic manifestations as well as on the so-called somatic compliance in hysterical illness;

— that the different constituents of the mental apparatus pursue aims as different from each other as drive satisfaction, regard for reality and moral concerns, has accounted for the inevitable presence of conflict in human life;

— that the mental mechanisms serving conflict solution are responsible for normal development as well as for pathology has narrowed the gap previously thought to exist between mental health and mental illness;

— that the common amnesia for early childhood covers decisively important events has accounted for the power of past over present in individual life;

— that the young child passes through a period of long-drawn-out complete dependency accounts for children being educable, i.e., for their compliance with parental demands for impulse control, which is a precondition for social adaptation;

— that this dependency on parental protection is not easily outgrown explains the religious needs of many individuals, i.e., a lifelong longing for the existence of an all-powerful, benevolent, protective, if super-human, being;

— that the frustrations of infantile sexuality within the family constellation are painful, upsetting, and inevitable accounts for many of the adult's failures in love relationships and sexual performance.

What these instances (as well as many others not listed here) serve to illustrate are two main points. One, that far from being a barren, esoteric theory, psychoanalysis is intimately concerned with the manifestations of life itself. Second, that it is this very concern with the major human problems which establishes the usefulness of psychoanalysis for other disciplines. What is referred to here is not only its obvious application to general medicine, psychiatry, and pediatrics, but its equivalent relevance for the humanities. Its studies of unconscious motivation, of impulse control, of displacement and transformation of drive energy, of sublimation establish links with pedagogics, sociology, anthropology, biography, culture, religion, art, literature, and others.

Whatever further tasks the future Professor of Psychoanalysis may have in mind, I believe he will find that the Sigmund Freud Chair offers a unique opportunity to forge and develop these links within the university setting.

OUTLOOK

Whoever is concerned with the past of psychoanalytic work cannot help speculating about its future as well. Knowing full well how unreliable all prediction is, I personally imagine that the future advances will proceed in two main directions: one more decisively toward the abnormal, the other toward a normal psychology.

There are, by now, many signs that one section of the international membership is determined to go far beyond the original area of psychoanalytic preoccupation, namely, beyond the disorders caused by inhibitions, symptoms, and anxieties, and to explore the failures, arrests, regressions, and defects of functioning, up to the complete break with reality and the complete dismantling of the mental apparatus. What these pursuits are expected to provide is new knowledge about the mental casualties which, so far, have defied explanation. What is tested by them at the same time are the limits beyond which the interaction between theoretical knowledge and therapeutic efficiency ceases to function. However strenuous the efforts of the analyst, not every bit of added insight into the psychotic breakdowns turns in his hands into a therapeutic weapon to combat the psychotic illnesses.

Another ongoing advance points in the opposite direction. Psychoanalytic treatment of the immature has revealed the hazards which threaten mental health on the one hand from the direction of the environment via the early deprivations, frustrations, object losses, traumatic occurrences, and on the other hand from inside the mental apparatus due to its complex structure which, by itself, represents the source of never-ending conflicts. However, the practicing analyst's experience in this respect is heavily weighted toward the patients' failures to cope with and overcome these obstacles. What reappears and plays its part during a psychoanalytic treatment is predominantly what has remained unsolved, conflictual, and pathological, not what has been dealt with satisfactorily and has become an uncontested part of the individual's personality.

It is here where the growing preoccupation with child analysis and direct child observation promises to redress the balance between knowledge of normality and pathology. If we borrow from the theory of the neuroses some well-developed concepts such as multiple determination of mental acts, compromise solution of conflicts, synthesis of psychic experience, etc., it becomes possible to describe all progressive development as an intricate pattern which owes its unfolding to the integration of the most diverse influences with each other. Innate givens, maturational advance, developmental growth, external and internal forces are seen to interact with each other until the final transformations are reached which qualify infantile elements for entry into the adult personality. Psychoanalysis has depicted progress of this kind with regard to the individual's sex and love life which advances in consecutive steps, under external and internal pressures, from infantile narcissism to adult postambivalent genitality. If we emulate this prototype, it proves not too difficult to construct equivalent lines of development for other essential adult characteristics, such as, for example, selfreliance, body management, secondary process functioning, relatedness to peers, objectivity, ability to work. It is, I believe, in this manner that a more or less comprehensive developmental psychology could be added to the existing body of psychoanalytic metapsychology.

CONCLUSION

During the era of its existence, psychoanalysis has entered into connection with various academic institutions, not always with satisfactory results. It also has, repeatedly, experienced rejection by them, and been criticized for its methods being imprecise, its findings not open to proof by experiment, for being unscientific, even for being a "Jewish science." However the other derogatory comments may be evaluated, it is, I believe, the last-mentioned connotation which, under present circumstances, can serve as a title of honor.

25

August Aichhorn

(1976 [1974])

It is rare that warm humanity, clinical intuition and ingenuity, and familiarity with an exciting new theory and
method are combined in one person as they were in August
Aichhorn. To have seen an unusual man of this kind at
work makes an unforgettable impression that his immediate co-workers and pupils have retained throughout their
lives.

Posterity does not accord every pioneer all the tribute
that he rightfully deserves. In today's world, hundreds of
social workers, officers of the court, psychiatrists, and psychoanalysts are concerned with the problems of youth. Yet

First published in German as an introduction to *Wer war August
Aichhorn: Briefe, Dokumente, Unveröffentliche Arbeiten,* edited by
Wiener Psychoanalytische Vereinigung. Vienna: Verlag Löcker &
Wögenstein, 1976. Also in *Die Schriften der Anna Freud,* Volume 10.
Munich: Kindler Verlag, 1980. The English translation is published here
for the first time.

many of them are oblivious of the fact that it was August Aichhorn who led the way toward the approaches they use and that the questions they attempt to answer go back to his fundamental book *Wayward Youth.*

26

Personal Memories of
Ernest Jones

(1979)

I have only one justification for talking tonight, but it seems to me that it is a good one: I have known Ernest Jones longer than any of the previous speakers, including his wife, and my friendship with him lasted for a period of fifty years. What I can mention of this here are no more than a few highlights, personal as well as professional. The two kinds are difficult to disentangle from each other, a fact which is rather characteristic for the circumstances of my life.

I met Ernest Jones for the first time in 1908 as a guest at

Presented at the special meeting of the British Psychoanalytical Society, held on January 17, 1979, in memory of Ernest Jones. First published in the *International Journal of Psycho-Analysis,* 60:271–273, 1979. German translation: Persönliche Erinnerungen an Ernest Jones. *Die Schriften der Anna Freud,* Volume 10. Munich: Kindler Verlag, 1980.

the dinner table of my home in Vienna. He was, then, a good-looking, personable young man and I, a school girl, quite impressed by him. His traveling companion was A. A. Brill from New York, and he and Brill were at the spearhead of a large number of later visitors. However, they were the first who spoke English, which made me decide to learn that language so as not to be prevented from understanding their conversations in the future.

In the years that followed, my contacts with Ernest Jones were few and far between, a fact easily explained by his move to Canada and other travels and commitments.

Then, at age eighteen, I spent my first holiday in England, partly with friends near Arundel, partly in a girls' boarding school on the south coast. When my boat from the continent docked, there was Ernest Jones on the landing stage, with a bouquet of flowers in his hands to welcome me. Naturally, I was flattered and impressed, though not without a lurking suspicion that his interest was directed more to my father than to myself, a circumstance to which I had become used. However that may have been, he certainly did not show any lack of attention. He put himself out considerably to fetch me from the places where I stayed and to show me the beauties of England which he loved. There was a never-forgotten trip in a boat going up the river Thames. There was a book, *The Highways and Byways of Sussex,* which remained in my possession for many years. He also took every opportunity to correct my English. (I only read quite recently somewhere that my father had been in the habit of correcting his German when he was in Vienna.) Time passed quickly in this way.

Unfortunately, this was the summer of 1914 and presently enjoyment was cut short by the outbreak of the First World War. Its place was taken by the doubts and worries how, whether, and when to reach home again. It was only due to the efforts of Loe Jones, Ernest Jones's former wife and a firm friend of mine, that I was put on the list of selected persons, women and children and some others, who were permitted to leave with the Austrian Ambassador. Return through Germany, fully at war, was impossible, of course. But Italy was by that time still neutral, and the Ambassador was lent a boat to reach Austria via Genoa. This was a romantic trip, on an overcrowded small ship, meeting a storm near Cape Finisterre, a gunboat at Gibraltar, and rather threatening escorting soldiers after landing. In any case, it took one home to four years of war and austerity, cut off from friends and the world beyond the Central Powers. Connections in Holland kept us in minimal touch with London.

In 1918, after peace was declared, Ernest Jones was the very first visitor who came from abroad. With him came the luggage which I had had to leave behind, a collection of summer dresses which, somebody suggested, might well have done for a retrospective exhibition of prewar fashions. I was glad to have them, in any case. To be in contact with the outer world again and to begin active cooperation was a great pleasure; so was the reunion of analysts at the International Congress in The Hague, Holland, in 1919. Those of us who came from Austria, Hungary, and Germany had to learn to communicate again and also to begin to tolerate the proper food to which Central-European stomachs had become unused. There are still photographs in my possession which show Ernest Jones, my father, and myself in front of the Dutch hotel and also at a banquet inside.

After 1919 began years of active common work for the psychoanalytic movement. Ernest Jones was extremely eager to establish a psychoanalytic literature in the English language, to make accessible to English readers what until then had existed only in German. Stimulated by him, and under his direction, Joan Riviere, Alix and James Strachey began their work, and, so far as it was done in Vienna, I was chosen to be their helper. Ernest Jones also planned that an international journal in English should be added to the *Internationale Zeitschrift* and should, for financial reasons, be printed in Austria. Many preparations were necessary for this, and a young Englishman was sent to Vienna by Jones to look after the details. Undisturbed harmony between the London and Vienna Societies was at its height at that time.

Nevertheless, while work continued, professional harmony did not do the same. With the arrival of Melanie Klein in London under the sponsorship of Ernest Jones, scientific differences made their appearance. Ernest Jones disapproved strongly of my early lectures on child analysis and complained in a letter to my father of their publication. He was, I believe, eager at that time to prevent the disagreements from increasing and, for scientific discussion of their causes, he advocated the establishment of exchange lectures between London and Vienna. He visited Vienna to give one of these; Robert Waelder went to London for the same purpose. Nevertheless, the controversies grew and deepened, without, though, ever touching or altering the bonds of friendship between us. We merely agreed to disagree.

To arrive at the next highlight:

In March 1938, Hitler and his army entered Vienna and this marked the end of peace for us and many others. Ernest Jones, moved by his concern for my father and prompted by his duty as President of the International Psycho-Analytical Association, traveled to Vienna immediately to convince himself of the seriousness of the situation. He found everybody deeply troubled, the Vienna Psychoanalytic Society dissolved, the Psychoanalytic Press invaded, its books confiscated. No one, with the possible exception of my father, needed convincing that for the Jewish members of the Society emigration was the only feasible solution. But the numbers were large and the question was not easy to solve how to find entry permits for them into countries, many of them as unwilling as they are now when it is a question of receiving the Vietnam emigrants.

This, then, was the moment when Ernest Jones did the near-impossible. He persuaded the Home Secretary to issue permits not only for my father and his nearest family, but also to his personal doctors, to the family help, and beyond this to a number of his psychoanalytic co-workers, the Bibrings, the Krises, and the Hoffers: altogether a list of some eighteen adults and six children. I have always had enormous appreciation for this achievement. I had, if possible, even more admiration for another task which he undertook. It cannot have been easy to persuade the British Society to open their doors to the influx of members from Vienna, i.e., to colleagues who held different scientific views from their own and could only be expected to disrupt peace and internal unity. I never knew how he did it; I was also careful not to ask too much. In any case, it happened. Not only did the British Society accord the incomers immediate membership and, where appropriate, training analyst status, they also assured their financial security by arranging a scheme whereby their private patients could be treated under the auspices of the British Society and Clinic. I have never ceased to be grateful to the British Society for their attitude at this crucial moment and the memory of it influenced many of my later actions. Above all, I was always careful that none of my later activities in England should in any way constitute an embarrassment to our hosts.

When relating Ernest Jones's rescue activities in Vienna, I did not mean to imply that they pleased everybody. Since selection had to be made, those who were not among the chosen felt understandably hurt, anxious, and offended. Not to be able to enter the country of one's choice had a different meaning at that time than it had at others. It meant separation from the colleagues one had been working with; it meant, at best, the search for another destination; and, at worst, being left to the mercy of the Gestapo which implied deportation to a concentration camp and, possibly, death. Fortunately none of the analysts of our Society had to meet that fate. There were three other rescuers adding their efforts to those undertaken by Jones. Marie Bonaparte provided visas for France to individuals under immediate threat; the American analyst Walter Langer, then in training in Vienna, undertook a hurried visit to the United States to collect affidavits for a number of colleagues; Muriel Gardiner gave affidavits of her own until the State Department refused to believe that even her ample means could guarantee the support of the numerous individuals sponsored by her.

Next, of course, came the war and Ernest Jones's retirement to Elsted in Sussex. I visited him many times in his beautiful home and exquisite garden and learned to know him in his new role as country gentleman. It has been mentioned here before that he was no gardener, at least not one to dig and weed. But he was certainly a gardener in the sense of knowing the Latin and English names of every tree, shrub, and plant. There was a great deal to learn from him in this respect, even if one also had to encounter his somewhat contemptuous attitude toward those who knew much less. I am quite sure that no other analyst can rival him in this knowledge.

What happened then was a most exciting event, namely, Ernest Jones's undertaking to write the biography of my father. I do believe that in the beginning he approached the task with some hesitancy, or even fear. However, this changed quickly and made itself felt as an intense and pleasurable preoccupation. There were some inaccurate, and even ludicrous statements made about this in some places. I remember a rather malicious American author asserting that this was done under my direction, and that I carefully scrutinized every page which he wrote. Whoever knew Ernest Jones personally knows very well that this was wholly fictitious. No one ever directed Ernest Jones, or gave him permissions, or even criticized him to his face. It was always the other way round. With this labor to which he had devoted himself as well, he was entirely his own master, choosing what to use, what to discard, how to arrange matters to achieve maximum information for the reader. His aim was to be factual and to adhere strictly to the truth. I would not be surprised to be told that his biography is one of the few ever written which achieved this aim.

His collection of material was simple and direct. He used to appear at our house empty-handed and depart with armfuls of documents, letters, handwritten notes, etc. It made little difference whether we were always willing to part with them. They went and found their place in Ernest Jones's study. They did not even always return. My brother Ernst recovered some of them after Ernest Jones was gone; others found their way into the Library of the British Society and Institute as gifts donated by Mrs. Jones. Some may still be floating around somewhere. In any case, they had served their purpose.

I paid a last visit to Ernest Jones when he lay fatally ill in a hospital. Our friendship, begun in 1908, ended with this very sad moment in 1958.

Editor's note: For other personal tributes not included in this book, see Anna Freud (1971c, 1972b, 1974c, 1978b, 1978d, 1979b, 1980).

27

Foreword to
Lest We Forget
by Muriel Gardiner
[1979]

Man-made catastrophes such as wars, revolutions, persecutions, and highjackings reveal not only what is worst in human nature, they also release, in some people at least, what is best.

The author of this book was not the only visitor from abroad who enjoyed the deceptive peace of Austria in the early 1930s. Like many others, she appreciated the beauties

---

Written after reading *Damit wir nicht vergessen: Unsere Jahre 1934 bis 1947 in Wien, Paris & New York,* by Muriel Gardiner and Joseph Buttinger. Vienna: Verlag der Wiener Volksbuchhandlung, 1978. It is included in French in a revised version of this book, *Le temps d'ombre: Souvenirs d'une Americaine dans la Resistance Autrichienne,* by Muriel Gardiner. Paris: Editions Aubier Montaigne, 1980. The English version is here published for the first time.

and amenities of Vienna, the easily formed friendships, and the sense of privacy and seclusion provided by the glens, meadows, and forests adjacent to the city.

Like many others of her compatriots, she also was caught up inadvertently in the political troubles which swept through Central Europe. However, she belonged neither to the hunters nor to the hunted, the persecutors nor the persecuted. The ugly scenes which followed Hitler's triumphant entry into Austria need have been none of her concern. Prudence, as well as the protection of her young daughter, would have advised that she follow the example of many other Americans who did not hesitate to return to their native country, in her case to the safe, comfortable, and luxurious background which the book describes so well.

Nevertheless, and in the face of all reason, she remained, apparently with the aim of finishing her medical studies, but even more to help her friend's political collaborators. And from these, her helpfulness and compassion began to spread: to their friends; to the friends of friends; to anybody in trouble, however remote and unfamiliar; until she was surrounded by a whole crowd of potential victims who looked to her as possibly their only hope of salvation.

Those of us who, at this period, were forced to share the experience of lying sleepless in bed in the early morning hours, waiting for the dreaded knock of the Gestapo at our doors, find it difficult or even impossible to imagine that anybody could voluntarily choose to face the same anxieties. Every hidden socialist or Jew searched for and found in Muriel Gardiner's apartment would have meant the end, not only for him but also for her; every mad dash to the border escorting refugees could have ended in disaster. Moreover, this was not all. There were all the other accompaniments of an underground existence: the inevitable failures; the disappearances which placed people beyond the possibility of help; the endlessly drawn-out waiting periods when nothing happened; the discomforts and deprivations of daily life; the frightening possibility of being duped by impostors and the humiliating experience of being taken for an impostor herself.

There are other and fuller accounts of the happenings of this period, recording the struggle and disorganization of the Social-Democratic Party of Austria or the plight of its Jewish population, or the exact number of individuals driven into exile, deported, or exterminated. The present book does not aspire to belong to their category. It is a rendering of personal experiences, trying to depict how history affects the lives of individuals, and it should be read for its descriptions of individual despair, of the tearing apart and attempted reunion of families, of the search for countries of refuge, the battle for lifesaving affidavits, and the never-ending planning and plotting which, often enough, had to be abandoned again as unrealistic and impossible to carry into action.

What are harsh realities at one moment in time may dwindle to distant nightmares forty years later. However, that is no reason to relegate them to oblivion. The present generation of readers, even if far removed from such experience, may welcome two lessons which can be learned from it: one, that it is possible even for single individuals to pit their strength successfully against the sinister forces of an unjust regime; and, two, that for every gang of evildoers who take pleasure in hurting, harming, and destroying, there is always at least one "just" man or woman, ready to help, rescue, and sacrifice his or her own good for their fellow beings.

Editor's note: For other prefaces not included in this book, see Anna Freud (1971b, 1973b, 1973c, 1974b, 1974d, 1975c, 1975d, 1975e, 1975f, 1975g, 1975h, 1976a, 1976b, 1977a, 1977b, 1977c, 1977d, 1978c, 1978e, 1978f, 1979a).

28

Foreword to *Topsy* by Marie Bonaparte
[1980]

Political events such as wars, overthrows of governments, and social revolutions not only determine on a large scale the fate of nations and individuals; they also intervene, as side effects, as it were, in long-established occurrences and bring what had been deemed unalterable customs to a sudden end.

The inhabitants of Berggasse in the ninth district of Vienna had for decades been accustomed to see doctors and scientists from foreign countries appear and disappear. They somehow understood that this was connected with the professor who lived in their street and from whom

Written in German for the new edition of *Topsy: Die Geschichte eines goldhaarigen Chows,* translated into German by Anna and Sigmund Freud in 1938. Frankfurt am Main: Fischer Verlag, 1981. It is here published in English for the first time.

apparently something new could be learned. What this was was of little concern to them. What impressed them far more was the regularity of these coming and goings, a punctuality that could be relied on with greater certainty than their clocks. It was this routine, by then a matter-of-course, which, like many other things, came to an end with Hitler's march into Vienna. With the appearance of a swastika and a National Socialist flag at the door of number 19, the foreigners disappeared and, like a flock of startled birds, returned by the next planes to the countries of their origin.

For Freud, the disappearance of his analysands meant a period in which he unaccustomedly found himself without work. Walks or drives through the streets of Vienna were in view of the new uncertainties not advisable. The threatening times and the questionable future were not conducive to scientific work; and plans were still too unsettled to prepare for emigration. In this state of loneliness and irresolution it was easier to revert to an old occupation, the work of translation, which had played a role at the beginning of his scientific career. Freud was a gifted translator, who could effortlessly read off a page of a foreign-language text in German, without having to search, like others, for the correct words and sentence structure. Moreover, a French author was present — Marie Bonaparte, whom Freud was only too eager to do a favor in gratitude for her unflagging helpfulness. A text presented itself: Marie Bonaparte's book on her dog.

Today we may assume that it was not only the person of the author but, above all, the topic of the book which influenced Freud's choice. What at that time, perhaps as never before, made for disappointment were people. Even the destruction of illusions during the First World War could not measure up to the impressions of unrelenting brutality and blind lust for destruction which no one could escape. Instinctual manifestations which, according to Freud, should have been banished to the unconscious and warded off by the higher agencies of the personality, suddenly emerged, unleashed and unrestricted in their search for gratification. In these circumstances it became easier to look away from one's fellowmen and turn to animals.

Freud's interest in the world of dogs was a late acquisition. It began in the twenties of this century as a relationship, built on mutual respect, with a large, not undangerous Alsatian dog that for more than ten years had shared the life of the family. This relationship deepened and grew more tender, in the affectionate care for his own animal which had been procured for him in Paris. Yo-Fie, a female Chow, in bearing and appearance not unlike a little lion, soon became his daily companion, accompanied him on excursions, patiently participated in all analytic hours, sat next to him at mealtimes. After the tragic loss of Yo-Fie, Lun-Yu, a Chinese dog of the same race, assumed the same role and later also accompanied him in the emigration. What Freud valued in his dogs was their gracefulness, devotion, and fidelity; what he frequently stressed and praised as a decided advantage over men was the absence of any ambivalence. "Dogs," as he used to say, "love their friends and bite their enemies, in contrast to men who are incapable of pure love and must at all times mix love and hate in their object relations."

Marie Bonaparte's love for her Chow was evident in

Topsy, a feeling that apparently touched a responsive chord in Freud. The work of translation he devoted to the book should at the same time be regarded as part of the gratitude and indebtedness which he endeavored to repay to Yo-Fie and Lun-Yu for many years of friendship.

Bibliography

AICHHORN, A. (1925), *Wayward Youth.* New York: Viking Press, 1935.

ALEXANDER, F. & STAUB, H. (1929), *The Criminal, the Judge and the Public.* New York: Macmillan, 1931.

ALPERT, A. (1959), Reversibility of Pathological Fixations Associated with Maternal Deprivation in Infancy. *The Psychoanalytic Study of the Child,* 14:169–185.

_____ NEUBAUER, P. B., & WEIL, A. P. (1956), Unusual Variations in Drive Endowment. *The Psychoanalytic Study of the Child,* 11:125–163.

BALINT, M. (1968), *The Basic Fault.* London: Tavistock Publications.

BERNFELD, S. (1925), *Sisyphus, or the Limits of Education.* Berkeley: University of California Press, 1973.

BIBRING, E. (1936), The Development and Problems of the Theory of the Instincts. *Int. J. Psycho-Anal.,* 22:102–131, 1941.

BRENNER, C. (1971), The Psychoanalytic Concept of Aggression. *Int. J. Psycho-Anal.,* 52:137–144.

BREUER, J. & FREUD, S. (1893–95), Studies on Hysteria. *Standard Edition, 2.**

*See footnote‡ (p. 367)

BURLINGHAM, D. (1972), *Psychoanalytic Studies of the Sighted and the Blind.* New York: International Universities Press.

―――― (1979), To Be Blind in a Sighted World. *The Psychoanalytic Study of the Child,* 34:5–30.

EDGCUMBE, R. (1975), The Border Between Therapy and Education. In: *Studies in Child Psychoanalysis: Pure and Applied.* New Haven: Yale University Press, pp. 133–148.

EDITORIAL (1931), Gegen Psychoanalyse. *Süddeutsche Monatshefte,* 28.

EISSLER, K. R. (1971), Death Drive, Ambivalence, and Narcissism. *The Psychoanalytic Study of the Child,* 26:25–78.

FERENCZI, S. (1920), Open Letter. *Int. J. Psycho-Anal.,* 1:1–2.

FREEMAN, D. (1968), Aggression: Instinct or Symptom. Lecture to the Australian and New Zealand College of Psychiatrists.

FREUD, A. (1927), Four Lectures on Child Analysis. In: *The Writings of Anna Freud,* 1:3–69.

―――― (1936), *The Ego and the Mechanisms of Defense.* New York: International Universities Press, rev. ed., 1966 [Volume 2].†

―――― (1965), *Normality and Pathology in Childhood: Assessments of Development.* New York: International Universities Press [Volume 6].

―――― (1968), *Indications for Child Analysis and Other Papers.* New York: International Universities Press [Volume 4].

―――― (1969), *Research at the Hampstead Child-Therapy Clinic and Other Papers.* New York: International Universities Press [Volume 5].

―――― (1971a), *Problems of Psychoanalytic Training, Diagnosis, and the Technique of Therapy.* New York: International Universities Press [Volume 7].

―――― (1971b), Foreword to *Teaching and the Unconscious Mind,* by J. C. Hill. New York: International Universities Press.

†The Volume numbers in brackets refer to *The Writings of Anna Freud.* New York: International Universities Press, 1966–1980.

_____ (1971c), The Seventieth Birthday: A Letter to Max Schur. In: *The Unconscious Today,* ed. M. Kanzer. New York: International Universities Press, pp. 5–7.

_____ (1972a), The Child As a Person in His Own Right. *The Psychoanalytic Study of the Child,* 27:621–625.

_____ (1972b), Muriel Gardiner. *Bull. Philadelphia Assn. Psychoanal.,* 22(2).

_____ (1973a), *Infants Without Families: Reports on the Hampstead Nurseries* (with D. Burlingham). New York: International Universities Press [Volume 3].

_____ (1973b), Foreword to *Sisyphus, or the Limits of Education,* by S. Bernfeld. Berkeley: University of California Press.

_____ (1973c), Foreword to *Don't Push Me, I Am No Computer,* by H. Beck. New York & London: McGraw-Hill.

_____ (1974a), *Introduction to Psychoanalysis: Lectures for Child Analysts and Teachers.* New York: International Universities Press [Volume 1].

_____ (1974b), Foreword to *A Child's Parent Dies,* by E. Furman. New Haven & London: Yale University Press.

_____ (1974c), On Hilda Abraham's Biography of Karl Abraham. *Int. Rev. Psycho-Anal.,* 1:15–16.

_____ (1974d), Preface to *The Standard Edition of the Complete Psychological Works of Sigmund Freud,* Volume 24. London: Hogarth Press.

_____ (1975a), Remarks on Receiving the C. Anderson Aldrich Award. *Amer. Acad. Pediat.,* 56:332–334.

_____ (1975b), The Nursery School of the Hampstead Child-Therapy Clinic. In: *Studies in Child Psychoanalysis: Pure and Applied.* New Haven: Yale University Press, pp. 127–132.

_____ (1975c), Vorwort to *Das Ich und die Abwehrmechanismen: Kindler Studienausgabe.* Munich: Kindler Verlag.

_____ (1975d), Foreword to *The Selected Papers of Ernst Kris.* New Haven & London: Yale University Press.

_____ (1975e), Foreword to *Studies in Child Psychoanalysis: Pure and Applied.* New Haven & London: Yale University Press.

_____ (1975f), Zum Geleit: Sigmund Freud Gesellschaft. *Sigmund Freud House Bull.,* 1(1).

_____ (1975g), Foreword to Pseudobackwardness in Children, by M. Berger & H. Kennedy. *The Psychoanalytic Study of the Child,* 30:279–282.

_____ (1975h), Foreword to *Female Sexuality and the Oedipus Complex,* by H. Nagera. New York: Jason Aronson.

_____ (1976a), Foreword to *The Hospitalized Adolescent,* by A. D. Hofmann, R. D. Becker, & H. P. Gabriel. New York: Free Press.

_____ (1976b), Foreword to *Obsessional Neurosis,* by H. Nagera. New York: Jason Aronson.

_____ (1977a), Vorwort to *Maria Montessori,* by R. Kramer. Munich: Kindler Verlag.

_____ (1977b), Foreword to The Referral of Nursery School Children for Treatment, by P. Wilson. *The Psychoanalytic Study of the Child,* 32:479–481.

_____ (1977c), Preface to The Vienna Symposium on Work in the Hampstead Child-Therapy Clinic. *Sigmund Freud House Bull.,* 1(2).

_____ (1977d), Foreword to *Psychoanalytic Assessment: The Diagnostic Profile.* New Haven & London: Yale University Press.

_____ (1978a), Die Bedeutung der Kinderanalyse. *Sigmund Freud House Bull.,* 2:8–12.

_____ (1978b), Edith B. Jackson: In Memoriam. *J. Amer. Acad. Child Psychiat.,* 17:730–731.

_____ (1978c), Introduction to *The Israel Annals of Psychiatry and Related Disciplines,* 16(2).

_____ (1978d), Mathilde Hollitscher-Freud, 1887–1978. *Sigmund Freud House Bull.,* 2(1).

_____ (1978e), On 'The Hampstead Bulletin.' *Bull. Hampstead Clin.,* 1:5.

_____ (1978f), Foreword to *The Child in His Family,* ed. E. J. Anthony et al. New York: Wiley.

_____ (1979a), Foreword to The Development of Blind Children. *The Psychoanalytic Study of the Child,* 34:3–4.

_____ (1979b), Agi Ben Moses. *Bull. Hampstead Clin.,* 2:163.

_____ (1980), In Memoriam Dorothy Burlingham. *The Psychoanalytic Study of the Child,* 35:x–xiv; also in *Bull. Hampstead Clin.,* 3:75–77.

FREUD, S. (1893), On the Psychical Mechanism of Hysterical Phenomena: A Lecture. *Standard Edition,* 3:25–39.‡

_____ (1896), Further Remarks on the Neuropsychoses of Defence. *Standard Edition,* 3:159–185.

_____ (1900), The Interpretation of Dreams. *Standard Edition,* 4 & 5.

_____ (1901a), On Dreams. *Standard Edition,* 5:629–686.

_____ (1901b), The Psychopathology of Everyday Life. *Standard Edition,* 6.

_____ (1904), Freud's Psycho-Analytic Procedure. *Standard Edition,* 7:249–254.

_____ (1905a), Fragment of an Analysis of a Case of Hysteria. *Standard Edition,* 7:3–122.

_____ (1905b), Three Essays on the Theory of Sexuality. *Standard Edition,* 7:115–143.

_____ (1905c), Jokes and Their Relation to the Unconscious. *Standard Edition,* 8.

_____ (1906), Psycho-Analysis and the Establishment of the Facts in Legal Proceedings. *Standard Edition,* 9:97–114.

_____ (1907a), Obsessive Actions and Religious Practices. *Standard Edition,* 9:115–127.

_____ (1907b), Delusions and Dreams in Jensen's *Gradiva.* *Standard Edition,* 9:3–95.

_____ (1907c), The Sexual Enlightenment of Children. *Standard Edition,* 9:129–139.

_____ (1908a), Creative Writers and Day-Dreaming. *Standard Edition,* 9:141–153.

‡*The Standard Edition of the Complete Psychological Works of Sigmund Freud,* 24 Volumes, translated and edited by James Strachey. London: Hogarth Press and the Institute of Psycho-Analysis, 1953–1974.

—————— (1908b), On the Sexual Theories of Children. *Standard Edition,* 9:205–226.

—————— (1909a), Analysis of a Phobia in a Five-Year-Old Boy. *Standard Edition,* 10:3–149.

—————— (1909b), Notes upon a Case of Obsessional Neurosis. *Standard Edition,* 10:153–320.

—————— (1910), Leonardo da Vinci and a Memory of His Childhood. *Standard Edition,* 11:59–137.

—————— (1911a), Psycho-Analytic Notes on an Autobiographical Account of a Case of Paranoia (Dementia Paranoides). *Standard Edition,* 12:3–82.

—————— (1911b), Formulations on the Two Principles of Mental Functioning. *Standard Edition,* 12:215–226.

—————— (1912a), The Dynamics of Transference. *Standard Edition,* 12:97–108.

—————— (1912b), Recommendations to Physicians Practising Psycho-Analysis. *Standard Edition,* 12:109–120.

—————— (1912c), A Note on the Unconscious in Psycho-Analysis. *Standard Edition,* 12:255–266.

—————— (1913a [1912–13]), Totem and Taboo. *Standard Edition,* 13:1–161.

—————— (1913b), The Claims of Psycho-Analysis to Scientific Interest. *Standard Edition,* 13:165–190.

—————— (1913c), The Occurrence in Dreams of Material from Fairy Tales. *Standard Edition,* 12:279–301.

—————— (1913d), The Theme of the Three Caskets. *Standard Edition,* 12:289–301.

—————— (1913e), On Beginning the Treatment. *Standard Edition,* 12:121–144.

—————— (1913f), Two Lies Told by Children. *Standard Edition,* 12:303–309.

—————— (1914a), On the History of the Psycho-Analytic Movement. *Standard Edition,* 14:3–66.

—————— (1914b), Remembering, Repeating and Working-Through. *Standard Edition,* 12:145–156.

—————— (1914c), On Narcissism. *Standard Edition,* 14:76–102.

_____ (1915a), Instincts and Their Vicissitudes. *Standard Edition,* 14:109–140.

_____ (1915b), Repression. *Standard Edition,* 14:141–158.

_____ (1915c), The Unconscious. *Standard Edition,* 14:159–215.

_____ (1915d), Observations on Transference-Love. *Standard Edition,* 12:157–173.

_____ (1916), Some Character-Types Met with in Psycho-Analytic Work. *Standard Edition,* 14:309–333.

_____ (1916–17), Introductory Lectures on Psycho-Analysis. *Standard Edition,* 16 & 17.

_____ (1917), A Difficulty in the Path of Psycho-Analysis. *Standard Edition,* 17:135–144.

_____ (1918 [1914]), From the History of an Infantile Neurosis. *Standard Edition,* 17:3–123.

_____ (1920), Beyond the Pleasure Principle. *Standard Edition,* 18:3–64.

_____ (1921), Group Psychology and the Analysis of the Ego. *Standard Edition,* 18:67–143.

_____ (1923a), The Ego and the Id. *Standard Edition,* 19:3–66.

_____ (1923b), The Infantile Genital Organization. *Standard Edition,* 19:141–145.

_____ (1924a), The Dissolution of the Oedipus Complex. *Standard Edition,* 19:173–179.

_____ (1924b), The Resistances to Psycho-Analysis. *Standard Edition,* 19:213–224.

_____ (1924c), Neurosis and Psychosis. *Standard Edition,* 19:149–153.

_____ (1924d), The Loss of Reality in Neurosis and Psychosis. *Standard Edition,* 19:183–187.

_____ (1924e), A Short Account of Psycho-Analysis. *Standard Edition,* 19:191–209.

_____ (1925a), The Resistances to Psycho-Analysis. *Standard Edition,* 19:213–224.

_____ (1925b), An Autobiographical Study. *Standard Edition,* 20:3–70.

_____ (1925c), Some Psychical Consequences of the Anatomical Distinction Between the Sexes. *Standard Edition,* 19: 243–258.

_____ (1925d), Preface to Aichhorn's *Wayward Youth. Standard Edition,* 19:273–275.

_____ (1926a), Inhibitions, Symptoms and Anxiety. *Standard Edition,* 20:77–175.

_____ (1926b), The Question of Lay Analysis. *Standard Edition,* 20:179–250.

_____ (1926c), Psycho-Analysis. *Standard Edition,* 20:259–270.

_____ (1927a), The Future of an Illusion. *Standard Edition,* 21:3–56.

_____ (1927b), Postscript to The Question of Lay Analysis. *Standard Edition,* 20:251–258.

_____ (1930), Civilization and Its Discontents. *Standard Edition,* 21:59–145.

_____ (1931a), Female Sexuality. *Standard Edition,* 21:223–243.

_____ (1931b), The Expert Opinion in the Halsmann Case. *Standard Edition,* 21:251–253.

_____ (1932), The Acquisition and Control of Fire. *Standard Edition,* 22:185–193.

_____ (1933a), New Introductory Lectures on Psycho-Analysis. *Standard Edition,* 2:3–182.

_____ (1933b), Why War? *Standard Edition,* 22:197–215.

_____ (1935), Postscript: An Autobiographical Study. *Standard Edition,* 20:71–74.

_____ (1937), Analysis Terminable and Interminable. *Standard Edition,* 23:209–253.

_____ (1939), Moses and Monotheism. *Standard Edition,* 23:3–137.

_____ (1940a), An Outline of Psycho-Analysis. *Standard Edition,* 23:141–207.

_____ (1940b), Some Elementary Lessons in Psycho-Analysis. *Standard Edition,* 23:279–286.

_____ (1950), *The Origins of Psychoanalysis.* New York: Basic Books, 1954.

_____ (1960), *Letters of Sigmund Freud,* ed. E. L. Freud. New York: Basic Books.

FRIEDMAN, M., GLASSER, M., LAUFER, E., LAUFER, M., & WOHL, M. (1972), Attempted Suicide and Self-Mutilation in Adolescence. *Int. J. Psycho-Anal.,* 53:179–184.

GILLESPIE, W. H. (1971), Aggression and Instinct Theory. *Int. J. Psycho-Anal.,* 52:155–160.

GOLDSTEIN, J., FREUD, A., & SOLNIT, A. J. (1973), *Beyond the Best Interests of the Child.* New York: Free Press.

_____ _____ _____ (1979), *Before the Best Interests of the Child.* New York: Free Press.

_____ & KATZ, J. (1965), *The Family and the Law.* New York: Free Press.

GREEN, A. (1975), The Analyst, Symbolization and Absence in the Analytic Setting. *Int. J. Psycho-Anal.,* 56:1–22.

HOFFER, W. (1950), Oral Aggressiveness and Ego Development. *Int. J. Psycho-Anal.,* 31:156–160.

KENNEDY, H. (1979), The Role of Insight in Child Analysis. *J. Amer. Psychoanal. Assn.,* Suppl. 27:9–28.

KESTEMBERG, E. (1972), Reporter: Panel on 'The Role of Aggression in Child Analysis.' *Int. J. Psycho-Anal.,* 53:321–323.

KLEIN, M. (1921–1945), *Contributions to Psycho-Analysis.* London: Hogarth Press.

KOHUT, H. (1971), *The Analysis of the Self.* New York: International Universities Press.

KRAMER, R. (1977), *Maria Montessori.* Munich: Kindler Verlag.

LORENZ, K. (1963), *On Aggression.* New York: Harcourt, Brace & World, 1966.

LUSSIER, A. (1972), Reporter: Panel on 'Aggression.' *Int. J. Psycho-Anal.,* 53:13–19.

MAHLER, M. S. (1968), *On Human Symbiosis and the Vicissitudes of Individuation.* New York: International Universities Press.

MASTERS, W. H. & JOHNSON, V. E. (1970), *Human Sexual Inadequacy.* Boston: Little, Brown.

MENNINGER, K. A. (1938), *Man Against Himself.* New York: Harcourt, Brace.

NAGERA, H. (1966), *Early Childhood Disturbances, the Infantile Neurosis, and the Adulthood Disturbances.* New York: International Universities Press.

PROVENCE, S. (1967), *Guide for the Care of Infants in Groups.* New York: Child Welfare League of America.

_____ & LIPTON, R. (1962), *Infants in Institutions.* New York: International Universities Press.

_____ NAYLOR, A., & PATTERSON, J. (1977), *The Challenge of Daycare.* New Haven & London: Yale Univesity Press.

RANGELL, L. (1972), Aggression, Oedipus and Historical Perspective. *Int. J. Psycho-Anal.,* 53:3-11.

_____ (1975), Psychoanalysis and the Process of Change. *Int. J. Psycho-Anal.,* 56:87-98.

SCHREBER, D. P. (1903), *Memoirs of My Nervous Illness [Denkwürdigkeiten eines Geisteskranken].* London: Dawson, 1955.

SPITZ, R. A. (1965), *The First Year of Life.* New York: International Universities Press.

STONE, L. (1954), The Widening Scope of Indications for Psychoanalysis. *J. Amer. Psychoanal. Assn.,* 2:567-594.

_____ (1971), Reflections on the Psychoanalytic Concept of Aggression. *Psychoanal. Quart.,* 40:195-244.

SYMPOSIUM (1954), The Widening Scope of Indications for Psychoanalysis. *J. Amer. Psychoanal. Assn.,* 2:565-620.

TYSON, R. L. (1978), Notes on the Analysis of a Prelatency Boy with a Dog Phobia. *The Psychoanalytic Study of the Child,* 33:427-458.

WINNICOTT, D. W. (1953), Transitional Objects and Transitional Phenomena. *Collected Papers.* New York: Basic Books, 1958, pp. 229-242.

_____ (1958), *Collected Papers.* New York: Basic Books.

_____ (1965), *The Maturational Processes and the Facilitating Environment.* New York: International Universities Press.

YORKE, C. (1965), Some Metapsychological Aspects of Interpretation. *Brit. J. Med. Psychol.,* 38:27-42.

Index